As For The Canadians

As For The Canadians

The Remarkable Story of the RCAF's "Guinea Pigs" of World War II

by

Rita Donovan

BuschekBooks

Canadian Cataloguing in Publication Data

Donovan, Rita, 1955-
   As for the Canadians: the remarkable story of the RCAF's Guinea Pigs
of World War II

Includes bibliographic references and index.
ISBN 1-894543-03-3

   1. Air pilots, Military—Canada—Biography. 2. Flight crews—Canada
—Biography. 3. Burn care units—England—East Grinstead. 4. Veterans,
Disabled—Rehabilitation—England—East Grinstead. 5. Guinea Pig Club.
I. Title.

UG626.D65 2000   362.1'9711   C00-901181-1

Cover image: Title: *Pedicled Airman #1, Royal Canadian Air Force Hospital,
East Grinstead, England*
Artist Name: Goldhamer, Flight Lieutenant Charles
Catalogue Number: CN11271
Copyright Canadian War Museum (C.W.M.)

Printed in Canada by Hignell Book Printing, Winnipeg, Manitoba.

BuschekBooks gratefully acknowledges the support of the Canada Council
for the Arts and the Ontario Arts Council for its publishing program.

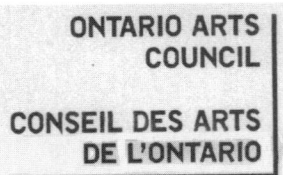

The Canada Council   Le Conseil des Arts
for the Arts   du Canada

BuschekBooks
P.O. Box 74053, 35 Beechwood Avenue, Ottawa, Ontario, Canada K1M 2H9
John Buschek, Editor

For Piper,
Thank you for being an inspirational figure in El's health journey.

For the Canadian Guinea Pigs,

your book.

In light of your family's R.A.F. connection, I thought you might enjoy my mom's book.
♡ + best wishes,
— Ellis

Contents

Photo Credits

p. 18 - Archibald McIndoe - photo courtesy *The Guinea Pig*; p. 20 - Drawing by Henry Standen courtesy Ann Standen; p. 23. photo of Ross Tilley - Uckfield Studios, provided by Jack Toper; p. 27 - photo of Gerry Dufort provided by Dufort; p. 28 - photo of Bill Martin provided by George Wilson; p. 31 - photo of C. A. L. Hurry provided by Ella Hurry; p. 33 - photo of Zdzislaw Krasnodebski courtesy *The Guinea Pig*; p. 35 - photo of Ed Smith provided by Smith; p. 40 - photo of Bob Fraser courtesy of *The Guinea Pig*; p. 41 - drawing of Bob Fraser by Henry Standen courtesy Ann Standen; p. 44 - photo of L. Somers courtesy *The Guinea Pig*; p. 47 - photo of Ken Fisher courtesy *The Guinea Pig*; p. 51 - photo of John Reynolds courtesy *The Guinea Pig*; p. 57 - photo of Paul Davoud courtesy Canada's Aviation Hall of Fame, Paul Davoud Collection; p. 59 - photo of Bill Newson courtesy Canada's Aviation Hall of Fame, William Newson Collection; p. 64 - photo of Wilson, Anderson and Kerr provided by Ruth Kerr; p. 65 - photo of George Wilson by Karsh, provided by Wilson; p. 69 - photo of John Kerr and Ross Tilley provided by Ruth Kerr; p. 74 - Pea-Nut Club emblem photo, from an article provided by Gordon Gentry; p. 76 - photo of Ray Leupp courtesy *The Guinea Pig*; p. 80 - photo of Bob Lloyd courtesy *The Guinea Pig*; p. 81 - photo of William Tanner provided by Lajeanne Tanner; p. 88 - photo of Bob Tait courtesy *The Guinea Pig*; p. 89 - photo of Reg Harrison provided by Harrison; p. 107 - photo of John Everett courtesy *The Guinea Pig*; p. 107 photo of Paul Branch provided by Ed Smith; p. 112 - photo of Ken Smyth provided by Debbie Smyth; p. 117 - photo of Bob McCallum courtesy *The Guinea Pig*; p. p. 127 — photo of Dr. Norm Park courtesy *The Guinea Pig*; p. 129 - photo of Fran Oakes provided by Enid Matheson; p. 130 - photo of Marge Jackson provided by George Wilson; p. 132 - photo of Dorothy Mulholland provided by Enid (Faulkner) Matheson; p. 133 - photo of Elaine Matheson provided by Enid (Faulkner) Matheson; p. 133 — photo of Enid (Faulkner) Matheson provided by Enid Matheson; p. 135 photo of nurses courtesy of Saskatchewan Archives Board, R98-147; p. 137 — photo of William Rhode provided by Rhode; p. 139 - photo of 'operation' courtesy the National Archives of Canada HQ-4782; p. 139 - photo of Nurse Jackson and patient courtesy Saskatchewan Archives Board, R98-147; p. 140 - photo of pedicle graft provided by Flora Duncan; p. 140 - photo of rotation flap graft provided by Lajeanne Tanner; p. 141 - photos of reconstruction of face and hands provided by George Wilson; p. 141 - photos of pedicle grafts provided by Henri Marceau; p. 145 — photo of Dr. Ross Tilley courtesy National Archives of Canada; p. 146 - photo of the Canadian Wing courtesy National Archives of Canada; p. 147 — photo of entrance to Canadian Wing courtesy National Archives of Canada; p. 148 — photo of Canadian Wing courtesy National Archives of Canada; p. 149 — photo of saline bath treatment courtesy National Archives of Canada HQ-3603; p. 150 - photo of an operation courtesy National Archives of Canada HQ-4783; p. 151 - photo of an examination courtesy National Archives of Canada; p. 152 — photo of nurses in Canadian Wing courtesy National Archives of Canada; p. 153 - photo of

Stanley Reynolds with the Alberta Order of Excellence provided by Reynolds; p. 158 - photo of "All Clear" Troupe provided by Stanley Reynolds; p. 163 - photo of Ken Davies courtesy *The Guinea Pig*; p. 172 - photos of shot-up Canadian Wing provided by Arthur Doyle; p. 176 - photo of Norman McHolm provided by McHolm; p. 179 - drawing by Henry Standen courtesy Ann Standen; p. 180 - photo of Lionel Hastings provided by Hastings; p. 190 - photo of E. Lacasse provided by Lacasse; p. 192 – photo of John Campbell Smith courtesy *The Guinea Pig*; p. 195 – drawing by Henry Standen courtesy Ann Standen; p. 196 - photo of Christmas 1944 (children) courtesy the National Archives of Canada, HQ 3570, provided by William Rhode; p. 197 - photo of Christmas 1944 (servicemen) courtesy National Archives of Canada HQ 3524, provided by William Rhode; p. 198 - photo of Stu Duncan provided by Flora Duncan; p. 200 - photo of John Harding provided by Harding; p. 216 - photo of Henri Marceau provided by Marceau; p. 219 - photo of John Southwell provided by Ed Smith; p. 224 - photo of lowering of ensign provided by William Rhode; p. 225 - photo of Dedication of the Wing courtesy Saskatchewan Archives Board, R98-147; p. 227 – cover drawing for initial issue of *The Guinea Pig*, by Henry Standen, courtesy Ann Standen; p. 254 – photo of Dr. Ross Tilley Public School provided by Rita Donovan; p. 260 – photo of Canadian Wing Staff provided by William Rhode; p. 260 photo of Dr. Tilley and nurses provided by Fran Oakes; p. 261 – photo of Lillian Hall and William Rhode provided by Rhode; p. 261 – photo of Bob Tait and Fergie Ferguson provided by Tait; p. 261 – photo of Hank Hastings and crew provided by Hastings; p. 262 – photo of the graves of Hank Ernst's and George Beauchamp's crew provided by Ernst; p. 262 photo of John Southwell and car provided by Southwell; p. 262 – Henry Standen drawing courtesy Ann Standen; p. 263 – photo of entrance of Canadian Wing provided by Gordon Gentry; p. 263 – photo of staff and patients courtesy Saskatchewan Archives Boars R98-147; p. 264 – photo of Lacroix wedding provided by William Rhode; p. 264 – photo of Stu Duncan in desert provided by Flora Duncan; p. 265 photo of Faulkner-Matheson wedding provided by (Faulkner) Matheson; p. 265 – photo of wedding guests provided by Enid (Faulkner) Matheson; p. 266 – photo of Dr. Norm Park and Johnny Kerr provided by Ruth Kerr; p. 266 – photo of Ed Smith with Mynarski bomber provided by Smith; p. 267 – photo of wedding group in 1972 provided by Enid (Faulkner) Matheson; p. 267 – group photo provided by Lionel "Hank" Hastings; p. 268 – group photo provided by Flora Duncan; p. 268 – photo of Jean Tilley and Mary Hastings provided by Hastings; p. 269 - photo of Garnett "Tar" Moore and George Wilson provided by Flora Duncan; p. 269 – photo of Dr. Tilley and George Wilson provided by William Rhode; p. 270 – photo of Duncans with Edna Martin provided by Flora Duncan; p. p. 270 – photo of Bill Martin and Hantons provided by Flora Duncan; p. 271 – photo of Lionel "Hank" Hastings and Ed Smith provided by Smith; p. 271 – photo of Jack Reynolds, Jack Harding and Hank Ernst provided by Ed Smith; p. 272 – photo of Hardings and puppets provided by Harding; p. 272 – group photo courtesy *The Guinea Pig*; p. 273 – dedication photo courtesy Saskatchewan Archives Board R98-147; p. 274 – Guinea Pigs with Tiger Moth provided by John Southwell; p. 274 – photo of Lionel "Hank" Hastings courtesy *The Guinea Pig*; p. 275 – three photos of Guinea Pig Pub provided by Gordon Gentry.

Acknowledgments

Any book that involves as many stories as this one does would have been impossible to write without the generosity of many people. Personal stories were provided by the Guinea Pigs themselves, or by their widows and family members. Stories were also provided by medical personnel. The author also interviewed, by phone, in person or on tape, several Guinea Pigs. Others sent tapes on their own. Stories were also gleaned from written accounts and audio-tapes located in the Guinea Pig holdings at the Province of Saskatchewan Archives in Regina. Finally, some stories were, literally, pieced together from snippets of news that appeared, over the years, in the indispensable *Guinea Pig* magazine, along with anecdotes from Guinea Pigs who remembered their colleagues. It is regrettable that there were many Guinea Pigs for whom no story was available. They are remembered, *en masse*, by their fellow Club members. Because of the varied nature of the source material, most quotations are un-referenced. The majority of these were given directly to the author or appeared as entries in *The Guinea Pig*.

The author would first like to thank all Guinea Pigs and their families who offered stories, articles, clippings, and cherished photographs—without them the book would have been diminished. The author would like to thank, in England: Mr. Jack Toper, Guinea Pig editor of *The Guinea Pig*, for his years of dedication to his unique magazine and for the photograph of Dr. Tilley; Mr. Bob Marchant, Curator of the Guinea Pig Museum, Queen Victoria Hospital, East Grinstead, for his correspondence and his information; Dr. T. Cochrane, Queen Victoria Hospital, for providing needed material; Mr. Gordon Gentry, Tunbridge Wells, for his interest in the project and for providing numerous articles and photographs; Mrs. Ann Standen, East Grinstead, for the generous use of her late husband Henry Standen's drawings.

The author would like to thank, in Canada: Dr. Leith G. Douglas, Toronto, for an interview in the middle of a busy schedule and for his good advice; Mr. Mike Filey, of *The Toronto Sun*, for information on the Christie Street hospital; Mr. Elward Burnside, Toronto, for his correspondence, video and information; Mrs. Phyllis Shanks, Edmonton, for her interest and for providing a book that was useful in research; Guinea Pigs Bill Martin and George Wilson, both of Calgary, for providing not only their own stories but for assisting the author in unearthing the stories of some of their colleagues; Guinea Pig Stan Reynolds, Jennifer Romanko and the staff of the Reynolds-Alberta Museum and Canada's Aviation Hall of Fame for their expertise and assistance in regard to particular photographs; Guinea Pig John Reynolds, of Regina, for sending not only his story but providing information about another Guinea Pig; Mrs. Mary Orr Hastings, of Regina, for allowing the author to quote a portion of her poem and for her hospitality in Regina; the following members of the staff of the Saskatchewan Archives, Regina, for their unstinting assistance during a research trip to their archives: Mr. Christopher Gebhard, Ms. Linda Putz, Ms. Shannon Stoffel, Mr. Bill Wagner. In Uxbridge, Ontario, the author would like to thank Mrs. Fran Thompson for permission to quote from her poem; Mr. Fred Brailey, Ontario, for his interest in the project and for sharing information and photographs; Mrs. Elizabeth Hicks, Ottawa, for her story about entertaining in the air force and for her enthusiasm; Mrs. Audrey Renton, archivist, Rideau Township Archives, for her interest in the project and for her many pieces of information; Mr. Vic Johnson, editor, *Air Force Magazine*, Ottawa, for making his files available and for his encouragement; Lt. Col. H. Wright, Ottawa, for sharing information of mutual interest; the staff at the National Archives of Canada, Ottawa, for their expertise and consultation; Mr. Ian Leslie and Ms. Fiona Smith-Hale at the National Aviation Museum, Ottawa, for their assistance; the staff of the Canadian War Museum, Ottawa, for information about war art.

On a personal note, I would like to thank M. M., for her courage; Norman Avery, Ottawa, author of aviation histories, for lunches spent commiserating on a sky full of stories; Frances Itani, author, of Ottawa, for reminding me about the cover image and for her e-mails which keep me going; John Barton, Ottawa, poet and museum publications coordinator, for his knowledge of aviation material and for putting up with me; Meridee Mascherin, Montreal, translator, for listening to me far too often and for her encouragement and hospitality during research trips to Montreal; Anna Carlevaris, St. Bruno, photographer and scholar, for long talks and years of mutual interests; my brothers and sisters, John, Martin, Dan and Dianne, for putting up with me longer than my friends have; my relatives—uncles and aunts who lived through this war and understood the importance of the project. I would also like to thank my parents, John and Anne, first for their wartime service to their country (John, air gunner, RCAF; Anne, sergeant stationed in London, Canadian Army), and for their support of this undertaking; my husband and editor John, for his patience with me and for understanding how this book grew and why; my daughter, Eleanor, a light, who has learned to read and knows the power of stories.

Finally, I must thank two people who were absolutely instrumental in the creation of this book: Lt. Col. Edward Smith, Ottawa, who was the first Guinea Pig I met, who opened his personal library to me, talked to me about the Club, and met with me whenever I needed information or a reminder of why I was writing the book; and Dr. Lionel "Hank" Hastings, Regina, who wrote the Summary of the Executive (Appendix A), and who offered me his expertise, advice, and files, as well as his fine memory, his time and his hospitality which enabled this book to move forward whenever the throttle was stuck, and whose love of, and respect for, the Guinea Pig Club, is infectious.

Lionel Hastings and Edward Smith are the guardian angels of this story. It is because of them that the book exists. That said, any inadvertent omissions, or errors in the text, are my own.

Introduction

The following is the story of a club. Already I have misled you as you, perhaps, conjure up images of leisure activities, a game of golf or cards, a group of people who come together to share a pleasurable pastime. The word "club", like so many other words in this story, will have to be re-defined so that, some fifty-five years after the end of the Second World War, these imprecise words can attempt to convey what it meant to be a young airman who might be on "ops" that night, hoping his "kite" wouldn't "prang" or get "coned", hoping he would make it back, instead, from a "piece of cake" mission. The empty bunks told a different story daily, but in all of the airman's dreams or nightmares never could he have imagined that a few seconds in the plane would alter him forever, change the way he saw the world, and the way the world saw him.

"Fried," they called themselves. "Fried" or "mashed" or "hash-browned." Choose one. It was your introduction into this most exclusive of organizations, The Guinea Pig Club. Remember, the language is important here. These men would be swift to remind you that it is they who call themselves Guinea Pigs, they who entered the Queen Victoria Hospital for a bit of "slabbing", going "for the chop" after being fried. In the argot-rich atmosphere of the air force perhaps it was inevitable that young men with quick minds and a quick turn of phrase would continue their banter even after horrifying injuries left them damaged and disfigured.

But the Guinea Pig Club is far more than banter. How else to explain an organization that has existed since 1941, that boasted over 640 members, some 176 of them Canadian, and that remains active to this day? How to explain the Canadian Wing, built and financed by Canadians and staffed with Canadian doctors and nurses who also took part in this wartime exercise of the human spirit?

Keeping in mind the mutability of language and of time, two points need comment. The first, to do with language: the Canadian Wing refers to two distinct things, the actual Canadian Wing of the hospital, which opened in July, 1944, and the Canadian Wing of the parent Guinea Pig Club, the branch that exists in Canada. The second point, regarding time, has to do with the structure of the book. Following Dr. McIndoe's edict that an injured airman was his patient from the moment he crashed, not the moment he entered the hospital, I have positioned the entries as much as possible, according to the date the men were injured, not the time they arrived at East Grinstead.

Language and time. Two factors that sabotage most attempts at recording history. This book has been a personal exercise in conceding to both language and time their various powers while attempting nonetheless to listen, to hear the voices still telling these stories. The airmen in this book deserve no less.

Language is what we have and as days pass there are fewer voices speaking the words. It is time, it is past time, to tell this tale. Our young airman has been reticent too long.

The Guinea Pig Anthem

We are McIndoe's army,
We are his Guinea Pigs.
With dermatomes and pedicles,
Glass eyes, false teeth and wigs.
And when we get our discharge
We'll shout with all our might:
'Per ardua ad astra,'
We'd rather drink than fight.

John Hunter runs the gas works,
Ross Tilley wields a knife.
And if they are not careful
They'll have your flaming life.
So, Guinea Pigs, stand steady
For all your surgeons' calls;
And if their hands aren't steady
They'll whip off both your ears.

We've had some mad Australians,
Some French, some Czechs, some Poles.
We've even had some Yankees,
God bless their precious souls.
While as for the Canadians—
Ah! That's a different thing.
They couldn't stand our accent
And built a separate Wing.

We are McIndoe's army,
(*as first verse*)

The Beginning

The Canadian men who were fated to become Guinea Pigs were fighting the allied cause in the skies. The casualties of the air war—the relatively new term for this technologically advanced form of warfare—would almost inevitably have suffered burns and disfigurement from exploding fuel tanks and fractures, breaks and lacerations from crashes. It is a fact of war that such inevitabilities were expected and planned for in the time leading up to the Battle of Britain.

The British Ministry of Health's Emergency Medical Service sought hospitals, preferably those away from target London, that could be converted or modified to accommodate these casualties. In East Grinstead, a small town some fifty kilometres south of London, stood the Queen Victoria Cottage Hospital. East Grinstead was a village dating back to the 1600s. It was friendly and comfortable, and this was to be as significant a factor in the survival of the men as was the hospital itself. It was to become "the little town with the big heart."

The hospital would have to be equipped to serve severely burned men. It is hard to understand, today, what an undertaking this must have been. Hospitals of the period treated burn victims with the known methods—escharotics such as gentian violet and tannic acid to close the wounds and prevent infection. A common sight was that of limbs rendered useless, encased in crusted sheaths of dried gentian violet. Amputation was also common.

The inability to properly treat burn victims was due in part to the relatively low number of burn patients. The First World War had brought its share, of course, and there were also civilian tragedies, but it was not until the Second World War that the doctors and surgeons would see the numbers and the kinds of burns, the "raw material" that would enable them to make advancements in this field.

So the hospitals they were hoping to set up would have to be ready to rebuild jaws and cheekbones, to fashion whole new faces and hands. This would be the work of plastic and dental surgeons. Essentially, a maxillo-facial unit would have to be built.

But where would they find such people? There were very few trained plastic surgeons in the British Isles at the time, it being, still, a somewhat rarefied profession. Sir Harold Gillies had done plastic surgery on some of the First War boys. He had performed early versions of the pedicle graft, in which a flap of skin is lifted from one part of the body, turned in on itself to form a tube, and attached to another part of the body. Such operations were not common. They would become highly visible routines at East Grinstead.

Sir Archibald McIndoe

As it turned out, one of the three plastic surgeons chosen by the Ministry was a young doctor by the name of Archibald McIndoe, a New Zealander by birth. Dr. McIndoe's appointment to the Queen Victoria Hospital is written up in the September 4, 1939, minutes of a meeting of the Board of Management of the hospital as:

> Mr. McIndoe has arrived to take over the Hospital on behalf of the Ministry of Health as a Maxillo-facial Hospital, although he has no written instructions.[1]

Perhaps prophetically, these words exemplified the many official responses to Archie McIndoe's style of operation. McIndoe didn't wait for officialdom. A civilian who refused an air force commission, McIndoe enjoyed both a charming and gregarious personality and a tenacity for autonomy when it came to the methods by which he ran his wards. He staffed his operating rooms with the best, a theatre nurse named Jill Mullins and a jovial, reassuring anaesthetist named John ("The Giant Killer") Hunter. These, together with an excellent medical support team of doctors, matrons, ward nurses and orderlies, were the backbone of the organization.

Sir Archibald McIndoe

Here was a man who was to become, to many of the British and allied Guinea Pigs, a kind of god, a larger than life figure who took them from physical and mental despair to the possibility of function, to the possibility, even, of hope.

When a man is lying in bed bandaged from head to toe, with eyelids gone, without a nose, it is hard to think of a useful life to come, harder still to believe there might be love and joy in his future. His life has crashed and burned and he is perhaps nineteen, perhaps twenty-one. Does he want to die? Quite possibly. He is in agony. If he is from a farm he remembers the merciful way a gravely injured animal is put down. Does he want to live? Hard to imagine when everything he once saw in his future, a few days ago, has disappeared in a blinding flash.

Yet there is someone beneath the bandages, someone the young man barely knows. The nurse who comes to moisten his lips, or to adjust his bandages, she seems to sense something. She has seen others like him. And she swears by the doctor who is making his rounds.

It would not be exaggerating to say that Archibald McIndoe was a visionary. It was McIndoe's creed that:

> The responsibility of the surgeon begins at the time
> of the accident and does not end until the patient is a
> fully functional, economic unit of society.

This statement predates our current theories of holistic medicine and whole-patient treatment by more than half a century, yet in looking at the patient as an entity that lives beyond the confines of the operating table McIndoe introduced a method that was to be the salvation of his men.

"The Maestro"—for they called him The Maestro and The Boss—had a plan, an unconventional one to say the least. In keeping with his philosophy regarding the duration of a physician's obligation to his patient, McIndoe challenged the "Ninety Day Law," a system whereby any airman absent from service for medical reasons for longer than ninety days received an automatic discharge. McIndoe decided that this was unreasonable given the nature of the absence. So he had the Ninety Day Law removed from within the walls of the Queen Victoria Hospital.

The next order of the day was to get rid of the hated hospital "blues" [garments]. McIndoe believed that if the patients were ever to be anything other than institutionalized, wasted men they would have to be treated as men, not as patients. A man lost his identity in the hospital blues. He lost attachment to his uniform, to the air. McIndoe felt that if anyone had earned the right to wear their uniforms it was these men. This suggestion was met with resistance among air ministry staff, but in a showdown in which McIndoe threatened to involve the media, McIndoe won. His men were permitted to wear their uniforms in the ward.

What else could he do to form a cohesive, functioning group? Something even more threatening to bureaucratic procedure than the uniform incident. McIndoe decided to abolish rank. This extraordinary step, like all the others, was done with the patient's welfare in mind. McIndoe had observed that NCOs seemed to recover better, and faster, than officers who were segregated. The camaraderie of other men, suffering the same way under the same conditions, seemed to play a role. Thus it was that, other than for medical reasons, McIndoe put everyone in the ward, and it was not uncommon to see a high-ranking officer with "scrambled eggs" on his hat, bunking next to a sergeant. To understand the magnitude of this arrangement one must imagine the combination of air force hierarchy and British class system. It was a bold and daring move.

But the public role of a man is only part of that individual. McIndoe had to see to their personal well-being too. After all, these were healthy young men who, normally, would have been

 going out for a drink and flirting with the girls. Archie McIndoe saw no reason for this to cease. He arranged for alcohol to be available on the ward. Beer was perpetually "on tap" in Ward III. As for the girls, well, Archie reasoned that any young man, scarred or unscarred, was interested in a pretty face. So he recruited the best-looking nurses he could find. After all, an attractive woman who would talk to and joke with a patient would make that patient far more likely to start feeling good about himself.

Remember: these early casualties were primarily veterans of the Battle of Britain, of Dunkirk, young fighter pilots who sat just above or behind the fuel tanks of their Hurricanes and Spitfires and ignited along with their firey planes. (McIndoe could tell what plane a man had been flying by the nature and severity of the burns.) Some of the most drastically disfigured Guinea Pigs were in this early group. And yet McIndoe expected them to get on with their lives.

But if Archie McIndoe, by will and vision, managed to keep his ward a "happy place", what, ultimately, was the good of that? It is true that some patients were there, on and off, for two to three years, but what would it all have been worth if the men could not, for example, leave the safety of Ward III, or Marchwood Park where they went for Occupational Therapy? What if the thought of meeting people *out there* in the world was too much for them?

The last ingredient in the inspired mix was the town. East Grinstead, the sleepy little town of shops, cinema and pubs, was to be the proving ground for the men. Early, very early on in their stay at the hospital they would be encouraged—participants might say forced—from their beds and wheeled, driven, shuttled down to one of the local pubs.

The Whitehall, for example, was extremely popular with the men. The genial host, Bill Gardiner, would pour a few pints and they would be served by a woman who had seen far worse than this lot. She would barely glance at the bandaged faces, the tubes that led here and there, the flaps and 'sausages' of skin that were growing out of chests and off faces. She placed the pint down and the young man, if he had anything to work with, even stumps instead of fingers, would pick up his pint with the rest. If his hands were useless, or gone, another man held the glass to his mouth, or the straw to his wired jaw. This was the pub. This was downtown East Grinstead, and the people beside them were locals. They took a liking to these young lads, and when the Allies came in larger droves as the war went on, they took a liking to them as well. They bought them a drink. Many a young man staggered back to the hospital and to the understanding countenance of the night duty nurse, who would bolster him with a cup of tea before tumbling him into bed. The people took these young men home to supper, out to dances and to the pictures. The medical staff took them into London to the theatre. In a bizarre way, many of the boys had never had it so good.

One wonders, though, whether it would have all worked out as it did were it not for the magical combination of Archibald McIndoe, the Queen Victoria Hospital, and the citizens of East Grinstead. It was this combination that gave the men, in 1941, the humour and the strength to form The Guinea Pig Club.

The Birth of the Club

There weren't many of them on hand that July morning in the small brown hut that was Ward III. Those who were there were quite probably hungover from the night before, having enjoyed the curious, surreal atmosphere that had turned a burn ward into a gentleman's drinking club. In the sober light of that Sunday morning a Czech fighter pilot, Frankie Truhlar, suggested a civilized glass of sherry might be in order.

There they sat, men who would have been shuffled off to a home or a chronic-care facility, who would almost certainly have been isolated from one another, were this the previous war. But this camaraderie born of nights at the pub, days of dressing changes, mornings and mornings of surgery, this was a good thing, wasn't it? It should be commemorated, they reasoned. After all, it wasn't just "anybody" who could sit in with this group. You had to have been fried magnificently, or mashed along with your plane. You had to have gone for the chop at the hand of Archie McIndoe. Perhaps you had more slabbing in store and were in the middle of your reconstruction. After all, you were a guinea pig, weren't you?

And so it was that the Club began, called by its original name: "The Maxillonian Club whose members call themselves the Guinea Pigs." The minutes of that first meeting indicate that the objectives of the club were "to promote good fellowship among and to maintain contact with approved frequenters of Queen Victoria Cottage Hospital." It was at this meeting that the classes of membership were outlined:

1) The Guinea Pigs (patients)
2) The Scientists (doctors, surgeons, and members of the medical staff)
3) The Royal Society for the Prevention of Cruelty to Guinea Pigs (friends and benefactors)

One can sense in these designations the exuberance of a college or university "club." They elected Archibald McIndoe president. The appointment of their executives is a by now famous story: F/O Bill Towers Perkins was chosen as secretary because his damaged hands prevented him from writing; P/O Peter C. Weeks was chosen treasurer because he was unable to walk and would not disappear with the funds.

The Club began innocently enough. It was a lark; it added an amusing formality to the drinking sessions. But Archie McIndoe and the Guinea Pigs were soon to realize that it offered them far more. The Maestro saw it like this: the lone airman in the iron-frame bed is feeling pretty bad. But something can be done for his eyes, immediately. Something can be done for his hands. Archie introduces him to another fellow who has also seen fire up close. The man has new eyelids, his cheek has been rebuilt, and in his scarred hands are a deck of cards. He will teach the new boy what he needs to know, how he will get every type of support except pity, because pity isn't support and this isn't a hotel for the self-indulgent and as soon as his hands are out of the bandages it will be his turn to deal.

While the majority of these early Guinea Pigs were with the RAF, "the Few," it must be remembered that many nations were flying with the Royal Air Force at the time. There were Czech and Polish pilots, French, Australian, and American airmen. And Canadian.

The Canadians were special. While there were Canadians involved all along, it was with the full activity of Bomber Command in 1943 that the numbers rose. So, inevitably, did the casualties. Fortunately, the Canadians were to have their own Archibald McIndoe in the person of their beloved "Wingco," Dr. A. Ross Tilley.

Dr. Tilley

Who was this enigmatic doctor the men reverently and affectionately referred to as their Wingco? A. Ross Tilley was born in Bowmanville, Ontario, in 1904, himself the son of a doctor. It is said that the young Tilley gave his first anaesthetic at the age of twelve, assisting his father. His formal training included graduation from the University of Toronto Medical School (1929), and further training in Vienna, the Royal Infirmary in Edinburgh, and Bellevue Hospital in New York. Upon completion of this period he set up practice in Toronto, joining 400 (City of Toronto)

Dr. Ross Tilley

Squadron as a Medical Officer in 1935 and studying plastic surgery with Canada's first plastic surgeon, Dr. Fulton Risdon.

As was the case with Archibald McIndoe, Ross Tilley was one of the few plastic surgeons in his country. Doctors with these special skills were going to have very large roles to play in the service of their countries.

In 1939, Dr. Tilley joined the active forces and became a captain in the Royal Canadian Army Medical Corps. He soon transferred to the RCAF Medical Branch and in 1941 became its chief medical officer overseas. In time wing commander, and later group captain, Ross Tilley went to East Grinstead. This was soon after the creation of the Guinea Pig Club, and Ross Tilley met the men in Ward III, the "Sty."

It would have been fascinating to have been present at the meeting of the two surgeons: Archie McIndoe, outgoing, charming, a man showing off his home turf; Ross Tilley, quiet, gracious, learning the language of the Sty. That these two men took a liking to one another is evident; that each saw the potential in the other is one of the happy occurrences of this story. For in 1942 Ross Tilley had settled himself in at the Queen Victoria Hospital, operating on the ever-increasing caseload of airmen who were entering the Guinea Pig Club.

The surgery was innovative: all forms of grafts were being employed, modified to each patient's particular situation: Tiersch grafts, flap grafts, stamp grafts, dermatome grafts, pedicle grafts.

Dr. Tilley worked on all areas but his specialty was hands, hands so damaged that in another time they would have been amputated [see the story of George Wilson].

One has to realize that unlike a single surgery to remove an appendix, plastic and reconstructive surgery involved a series of operations that slowly, graft by graft, built back a nose, or the skin of a hand. Success was measured incrementally, with a set of usable stumps slowly returning to functioning, articulated limbs.

The number of victims increased with the number of bombing runs. Whitleys, Halifaxes and Lancasters crashed and burned as readily as did Spitfires, Hurricanes and Typhoons. It meant, sometimes, two or more members of the same crew sharing the hospitality of the Sty.

Ward III was overcrowded and with no immediate end to the war in sight, something had to be done. Dr. Tilley was in a position to know what was needed, and he used his influence with those in authority. The result was that the Canadian government decided to build a Canadian Wing on the hospital. This was to be an all-Canadian operation from the ground up: a fifty-bed ward was to be constructed by Canadian Army Engineers, staffed by Canadians Dr. Tilley and Dr. Norman Park, his anaesthetist, and Canadian surgeons, doctors, nurses, orderlies and dieticians. It would handle the Canadian boys, and any overflow from the parent ward, and after the war it would be turned over to the Queen Victoria Hospital and the people of England as a permanent memorial to the men who passed through its doors. The ward would open in July 1944. By this time Dr. Tilley would have received the Order of the British Empire.

But who was the man, the full-time surgeon/mentor/father-figure to these young boys away from home? It is difficult to think of pilots, navigators, wireless operators, flight engineers, bomb-aimers and gunners as boys. Their function was that of men, their responsibilities huge and far-reaching, but it serves us to remember that most of these airmen were eighteen to twenty-one years old.

In our present day and circumstances such young men would be in school, or working their first jobs. But *these* young men grew up in their cockpits and turrets as they made decisions that affected one another's lives.

Yet while they rapidly came of age in some respects, in others most were boys whose first trips away from home had been the trip down to the local manning depot. Many had joined up from their mothers' kitchens. Many had yet to have a steady girlfriend. And there was plenty of time to think about what you didn't have or what you might not get while lying in a burn ward waiting for an operation.

Dr. Ross Tilley was there, a quiet man of great authority, a calm, athletic, humorous man who could sit you down and talk to you or just listen as you went on. He was a constant in a world that had so rapidly changed. He was an excellent surgeon who told you he could repair your useless arm and you believed him. And when your hand, still bandaged, was doing a little better, he was the man who accompanied you to the pub and watched with a smile as you successfully negotiated the pint to your lips.

As the Guinea Pigs will readily admit, Dr. Tilley was more than a surgeon. Dr. Tilley, like Dr. McIndoe, was a fierce advocate on behalf of the men in his care. And like Dr. McIndoe, Tilley tapped into the curious energy that came from the Guinea Pig Club, realizing that along with proper medical care it was the ticket to the reintegration of these men into society.

Guinea Piggery

There were no psychiatrists at the Queen Victoria Hospital. There was one who visited, once, and it is said that after he wandered around observing he commented that, basically, his services weren't needed.

Which is not to say there wasn't private anguish and terrible pain. Many Guinea Pigs have said they don't know how they got through the first few days after their crash. Others would admit to challenges that exist to this day. But the self-pity, the giving up and despairing, was nowhere on Ward III, and it would be kept at bay in the Canadian Wing as well. One phrase that echoed through both halls was that "there was always someone worse off than you were." This was, in most cases, correct, and— ironically—the most severely injured and disfigured individuals were often the most cheerful. It is as if, through this baptism by fire, they had in the truest sense been "born again" to the importance, simply, of being alive. And by the example of their lives they echo Archibald McIndoe's quote, which has become a credo for the Club:

> We are the trustees of each other. We do well to
> remember that the privilege of dying for one's country
> is not equal to the privilege of living for it.

As has been said, words have to be defined and re-defined in this story. The Canadian Wing is not only the physical extension of a hospital, it is also what would become the Canadian branch of the parent Guinea Pig Club. The members of this Canadian Wing include allied non-Canadians who settled in Canada sometime after the war as well as Canadians who live in the United States.

Men started burning prior to the July 1944 opening of the Canadian Wing of the Queen Victoria Hospital. These early Guinea Pigs were housed primarily in Ward III. Dr. Tilley was there as of 1942. And, of course, Archie McIndoe was there.

It is time to meet some of the members of the Club.

Guinea Pigs (1941–1942)

Gerald Dufort

Gerald Dufort

Not strictly a member of the Canadian Wing of the Guinea Pig Club, Gerald "Gerry" Dufort was very probably the first of the Canadians in Ward III, entering the Queen Victoria Hospital in October of 1941 after having crashed his Whitley on October 16, in England. A Montrealer serving with the RAF, the young sergeant air gunner was pulled from the burning wreckage of his plane. He was sent first to Durham County Hospital where he received sulphanimalide powder for his burns, Canada's Red Cross contribution to the healing process. From there he went to Lincolnshire and finally to East Grinstead.

He would have much work done at East Grinstead. There were new eyelids to be built, the nose needed work, and new lips had to be cut to fashion a new mouth. Dufort had had the benefit of early contact with Archie McIndoe, Ross Tilley and the Sty. He had the saline bath treatment, and early grafting. Despite the severity of his burns, he was doing well in Ward III.

Gerry Dufort befriended Guinea Pig Bill Martin when Martin arrived in the Sty. Dufort can be spotted, in early ward photographs, in his silver lounging robe. The engaging Dufort was also known to sport a cigarette holder and to go on and on about the eccentricities of the English. It seems somehow fitting that he settled in England after the war, married an English girl and now counts himself a proud member of the parent Guinea Pig Club.

Dufort maintains his ties with Canada, his friendship with Bill Martin, and his loyalty to the Guinea Pig Club. As he says:

> Belonging to the Club has meant a great deal, and
> the reunions every year [the British Club celebrates

every year; the Canadian Club now every two years] have been the basis for lifelong friendships.

As well, Dufort admits:

> The Canadian Wing of the hospital has always been much appreciated, the memory of Ross Tilley and company always maintained.

William E. Martin

William E. "Bill" Martin is another Quebecker who was an early entry into the Club. His story of Guinea Piggery begins in Malta where on October 16, 1941, the same day as Gerry Dufort, this F/O air gunner crashed and burned. Two members of RAF ground crew, one of whom received the George Medal, Britain's highest civilian honour for bravery, pulled him from his burning Blenheim. Martin was rolled in the dirt and the fire extinguished. He was in bad shape:

William "Bill" Martin

> I had burns to my face, hands, arms, back and I had multiple fractures. All my ribs were broken and some went through my lungs.... I spit out all my teeth.

He was then taken to No. 90 General Hospital in Imtarfa. Unfortunately for Bill Martin, the hospital was not equipped to deal with burns in a modern or enlightened manner. He was "strapped and wrapped" because of his fractures and burns and given the standard treatment—gentian violet applied to the wounds to counteract infection and tannic acid sprayed on the surface. The result of this treatment is akin to tanning leather; a hard crust forms causing limbs to become virtually useless. In Martin's case, the infection began oozing through the cracks in the tannic acid. He was taken to the operating room where, under general anaesthetic, the tannic acid was scrubbed off. Then it was back to the bandages. Martin describes the rest of his treatment at this hospital:

One day the head surgeon decided that he was going to graft the back of my hand, regardless of the infection that was still prevalent in my system. Needless to say that within four days, the stench was so unbearable that the nursing sister decided to take off the pressure bandages, and of course the graft had not taken. All that was left on the back of my hand was a great array of stitches. They wiped off the graft with a piece of gauze leaving me with open flesh on the back of my hand as well as the open wound of the donor area. The would-be plastic surgeon never did return. I had been his guinea pig.

One can hear the anger and dismay in the voice of this early airman. The reaction to this unrest—Archie McIndoe and Ward III—must have seemed a godsend.

But it would take Bill Martin a while to get to East Grinstead. In one of those cases of unrequested world travel, he was discharged on Christmas Eve 1941 and transferred to the Luqa, Malta, bomber station to await transportation to the United Kingdom. It was January 14, 1942, when he boarded the *Berkenshire* for transport to Alexandria. He was put in hospital for two days in Alexandria, then transferred to the RAF station at Abequir, Egypt, where he spent three weeks in a tent. He then boarded the *Louis Pasteur* and eventually journeyed to Capetown, then Freetown, finally docking in the Clyde, at Greenoch, Scotland. From there it was on to the RAF Hospital in Halton, Buckinghamshire, which he arrived at on April 22, 1942. On that day Bill Martin learned that his brother Emmerson had gone missing in a "Wimpey" [Wellington] flying from Malta to Egypt.

At Halton, Bill Martin was again poked and prodded by doctors but was left in the dark as to his future treatment. Threatening to leave, he was brought up before the chief surgeon. There was a civilian doctor present, and he examined Martin. By this time more than mistrustful of doctors, Martin demanded, "Who are you?"

Martin tells it like this:

He advised me that his name was Archibald McIndoe...a plastic surgeon. I recoiled at the term plastic surgeon and told him I wanted nothing more to so with his ilk. I asked to see a Canadian in authority to discuss my future. He then stated that he had a

Canadian surgeon working with him in East Grinstead who would be able to help me with all my problems. So I said, "What are we waiting for? Let's go."

Martin was about to encounter not only Ross Tilley but the fabled Ward III. Given back his uniform, he was transported to East Grinstead where one of the first people he met was none other than Gerry Dufort:

> The first patient I met was a French Canadian from Montreal who had heard my Canadian accent and, donned in an elaborate dressing gown and coloured p.j.'s, came strolling over to my bed to inquire where I was from and where I had been injured.

It was the beginning of their long friendship.

Martin was to meet Dr. Tilley the following day. He remembers it this way:

> [Tilley] sat down with us and diagnosed our problems man-to-man. We weren't treated as cast-offs. We were treated as equals.

Tilley quickly assessed the situation. Martin would need radiation treatment to soften the scar tissue which would then be removed. The nose would be straightened, the mouth redesigned, the upper and lower lips replaced. But the first operation, following the radiation treatment, would be on the right hand to repair the previous surgeon's work. Tilley hoped to have Martin regain the use of that hand.

Bill Martin trusted Tilley and the result was "a complete graft of the back of my hand and the webbing between the fingers completed in one operation." It is no wonder that he referred to Dr. Tilley as "an artist."

Bill Martin stayed at the hospital for eight months and had seven operations. "Part of my nose came from my thigh. Part of my cheek came from my stomach. Part of my upper lip came from under my arm." Martin returned home after the war to marry Edna, and they are now proud grandparents. He would become very active in the postwar Guinea Pig Club, attending reunions and serving on the executive. He is justifiably proud of his participation in the Club, noting that some ninety-eight percent of its members have gone on to lead highly successful lives.

C.A.L. Hurry

Another very early Guinea Pig was C.A.L. "Lyall" Hurry. Originally from Newcastle, Hurry was a Hurricane pilot involved in the Battle of Britain. Sergeant Hurry took part in operations with 43 and 46 Squadrons, RAF. On August 8, 1940, his Hurricane was slightly damaged during combat south of the Isle of Wight. Hurry was unharmed. On September 15 flying from North Weald, his Hurricane was damaged following combat over London. Again Hurry was unharmed. But on September 18 his Hurricane was shot down in combat, crashing at Sillingbourne, Swale. Hurry later said:

> I forgot to look over my shoulder. There was another 109 behind me, and I was on my own.

Burned and wounded, Sergeant Hurry bailed out, . A piece of fuselage panel from Hurricane P. 3816, C.A.L. Hurry's plane, resides in the Kent *Battle of Britain Museum*, Hawkinge. His photograph hangs in the Mayor's Parlour of the Swale Borough Council, and historical reports of his exploits have appeared in the *Daily Mail* and the *Daily Express*. C.A.L. Hurry, AFC, went on to be the personal pilot to Sir. Roderick Hill, Air Ministry, London.

C.A.L. "Lyall" Hurry

Lyall Hurry moved to Canada in the postwar period and counted himself an active member of the Canadian Wing. He and his wife Ella had two sons. C.A.L. Hurry died in 1995, completing a life lived by his squadron's motto: *Gloria Fini*. Glory is the End.

Looking at the dates of C.A.L. Hurry's brushes with mortality one can appreciate the frequency of these sorties. The Battle of Britain taxed its "few" with tremendous responsibility.

Zdzislaw Krasnodebski

This responsibility is evidenced by another Battle of Britain veteran, a Polish fighter ace named Zdzislaw Krasnodebski (another Guinea Pig who would later become a Canadian). Polish fighter pilots had already been put to the test over the skies of their homeland. Krasnodebski, the commander of a fighter squadron in 1939, was told at the time to transfer his unit from Okecie, near Warsaw, to a temporary field. From this temporary landing field they flew over Warsaw and into combat with German planes.

One can appreciate how early this occurred. On September 3, 1939, following a dogfight with Messerschmidt 110s, Krasnodebski was to have his first experience in a burning aircraft:

> Returning to the area of recent battle, I perceived a solitary Messerschmidt. I knew only too well by now that this machine would prove faster than mine—I could not, therefore, hope to approach him from behind and reach a distance short enough for a successful shot. I decided to attack head-on. We flew directly at each other—I held my fire, hoping to open up from a position close enough to allow my two machine guns to have the maximum effect. The German had a much greater strength, being in the possession of four machine guns and two cannons— he opened fire much sooner. When I saw the traces of his shots in the line of my flight I turned my craft abruptly upwards to escape the range of his fire—that very moment my plane received a direct hit and turned into flames.

Krasnodebski jumped from the plane. His parachute opened, and from his vantage point he watched his craft:

> spinning downward, dragging a ribbon of smoke and fire behind it—in a moment it would crash against the ground and become just a shapeless mass of metal.

He did not have long to ponder this, as the Messerschmidt turned and headed back in his direction. One of Krasnodebski's friends had met his end as a parachuting target. Fortunately for Krasnodebski an allied aircraft came to his aid, scoring a direct hit on the German plane.

This close call did not deter Krasnodebski from his desire to fight. He travelled to France and flew there, and when France fell, he made his way to England where, in 1940, he was stationed at Blackpool. There he organized and commanded the famous 303 Polish Fighter Squadron, which flew Hurricanes out of Northolt. The squadron was successful but the cost was high. On one day in particular, a day Krasnodebski would long remember, only five of their twelve aircraft returned from operations. One of the planes that did not return was Zdzislaw Krasnodebski's.

They were to have attacked a bomber formation heading for London at 20,000 feet. Going after an enemy bomber, Krasnodebski was hit:

> I noticed brightly burning gasoline pouring out of the severely bullet-punctured tank into the cockpit and filling it with flames. I opened the cockpit, rapidly undid the belts, disconnected the radio, the oxygen mask, and jumped. Doing this, the memory of my previous experience of the parachute jump was back; [it] came to me in a flash—I decided not to open my parachute then in order to get out, as quickly as possible, from the shooting range.

After he opened his chute and was drifting toward the earth, he became aware of the pain in his burned hands and legs. He found he was still a target of sorts in that the Home Guard had their rifles trained on this burning parachutist in the unfamiliar (Polish) uniform who hardly spoke a word of English.

Above right: Zdzislaw Krasnodebski with Sir Archibald McIndoe

Krasnodebski, later Group Captain Krasnodebski, was taken to East Grinstead, where Archibald McIndoe and company repaired him. "Before a year was out, I was ready to fly again."

Group Captain Krasnodebski, "Kras" to the early Club members, and his wife Wanda settled in Canada after the war where he remained a proud member of the Guinea Pig Club until his death.

Tadeusz Podbereski

Another man who put his trust in Archie and the team was Tadeusz "Teddy" Podbereski, a Polish Guinea Pig who would come to Canada after the war and eventually join the Canadian Wing. Teddy Podbereski's encounter with the Maestro went something like this:

> "Teddy, what kind of a nose would you like me to fix for you, a Roman one, perhaps?"—And he was serious, I know! I was lost. I raced through my whole life and, finally, I said: "I have always been an ugly duckling so I might as well stay that way; I will feel more secure with a normal nose." I gave him an old photograph and although the Great Man was not pleased, he was loyal. He transplanted my hip bone to my forehead and nose and the results are there today.

Podbereski became fascinated with plastic surgery to the point of pondering the possibility of studying medicine after the war. He was dissuaded when he understood the depth of study. But it was Archibald McIndoe's letters of recommendation that got him into school in Britain and into a career in Quebec where he married and had a family. He later moved to Ontario. He continued to keep in touch with the Guinea Pig Club until his death.

Gordon Frederick

Gordon "Freddy" Frederick was in a Hampden torpedo bomber when the plane crashed into a gasoline dump in 1941. Severely burned in both the eyes and nose, he nonetheless was able to see the skin on his hands hanging from his fingertips "like inside-out gloves." He was taken to East Grinstead where, five days after being operated on, he was taken to a concert in town. "I was a shocking sight," he realized. Yet, he *enjoyed* the concert. He had passed the big test; he had "seen and been seen."

Freddy Frederick recovered and returned home. The Cambridge engineer married Lynne and had a child. He died in July 1994.

Edward W. Smith

Edward "Ed" or "Smithy" Smith is an example of someone who returned to his duties after his stay in East Grinstead. Edward Smith, of Sherbrooke, Quebec, joined the RCAF on July 4, 1940. He had been working at an accounting job when duty called. His father preferred that he enter the air force because, as a First War veteran, he had dreaded the thought of his son in the trenches.

Smith was selected for pilot training and received his wings in February 1941.

Then it was off to Halifax where he boarded an armed merchant ship headed for Europe. He stopped off in Iceland to transfer to another ship. The merchant ship that had ferried him over was returning to Halifax when the following day it was torpedoed with a loss of all hands.

Ed Smith

Edward Smith was posted to 102 Squadron in Yorkshire, flying Whitleys, and began the first of sixty ops over enemy territory. His first encounter with the kind of "dicey" conditions that often gained one entrance to the Guinea Pig Club occurred in the summer of 1941. Smith was flying over Dunkirk when he met with ack-ack fire which hit the fuel tanks. This was an older Whitley bomber, one not equipped with self-sealing tanks. But Smith pressed on to Frankfurt, the target, and dropped his bomb load.

On the way back over the English Channel they ran out of what little petrol was left in the tanks. The wireless operator sent a distress signal giving their location, and "Smithy" managed to land the aircraft on the water. Smith got to sit in the dinghy waiting and hoping for rescue. Six hours later a search plane spotted them and arrangements were made for them to be picked up. Fortunately, there were no injuries. The men thus joined the Goldfish Club for landing on the water.

The men were given a week's leave and then it was back on ops. The target, again, was Frankfurt. They made their way across, successfully dropped their bombs, and were almost back to their base at Topcliffe. Smith was making the final approach to land. As was the policy, only at the final moment were the drem lights switched on, to minimize the possibility to attack. That brief illumination was enough light, and enough time, for a German night-fighter to blow the port rudder off the Whitley and set fire to the engines.

They were too low to bail out. The crash killed over half the crew: the co-pilot, the navigator and the wireless operator. The air gunner was unharmed. Ed Smith was thrown out of the cockpit. He was in flames. The gunner put the flames out but Smith had been severely injured. He had badly burned legs, hands and head, and he had a broken jaw.

He was brought to an army hospital north of the base. There his immediate burn needs were seen to, although the treatment was the usual gentian violet. He woke up a week after he arrived and witnessed the brown-coloured burnt skin on his body and on his face. His jaw was also wired. He was transferred to Rauceby Hospital where he had the strange wartime experience of spending his twenty-first birthday in a ward with strangers. One of the nurses brought in two bottles of Guinness so he could celebrate, perhaps inadvertently preparing Smith for entry into Ward III and the Sty.

Soon after this, as luck would have it, Archie McIndoe took a trip to Rauceby looking for potential patients. He studied Smith's hand. The burns were healed, but the gentian violet had done its work and the hand wouldn't close. Without the ability to grip the controls Smith would be unable to fly an aircraft. Archie felt there was something that could be done, which filled Smith with hope because, "I'd never heard of plastic surgery."

McIndoe arranged for Ed Smith to come down to the Queen Victoria Hospital. He arrived in January of 1942. There he received preliminary grafts. He also got acquainted with life in the Sty. As Smith recalls:

> I remember going into Ward III, the hut. I was shown my bed by one of the nursing sisters. Then someone came up and said, "Would you like a beer?" I'd just come from an RAF hospital, which was very disciplined. And I walk into this hospital and the first thing I'm asked is, "Would you like a beer?" And I said, "I'd love one."[2]

While waiting for the second round of surgery he returned to his squadron and took a ground job. Then it was back to the

Queen Victoria Hospital where Dr. Ross Tilley, hand specialist, removed the stiff flesh and grafted the hand with a piece of skin from Smith's leg. This was a full free graft, performed with the use of a cutting tool called a dermatome. It was this graft that would allow Smith to regain the full use of his hand.

He stayed a short while longer and then was back on ops, finishing his tour flying Halifax bombers. After this tour Smith was screened and sent to Scotland to instruct. Here he had the opportunity to add a bar to his Goldfish Club insignia when a port engine died on take-off with a student pilot at the controls. Smith took over and landed the plane safely in a bay.

He was sent to Canada for a month but returned for a second tour of operations. This time he flew Halifax bombers with 424 Squadron.

Smith met Jane McDonough, of Glasgow, the woman he would marry, while in Scotland near the end of the war. But though the war would end and they would return to Canada, it was not to be the end of Smith's flying career. As Lt. Col. Edward Smith, DSO, CD, says, the idea was to: "fix you up so that you could be sent back on flying. I was sent back flying—thirty years!"

Ed Smith's illustrious post-war flying included secondment to the United States Air Force, where he participated in 50 humanitarian missions during the Berlin airlift. He also was a pilot at Test and Development, at Rockliffe in Ottawa, during which time he took part in exercise "Muskox" in the Arctic, flying troop-carrying gliders which were "snatched up" from the ice by means of a cable and hook by a DC-3 in full flight. This exercise made him the first glider pilot to cross the Arctic Circle. As well, he was in command of the RCAF's first round the world flight, personally flying Prime Minister Lester B. Pearson to the New Delhi Commonwealth Conference in 1950.

Smith was promoted to squadron leader and spent the years 1950-1953 in Vancouver as officer commanding, 442 Auxillary Support Units. Following this, Smith transferred to the All Weather OTU at North Bay and was promoted to wing commander to command 428 All Weather Fighter Squadron. In 1958 he transferred to Cold Lake to command the All Weather OTU. Smith continued in a career that saw him transfer to Allied Air Forces Central Europe in Fontainbleu, France, in 1964, as staff officer ground environment. Back in Canada at the end of that year, he was appointed Deputy Director Bilingualism at Air Force Headquarters. He retired from the force in 1970, but like many Guinea Pigs he continued to search out new challenges, new careers.

Smith worked for the Department of Energy, Mines and Resources as Director of Security, and for Statistics Canada as a Senior Labour Force Survey Interviewer. He also found time to earn a degree in political science from Carleton University.

Ed and Jane Smith raised a family. Their daughter Rosemary is a graduate of McGill University and their sons, Donald and Kevin, are both graduates of the Royal Military College. Today, Ed and Jane Smith live in Ottawa.

Edward Smith's story underlines the purpose for treating these men. The primary justification was that a flier be back in the sky as soon as possible. Already we see that were it not for the type and variety of operations being performed at the Queen Victoria Hospital by Archibald McIndoe and Ross Tilley, men like Edward Smith would not have been able to return to active duty. So the innovative surgery techniques were fulfilling the military's objective while they were also giving men back their pride, their jobs and their lives.

But while some men survived their crashes, and their surgeries, and went back on ops, for others it was not to be.

Richard L. Turnbull

For Richard L. Turnbull, the entry fee for membership in the Club was a chance flight in a Wellington one January night in 1942. Turnbull had arrived in England in 1941. The wireless operator/air gunner was with 405 Squadron flying missions that bombed the docks at Dunkirk. He had also gone on ops over Berlin, "The Big City", as well as sorties over Wilhelmshaven, Emden, and St. Nazaire.

Then on the night of January 17, 1942, when he and the crew were on leave, he received word from a navigator that the CO wanted to go out that night. Would he volunteer to go? Richard Turnbull volunteered.

After crossing the English coast heading toward Bremen, the navigator sent the message that there was trouble in the starboard engine. He suggested they turn back to base at Pocklington. The "trouble" was a fire. They tried to turn back, hoping, if not to get back to base, to at least position themselves to be able to bail out over land.

Turnbull was getting into his parachute. The plane was in a glide, and according to the readings, they were still at 2,000 feet. But the altimeter was wrong—and they hit the North Sea hard. Turnbull was thrown forward smashing his face on an extension of the instrument panel. The water flowing over the wing "looked like oil." Turnbull says:

> It was fortunate I was thrown forward as the plane went straight down, and I was washed out as the canopy over the cockpit broke away. As I reached the surface the dinghy flipped over on top of me when the line broke which held it to the aircraft. The aircraft was sinking. At about the same time, the navigator, Flt Lt. Scrivens, came alongside so we got into the dinghy This was about 6:00 a.m.

The two survivors floated in the frigid North Sea waters. They were 14 hours in the dinghy, and one wonders what they did or said during that very long vigil.

As fate, or luck, or whatever providence one believes in would have it, there was a convoy returning from the North. The *HMS Leeds*, a destroyer, spotted the bobbing dinghy, and the men were picked up. They were put ashore on the Isle of Sheppy at the entrance to the Thames. There they were placed in a civilian hospital. Turnbull remained for a week to ten days. His major injury was not burns. His face had taken the brunt of the impact, his nose displaced to one side of his head. While in hospital a Russian doctor decided to do something about Turnbull s nose and manipulated it back into place.

Soon Turnbull was off to East Grinstead and Ward III where Archie McIndoe observed and followed up on treatment of the nose as well as treating the flier for "immersion foot," exposure of the foot to water for long periods of time.

Turnbull went up before the Review Board and was sent back on ops. Now in a Halifax, Turnbull spent time flying familiarization flights with various "sprog" (new) crews before crewing up and transferring to the south of England for coastal patrol work covering the Bay of Biscay.

Turnbull is philosophical about his lot. "I have led a charmed life through my experiences in the air force overseas." Besides surviving the North Sea crash that claimed the lives of most of the crew, he also avoided another brush with mortality. Back in

Yorkshire he was hospitalized with bronchitis. He missed his last op. On that flight, the entire crew was lost.

In cheating fate out of a W/O A/G, Turnbull survived to go home to Canada where he instructed in Winnipeg and eventually helped close stations in Winnipeg, Claresholme, Reinhold and Calgary. There he was discharged in 1946.

He would eventually make use of the services of the Christie Street hospital in Toronto where so many Guinea Pigs went for treatment after the war and where Dr. Tilley offered both a medical and an emotional bridge from East Grinstead to Canada. Because Tilley and the Guinea Pig Club were continuity. They gave a man a context. As Turnbull says, undoubtedly echoing many other fliers, "I'd been all over Europe but not on it." There was the service, and there was the Club.

Richard Turnbull married Loree, and they had a family. He enjoyed a career in the office equipment field and has attended many Guinea Pig Reunions.

Richard Turnbull was fixed up and then sent before the Review Board. He was pronounced fit to fly. One wonders how some of the men were able to handle this, yet as said before the military reason for repairing these men was so that they could go back and fight again. While some men could not return due to the extent of their injuries, many did return to the skies. In fact, it was not uncommon for a Guinea Pig return to flying, or at least to a ground job, between operations.

And, at East Grinstead, there were always other possibilities.

Robert Alexander Fraser

Bob Fraser

The trust in McIndoe and the Sty would be experienced by another early Canadian Guinea Pig, Robert Alexander "Bob" Fraser, who had trained as a fighter pilot, flying Spitfires. In 1942 his Spitfire was involved in a collision with a plane that had landed across its path. The result was dire. Bob Fraser lost his right arm in the crash and suffered severe facial injuries when his head hit the instrument panel.

He found himself in Ward III. There he received bone grafts to his nose and had other extensive facial repairs. While in the Sty he took the opportunity to introduce his British counterparts to the wonders of peanut butter and Laura Secord candies, undoubtedly secured from home. His British hosts would later refer to Fraser as a "character," which was something, coming from Ward III.

Typical of both Guinea Pigs and Canadians, Bob Fraser did not let his serious injuries cramp his dating style. He met and married his English wife, June, and took her home to Canada. He also took home an artificial arm which he soon disposed of, stating that it was "about the most damn useless thing ever invented."

The Frasers settled in Montreal after the war where Bob began teaching at Sir George Williams University (now Concordia University), at various times instructing in English, History and Political Science. This profession was to prevent him from attending the reunions of the parent Guinea Pig Club in East Grinstead, as, traditionally, they occurred in September when Fraser's teaching schedule was annually gearing up. He did attend Canadian reunions, however, and kept the Club informed of his life as a professor. Fraser was on staff during the infamous occupation of the computer centre at the university in the turbulent 1960s during which the computer centre was burned and destroyed. This prompted a drawing by Henry Standen, editor of *The Guinea Pig*. While on staff Fraser also was active in the 102 University Squadron for Officers and Officer Cadets, where he was promoted to Lieutenant Colonel. Bob Fraser took early retirement due to ill-health in 1973. He died in January of 1984.

Sydney Noyes

Sydney "Syd" Noyes arrived at East Grinstead in the summer of 1942 suffering from deep scar tissue, the result of a crash. The tissue on his hands had rigidified their movement. This was a standard outcome of standard treatment. At the Queen Victoria Hospital Noyes underwent a series of operations that would gradually bring mobility and function back to his hands. However, there was the intervening time between operations to be dealt with. As stated, the purpose was to get the boys up and around and flying, or up and useful, or at least up and home. Between operations, many of the men were quite capable, and Archie McIndoe saw a potential that could be tapped.

Accordingly, patients were "loaned out" to industry. There were many reasons for this. First of all the patient, who wished to remain mentally and physically active, was working, was focused on something other than his own worries and pain. Second, the patient was contributing, positively, to society where he, eventually, would return. A third reason was to be of benefit not to the patients but to the factory workers. There was a dissatisfaction among munition employees over the long hours of work and the modest wages. If they were suddenly to come face to face with some of Archie's boys, they might end up feeling rather fortunate.

McIndoe sent Canadians Syd Noyes, Jimmy Morrison, and Bill Martin, and three badly disfigured British Guinea Pigs, to Carrier Engineering in Wembly. The peacetime Carrier Engineering company manufactured heating and air conditioning units. The wartime company built air-sea rescue launches.

Syd Noyes, badly in need of therapy on his hands, was trained as an electric welder. He worked alongside an attractive factory girl. There were definite perks to the job.

Flying Officer Syd Noyes recovered from his wounds and his operations, returned to Canada, and became a postmaster in a town outside of Saskatoon.

Lorne Maxwell Cameron

Lorne M. Cameron of Roland, Manitoba, was a fighter pilot with 401 Spitfire Squadron. In 1942 he was shot down, and his injuries led him to East Grinstead where he was treated. While recuperating he was sent to a hotel in Torquay, Devon, which aided his rehabilitation. It was with sadness that he later learned that the hotel had been bombed, killing some forty to fifty defenceless airmen who were recuperating there.

Cameron returned to his squadron, eventually earning a DFC and becoming CO of the station. (He was fellow Guinea Pig Frank Hubbard's CO while he was stationed with 401.) Wing Commander Lorne Cameron returned to Canada listed as one of Manitoba's "war aces." He married Norma Claire, and in subsequent years was a tireless worker for Ducks Unlimited. A waterfowl conservation project at Shoal Lake, Manitoba, bears his name. Lorne Cameron died in 1997.

Orvel Dove

Orvel Dove was a young pilot with RAF 256 Squadron, a night-fighter Beaufighter squadron stationed at Squires Gate, Blackpool. Dove had joined up on September 13, 1940.

On February 10, 1942, after testing aircraft, he was in a car on the base. Unfortunately, a wayward aircraft collided with the vehicle. Dove suffered a broken femur, and a badly bashed up, slit head. He also lost three fingers.

He was taken to East Grinstead where he enjoyed the hospitality of Ward III. Dr. Tilley worked on Dove. The pilot was impressed with Tilley's abilities as a surgeon but was even more impressed with his ability to instil the notion that there was "still life out there."

Dove admits he was shocked when he first saw some of the other boys. He found it extraordinary that Tilley could get these devastatingly injured men to think positively:

> I felt that the friendships and the ability of the really injured ones to put their lives back together again was remarkable.

Orvel Dove was fairly mobile, so he walked around the town of East Grinstead. He could not get over how young the patients were.

Dove recovered from his wounds, but he did not go back on ops. Instead, for the remainder of the war he was stationed with Ferry Command, ferrying single-engined aircraft. He was discharged on September 13, 1945, five years to the day after he joined up. Orvel Dove married Olive after the war. They live in Kamloops, British Columbia.

Lawrence J. Somers

Unlike Orvel Dove, Lawrence "Larry" Somers was not to see the inside of the Queen Victoria Hospital until war's end, but his personal battle in the skies came to a crashing end on June 2, 1942.

Larry Somers, of Simcoe, Ontario, was a Spitfire type. On June 2 he was on his 110th mission. His aircraft was flying with forty-six others on a fighter sweep. They found themselves in contact with at least thirty enemy fighters. In due course Somers discovered his tank was hit.

Separated from the main group, twelve of the fighters tried to head home, but again Somers was hit. This time the bullets ignited the petrol that had spilled in the previous dog-fight.

Lawrence Somers

He was on fire. The plane was going down. Somers had to contend with his burns, with blinding smoke and with parachute silk. Then the world changed and he was, somehow, climbing into the rubber dinghy.

Now all he had to do was wait to be rescued. He was, after all, in the English Channel. Somers waited, floating helplessly for two days, his burned hands useless with the paddle. He was so close to home, yet he might as well have been a world away:

It was maddening. There I was, burned and suffering from exposure, floating around in sight of Beachy Head. At last I was picked up—by the Germans!

Thus began an odyssey that took Somers to Boulogne, then to St. Omer Hospital, where he was under the care of German doctors. His first four "postings" would be to hospital camps, and he would eventually endure the hospitality of ten different camps.

Somers had nothing bad to say about his care under German doctors; however, his interrogators were another story. By refusing to divulge anything other than his name and number while at the second hospital, he was denied a change of dressings for five days. Only someone who has been burned can truly appreciate how terrible a punishment this is.

Somers later was moved to a hospital staffed by British doctors. It was there that, during a routine change of dressings, it was discovered that there was a bullet hole through the top of his left ear. Somers must have had remarkable resilience for he was then taken to Stadtroda, where, as a mobile patient, he was able to assist in the care of Canadians wounded at Dieppe.

The war went on for this POW. As the Russians advanced from the east, Somers was one of the many allies forced to march

150 miles on foot and then spend three days travelling by truck, to a new location. When the allies pressed forward from the west, Somers was forced to march *back* some 200 miles!

Larry Somers finally got to East Grinstead in 1945. He had had some preliminary surgery done earlier, by an army doctor taken at Dunkirk:

> Whilst I was in the prison camp, I had some plastic surgery done on my burned eyelids...but as his instruments were a bit far gone (plating peeling off the scalpels and that sort of thing) he wasn't able to give of his best. However, all ended well when the war was over and I was brought across to East Grinstead where Ross Tilley did all that was needed.

This serves as a reminder of McIndoe's dictum that an airman became his patient the moment he was injured and remained so until he had returned to being a fully-functioning member of society.

Larry Somers was part of a fraternity even while in a German military hospital. And, true to the Guinea Pig form, it was not his circumstances that got to him as much as it was the topic of conversation:

> I was taken off to hospital and was well cared for. I have no complaints on that score. Mind you, I got very fed up with having to listen to the other patients— Luftwaffe characters—trying to tell me that the Spitfire was no good, that the Focke-Wulf was the fighter plane.

Larry Somers eventually returned to Canada, married Peggy, had a daughter, and studied Veterinary Medicine, earning a Doctor of Veterinary Medicine. Dr. Somers practised in his chosen field until ill health forced his retirement and, after a long illness, his death.

Larry Somers' extensive experience (110 missions) was no guarantee of safety. A career (or a face, or a life) could go up in flames in an instant.

Howard L. Phillips

Howard "Tex" Phillips was a Texas native. In 1941 he travelled to Detroit and then into Canada at Windsor to join the RCAF on January 12, 1941. He was classified for pilot training and did his Elementary Flying Training (EFTS) at Regina and his Service Flying (SFTS) at Yorkton, Saskatchewan. In November 1941 he received his pilot wings.

He was posted overseas and did his advanced and operational training and then joined 112 (Kittyhawk) Squadron which operated out of the western desert in North Africa. Phillips was involved in a crash in 1942 that sent him to hospital in Cairo with burns to the hands and face, and burns to the legs. Both jaws had been broken, and he had also cracked a vertebrae in his neck. Some preliminary plastic surgery was done in Cairo, but he returned to England in February 1943 for three months at East Grinstead where the bulk of the work was done.

He was soon considered fit to fly and was sent to an OTU for trial testing on Spitfires. He returned to operational flying on Spitfires, flying with 412 Spitfire Squadron at Biggin Hill, with 126 Wing. His squadron participated in the preparation for the D-Day landing in Normandy, attacking targets in Belgium and France and providing cover for bombers.

On D-Day + 12 his squadron was sent to France to provide close air support for the army with the 2nd Tactical Air Force. His squadron followed the army through France, Belgium and into Holland. While in Holland in November 1944 after a total of 178 missions, he was relieved of further duty and returned to Canada as a Flight Lieutenant. He spent some leave in Canada and the United States and then went to hospital in St. Thomas, Ontario, for some follow-up surgery.

Howard Phillips returned home to Texas to farm. He is presently retired and living in Green Valley, Arizona, with his wife Virginia.

John Broughton

John "Johnny" Broughton was born in Creelman, Saskatchewan. He enlisted in the RCAF and trained as an air gunner. Broughton was badly burned in a crash at OTU sometime in mid-1942 and was sent to Princess Mary's RAF Hospital. There he briefly met Jack Reynolds, a fellow Guinea Pig. Broughton would actually get to Archie, Ross and Ward III in January 1943, while Reynolds would follow in April. The two men passed time together in the Sty or in the annex between operations. Both remained at East Grinstead until January 1944.

For Broughton, it would be more operations back at Toronto's Christie Street Hospital following his return to Canada. After his discharge from the service he returned to Creelman where, for a short time, he ran a small café. It soon became clear, however, that the severity of the burns to his hands made this career impractical, so he went to work for the meteorological branch of the federal government in Regina and later in Thunder Bay and Winnipeg. His later career included working for a timber company in northern Alberta. Broughton continued an active life and career until his death.

Kenneth R. Fisher

Kenneth "Ken" Fisher joined the RCAF in March of 1941.

He went over to England where he took his final training at No. 14 OTU Cottesmore, Rutland.

Ken Fisher

It was during this training that he gained his entrance to the Guinea Pig Club. On August 31, 1942, during a low-level bombing exercise, Ken Fisher sustained third degree burns to his right hand and second degree burns to his face and left hand when the Hampden he was piloting crashed. Fisher describes it like this:

> It was a warm day. They never thought about it then. They came and checked with me [afterward] and asked what happened. I thought, maybe, it was a skid around on a turn, but all the wreckage was in a straight line so it wasn't that. What it was...I was going down the road and all of a sudden I got an updraft on the right wing and the left wing dropped. Cracked it immediately. The right engine went up in flames.

They lost a man in that crash, the observer. As with Edward Smith, Fisher was also taken to Rauceby. The RAF hospital was, at this point, equipped with saline treatment for burns. Fisher remained at Rauceby for about six months while his wounds healed. He was then transferred to East Grinstead where in Ward III he met the Canadian contingent of Dr. Ross Tilley, and nurses Marge Jackson and Fran Oakes. He would remain there for another six months before being transferred back to Canada. At the Christie Street hospital he had more work done on his right hand. Ultimately he lost various fingers in an effort to enable him greater use of the hand. Fisher stayed in the RCAF until his discharge in 1946, but the accident at OTU changed his life forever.

Yet Fisher remembers the people at East Grinstead with immense fondness. As one of the more mobile members of the Guinea Pig Club, he was able to stroll through town and observe the great compassion that was shown to the burn victims. That memory, as well as the companionship of this group of men, endures to this day.

Ken Fisher and his wife Isabel live in Regina. He has been an active member of the Guinea Pig Club, serving on its executive.

What strikes one as amazing is the general lack of bitterness in any of the stories one hears. In my interview with Mr. Fisher there was never a note of bitterness over the fate of being so severely injured in a training exercise. Bodies burn as effectively on a simulated bombing run as they do on an actual op, and without the training runs the others do not exist. Intellectually, this is perfectly acceptable logic. But it is the lack of self-pity in the voice that stays with the listener. If anything, there is humour. It is impossible to get two or three Guinea Pigs in the same room and not hear laughter. Whether the discussion is about the arc the kite made as it circled down to crash, or the particular flammability factors of one's assigned plane, or the antics that went on in the ward, there is a good deal of laughter.

As 1942 came to a close, the in-house members of the Guinea Pig Club celebrated in Ward III. Back home families were listening to the sounds of Bing Crosby and Glenn Miller. Theatre houses were showing pictures like *Casablanca*.

But 1942 had also seen the beginning of something that would have a bearing on the Guinea Pig Club. It saw the instalment of Bomber Harris as head of Bomber Command. Arthur Travers Harris. "Bomber" in the headlines, took over Bomber Command on February 22, 1942, and set about bolstering a depleted and inadequate force. He had little to work with. With only a few hundred planes at his disposal, he could hardly hope to attain the force he envisioned. These planes: Stirlings, Halifaxes, and Lancasters were an improvement on the Hampdens in size and bomb load capability, but Harris needed numbers.

Unfortunately, Bomber Command was not seen as a priority. Money was earmarked for Royal Navy defense. Allotting the sums Harris wanted for a largely unproven *offensive* strategy was met with resistance.

Harris, a proud, supremely confident man, decided that what was needed was a show of force. He planned a raid. Not just any raid but the largest air raid ever mounted. One thousand bombers. A thousand bombers over one target! Never before had this been tried. It was incredible. It was also improbable—Harris's force was under five-hundred planes.

But Harris was determined. He asked Coastal Command to take part. They agreed. He scrounged every plane, every crew member on his way in or out of ops. So sure was Harris that when the Admiralty took Coastal Command out of the raid at the last minute Harris forged on, finding the last few men and machines. And on May 30, 1942—target Cologne—the planes took off. It was a style of raid that would be repeated throughout the remainder of the war, the planes in formation, the force a visually, aurally fearsome thing.

The operation was a success. The world heard about it in the newspapers and on radio. It was the beginning of Harris's true tenure with Bomber Command.

And as the folks back home were dreaming along with Humphrey Bogart and Ingrid Bergman in *Casablanca*, plans were being made for another meeting in Casablanca.

At the beginning of 1943, Churchill met with Roosevelt and the combined Chiefs of Staff, to discuss allied strategy. The so-called "Casablanca Directive" planned invasions (Sicily) and the organization of a military force at the ready to invade France the following year. Most significantly for the airmen to come they planned a Bomber Offensive that would hit Germany in its war-materials production centres. The Bomber Offensive was also designed to undermine the morale of the German population. RAF Bomber Command (Harris) and the 8th United States Army Air Force (USAAF) would carry out "round the clock bombing" (the Americans by day, the British by night).

Harris favoured widespread urban bombing over a few specific targets. His own memoirs state that he saw his directive as allowing him "to attack pretty well any German industrial city of 100,000 inhabitants and above."[3.]

Much would be achieved in 1943, but, as always, there would be a human cost.

DANGER! MEN AT WORK! GUINEA PIGS WERE ENCOURAGED TO WATCH OPERATIONS

Guinea Pigs (1943)

John A. Reynolds

One of the first people to acquire membership in the Guinea Pig Club in 1943 was John A. "Jack" Reynolds. Reynolds had been in the service since June 12, 1941, when he enlisted in Regina.

John A. "Jack" Reynolds

After basic training in Penhold, Alberta, he went on to No. 3 SFTS at Calgary where he was assigned guard duty. He eventually entered No. 2 Wireless School and in September 1941 started Course No. 24. By January 1942, his course completed, he was posted to No. 2 Bombing and Gunnery School in Mossbank, Saskatchewan. Upon graduation he was posted to RAF ferry command in Dorval, Quebec. The summer of 1942 was spent ferrying aircraft from Canada to Britain and in October of 1942 the crew was posted to Britain.

The first order of business was to complete a conversion course to British aircraft. At No. 15 OTU, Harwell, Reynolds and crew flew Wellingtons, a plane about which Reynolds was to quip, some fifty-six years later, "They burn good."

Unfortunately, on November 23, they were involved in a crash which resulted in the disability of their pilot. Without a skipper, the crew put in time until a new pilot was found between Christmas and New Years 1942. They were to complete their course and then go on ops.

But it was not to be. On January 8, 1943, their Wellington crashed and burned. Wireless Operator/Air Gunner Reynolds suffered third degree burns to his face, left hand and left leg. He was taken first to the station hospital, then to a civilian hospital in Oxford and then to Princess Mary's RAF Hospital in Buckinghamshire. He spent three months there. Around this time he was visited by Archibald McIndoe, who in turn invited him to the Queen Victoria Hospital at East Grinstead. Reynolds, having received good care at the RAF hospital, was initially reluctant to leave. But once he arrived he realized that something was different about the place:

> My first contact at the East Grinstead hospital was with the patients in the ward, many of whom were Canadian airmen. I could not help but be impressed by their attitude, and I quickly realized that many were more seriously burned than I. The situation was hard to understand until I was first examined by, and talked to, Dr. Tilley.

Tilley examined Reynolds' burns while he soaked in the saline bath. By the next morning, Tilley had already started grafting.

John Reynolds would spend some ten months in Ward III, having numerous operations to make his eye capable of closing, to straighten his burned leg, to tidy up his face and give him an eyebrow.

He left East Grinstead in January of 1944, returning to RAF Ferry Command in Dorval, Quebec, where he performed administrative duties and underwent more operations under Dr. Hamilton Baxter at the Royal Victoria Hospital, Montreal. By December 1944 Reynolds was back flying for the RAF, first ferrying aircraft to the Middle East and Britain, then posted back to the RCAF and finally discharged on September 27, 1945. There was one more surgery in Montreal and then home to Regina and a post with Veterans Affairs. He married and had a family.

John Reynolds credits Dr. Tilley with far more than rebuilding his face, hands and legs:

> I watched him rebuild the faces, noses, ears and fingers of severely burned airmen, not only Canadians but many allied airmen. Much greater than the plastic surgery he performed was the confidence he instilled in each of us.

Reynolds goes on to note that much of his post-war career with DVA involved work that required him to deal with the public. Reynolds summarizes it this way:

> My being somewhat scarred has never at any time been of concern, and I have to thank Dr. Tilley....

Jack Reynolds has been active in the Guinea Pig Club, serving on the executive.

Herbert Aldridge

Herbert "Bert" Aldridge, of Toronto, was a navigator serving with 464 Australian Squadron in 1942. They were attached to the RAF at Feltwell, Norfolk, flying Venturas on daylight raids. On January 20, 1943, Aldridge was on a low-flying practice run when the plane hit an oak tree near West Stow, Bury St. Edmunds. That Aldridge would survive this is one of those stories of luck. Normally, as a navigator, he would have been in the nose of the plane, but this day he was taking advantage of an absent mid-upper gunner to do his map-reading from that position. The pilot and the wireless operator were killed.

What happened to Aldridge was interesting. He did not remember what had occurred despite being conscious and talking for an hour and a half to the man who came along and rescued him. According to the gentleman, Mr. Charles Follett, the plane smashed nose first into the ground and disintegrated while the fuselage continued on about another fifty feet, minus wings and engines. The fuselage wrapped itself around a tree, at which point the side door burst open and Aldridge was shot out. He missed hitting any trees and travelled another twenty yards before ending up in a gravel pit, followed by a petrol tank which was spewing petrol.

Follet found Aldridge and thought he looked pretty bad. His eyes were shut from the crash, and he was crawling around trying to get away from the petrol tank. It took over an hour and a half for the ambulance to arrive, hence the long talk that Aldridge wouldn't remember.

Aldridge categorized his injuries as minor: a head concussion, fractured nose, and cuts and bruises. He was taken to a civilian hospital at Bury St. Edmunds and then transferred to RAF hospital, Ely, before going back to flying, this time with New Zealand 487 Squadron, Methwold and Sculthorpe. Here they flew Venturas and Mosquitos.

Toward the end of 1943, Aldridge was sent to East Grinstead so that Dr. Tilley could work on his nose. He was surprised when he met his first Guinea Pigs:

My first introduction to burns cases was while waiting for the East Grinstead train at Victoria Station in

London when three disfigured airmen…left the incoming train, joking. Later, on seeing further burned and injured patients at the hospital and particularly when examined by the Wingco I felt embarrassed and humble, not because of the Wingco, who was understanding and displayed the master's touch, but because of my own feelings: "what the hell am I doing here simply for a nose straightening?"

While at the hospital Aldridge had time to note the "deep personal concern and caring" shown by all the staff. He also witnessed "the acceptance in town of a pig's disfigurement" and saw it as a big step toward the eventual rehabilitation of that man.

After he left East Grinstead, Aldridge went back to the squadron, and was later posted to 90 Squadron, RAF Tuddenham, where they flew Lancasters. Aldridge finished his tour there, with a Canadian crew.

Returning home to Canada in 1945, Aldridge studied business administration. He also married Jeanne and they had two children, a boy and a girl. He became a mortgage banker and enjoyed a long and successful career. Bert and Jeanne Aldridge live in Toronto.

Two Guinea Pigs (Henry Ernst and George Beauchamp)

Henry "Hank" Ernst and George Beauchamp are two members of the Club who crashed and burned together. They also share the experience of having to reconstruct their stories while taking into account various lapses of memory. Ernst admits that his memory of the crash was affected *by* the crash while Beauchamp states that he has little memory of the first three months following the downing of their plane.

Henry Ernst enlisted in the RCAF on Remembrance Day, 1941. A native of Mahone Bay, Nova Scotia, Ernst had previously enjoyed a peaceful rural upbringing before heading to Halifax to find work. He landed a job at Imperial Tobacco, the sort of solid company which, ideally, would have provided him with lifetime employment.

However, it was not to be. With the declaration of war Ernst followed the lead of his older brother and joined the RCAF. Halifax was a centre of military activity, and one might wonder why he hadn't opted for the Navy. But, as Ernst says:

My decision not to join the Navy went back to my exposure to the rough life fishermen had on the cruel Atlantic.

So, an airman was born. After taking the train to No. 1 Manning Depot in Toronto, Ernst quickly settled into military routine. He was posted to the equipment depot at Moncton where he worked as an equipment assistant. A call came down for gunners, though, and Ernst answered it, heading to Mont Joli for training in the summer of 1942. While on training Ernst was involved in a take-off crash of a Fairey Battle but emerged unscathed.

He was then on his way to Bournemouth and was posted to 420 Squadron, at Middleton St-George, flying Wellingtons. Here he served as a "floater," replacing crew members as needed. He was needed the night of January 29, 1943. The target: Brest. Hank Ernst tells what occurred then:

> Halfway to target, Command updated weather conditions, and we were informed the target area was 10/10th cloud. A short discussion and we decided to continue. The maximum weight or load for the Wellington Mark III was 2,000 pounds, which we had. I am not positive about this point, but I believe that with this load the bomb bay doors were removed. In any case our aircraft had no doors and was open to the elements such as icing and freezing.

They were coming up on target. Ernst remembers:

> Prior to making our run over the target the bomb-aimer fused the bomb. [The fuse was to] detonate on impact, and once this has been completed there is no way to defuse it. To our dismay and concern the mechanism did not rid us of our live bomb. All action—wiggling, diving and pulling out, flying at an altitude we thought below freezing—would not rid us of our problem.
>
> Now fuel was becoming a serious concern. We decided to head toward the southern coast of England, put the aircraft in George [automatic pilot] and bail out over England. In our confusion, excitement and panic we crossed the restricted area, and English guns

opened up on us. We managed to escape their fire and headed for Exeter, the nearest air drome situated in a valley (I think) with hills of 700 feet. (While en route to Exeter our live bomb fell on England.) The ceiling was down to 500 feet, making the approach to the airport impossible, and we hit the hills.

The hills were at about 700 feet. The crash killed pilot W/O Sanderson, Flt. Sgt. Downton, Sgt. Sealey and Sgt. Bittner.

Hank Ernst and George Beauchamp survived. How? Well, here memory shuts down. It is clear that they were both pulled from the burning plane by a third party. George Beauchamp believes it was a Czech soldier. Ernst also maintains that the fellow was Army. Whoever he was, he took two burning men from their plane while live ammunition exploded around them.

Ernst remembers waking up in a hospital in Exeter some days later. Beauchamp does not remember anything much for the first three months. They were given the standard gentian violet treatment.

The burns were bad. George Beauchamp had grave burns to his body. Hank Ernst had second degree burns to his hands and face and third degree burns to his leg, making his affected area head, hips, neck and ankle.

They were "saved" again when either Dr. McIndoe or Dr. Tilley recommended them for transfer to East Grinstead. This was a long uncomfortable ride for both men.

They arrived. There they experienced the godsend of the saline bath treatment which, over time, loosened up and helped remove the gentian violet crust. Both men would have extensive surgery. George Beauchamp remembered flap grafts and a Thiersch graft on his elbow. Both men would carry the results of that January 29 crash with them, neither going back to operational flying, both seeing the insides of convalescent hospitals for some time to come. As recently as 1993, Hank Ernst underwent an operation for an injury sustained during the crash some fifty years previous—an apparent broken neck!

Ernst settled in Calgary and married Rosemary. He worked for many years for Air Canada before opening his own used car business. He has served on the club executive.

Beauchamp married Margaret and made his home in California.

Both men remember Dr. Tilley with fondness and admiration, Ernst saying that Tilley was like a father to his patients:

He cared about them, worried about them and looked after them physically and mentally.

James G. Adams

James G. "Gibb" Adams received treatment at the Queen Victoria Hospital after a crash on January 29, 1943. He remained in hospital there until July 1943. He currently lives in British Columbia.

Paul Y. Davoud

Paul Yettvart Davoud was born in Provo, Utah in 1911. As a young man he moved with this family to his mother's hometown of Kingston, Ontario where he began his military training at the Royal Military College (1928-1932). During the summers when school was out, Davoud used the time to train at RCAF Camp Borden, and by 1931 he was a provisional pilot officer and had received the Sword of Honour as best all around cadet.

One might envision a career in flying based on this early exposure, but no one, perhaps not even Davoud himself, would have suspected the truly impressive career that lay ahead.

In the early 1930s, as the RCAF did not have an abundance of permanent commissions available, Davoud sailed to England where he accepted a permanent commission with the RAF. He would remain there until 1935. He returned to Canada following this to work for Canadian Airways, Ltd., and stayed there until 1938. He then did some bush flying for the Hudson's Bay Company, actually going on to organize and operate a northern air service for the fur trade department. He would remain with the Hudson's Bay Company until 1940 when the air force again beckoned.

Above right: Wing Commander Paul Davoud meeting King George VI and Queen Elizabeth

Paul Davoud was posted to Trenton, Ontario, as assistant chief flying officer. From there he went to the U.K. in June 1941 and was awarded the rank of squadron leader in charge of 410 Night Fighter Squadron. Within the month he was a wing commander with 409 Night Fighter Squadron which flew Beaufighters and later Mosquitos.

Davoud continued ops with 409 Squadron until February 1943 when he joined the Guinea Pig Club. His Beaufighter engine developed trouble, and he crashed on landing. There were some serious burns to deal with, so he was sent to East Grinstead. Under the attentive care of the medical team, he recovered and was back on active flying duty within four months.

There were to be many other highlights in this remarkable career. In June 1943, Davoud was posted to command 418 Night Fighter (Night Intruder) Squadron, the first Canadian to hold the position. Davoud's influence saw his squadron excel to the point of becoming, eventually, the top scoring fighter squadron, night and day, in the RCAF. It was during this period that he was awarded the Distinguished Service Order (DSO) and the Distinguished Flying Cross (DFC). According to one citation, Davoud is listed as:

> ...a forceful and courageous leader whose personal example and exceptional ability have been reflected in the fine fighting qualities and efficiency of the squadron he commanded.

The squadron actively benefitted the civilians, countless of whom were saved from V-1 buzz bomb attacks by the cool-headed precision of this attack squadron.

By February 1944 Davoud was a group captain with 143 Fighter Bomb Wing. This comprised three wings of Hawker "Typhoons" on an assignment that would involve the operation of a maximum Army support program prior to, during, and following the invasion of northwest Europe. The Typhoons were becoming regarded as the optimum fighter/bomber in the allied force, a fact Davoud demonstrated to General Eisenhower in April 1944. Eisenhower was impressed, both with the Typhoon and with Davoud, sending the airman a personal thank you.

From January 1945 until June 1945 Davoud was group captain operations on the headquarters staff of 83 Group, 2nd Tactical Air Force RAF, in an assignment which involved the operation and control of 600 fighter and fighter/bomber aircraft and the detailed planning of their role in the crossing of the Rhine and subsequent support roles. During his tenure there he would also see himself made an Officer of the Order of the British Empire (OBE Military). He was made a Commander of the Order of Orange Nassau (Netherlands), and he was also awarded the croix de guerre (France) and the Legion of Honour (France.)

Davoud's aviation career continued after the war. He held responsible positions with Trans Canada Airlines; Canadian Breweries/Argus Corporation; Field Aviation; Kenting Aviation; Orenda Engines, Ltd.; and De Havilland. He also had a position with the federal government as Chairman of the Air Transport Board and, later, a position with the Government of Ontario as Director of Aviation Services for the Ministry of Transportation and Communications. He was awarded the McKee Trophy, Canada's highest civil aviation award, in 1985. The same year, he was made a member of Canada's Aviation Hall of Fame. He died in 1987. His name lives on in the Paul Davoud School at CFB North Bay.

William Newson

Another of the more illustrious air force careers belongs to William Newson. William "Bill" Newson was born in 1917 in Calgary. He spent his early years in Edmonton and then went on to Kingston's Royal Military College where he graduated in 1939 with a degree in civil engineering.

William Newson

Newson was a born leader who excelled at all of his endeavours. He joined the RCAF and took his flying instruction at Camp Borden and Trenton, where he received the Sword of Honour upon graduation. He also completed a specialist navigator's course.

Then it was on to 11 Bomber Reconnaissance Squadron at Dartmouth, Nova Scotia, to escort convoys and to take part in coastal operations. Transferred over to England, he joined the RCAF 408 Squadron and commenced a tour of operations that would include two sorties in which his plane was seriously damaged. He was injured in one of the encounters and became a member of the Guinea Pig Club. During this period he was awarded the DFC for his courage and leadership.

In June 1943 Newson became commander of 431 Squadron. He completed his first tour of thirty ops over enemy territory in February 1944. His leadership and courage succeeded in garnering him a Bar to his DFC. Newson followed this up with a six-month stint as group captain and commander of RAF Station Leeming, but by the autumn of 1944 Group Captain Newson was commander of 405 Pathfinder Squadron. This involved thirty-two more ops (another operational tour), and during this time Newson was awarded the Distinguished Service Order (DSO).

Newson remained in the post-war air force, commanding RCAF Lachine, Quebec. He later attended RCAF Staff College and also served at Air Force Headquarters, Ottawa. In 1949 he was named commanding officer at RCAF Station Centralia, Ontario, and then commanding officer at Training Command Headquarters, Trenton and eventually commanding officer of 2 Fighter Wing in Grotsenquin, France. In 1959 he was commanding officer of RCAF Station Namao, Alberta, and in 1960 was commandant of the Air Force College in Toronto. The year 1964 saw him become commander of the 36th NORAD division, Topsham AFB, Maine. By August of 1968 he was Assistant Chief of Staff Air Operations at Allied Forces Central Europe, Brunssum, Holland.

General William Newson's varied career continued until his retirement in 1972. This accomplished gentleman, a member of Canada's Aviation Hall of Fame (1984) is remembered by fellow Guinea Pigs as "an enormous, gentle and unassuming man."

Bill Newson, DSO, DFC, CD, B. Eng., and his wife Alice had three children. He died in 1988.

Douglas Thompson

Flight Lieutenant Douglas Thompson was also able to benefit from Tilley's gifts, but getting to East Grinstead was by way of a circuitous route.

Douglas Thompson joined the RCAF in 1941 and trained as a Lancaster bomber pilot. He was sent overseas in the fall of 1942 and joined 106 Squadron attached to the RAF.

It was on the night of February 4, 1943, on a mission to bomb Turin, Italy, that Thompson and his crew encountered tragedy. They met with resistance while on the mission, and two engines were knocked out. The plane began to lose altitude. Desperate, the crew jettisoned everything they could to maintain an altitude that would take them over the Alps. They were just beginning to gain a bit of height when they crashed into the side of a mountain in the French Alps. Several crew members died instantly. One of four men thrown free of the plane, Thompson regained consciousness and saw a fellow crew member trying to pull someone from the plane. Thompson was moving toward them when the burning plane exploded and he lost consciousness again.

He awoke in a hospital in Paris, under the care of a German doctor and nurse. Thompson was horribly burned. He could not speak as his mouth was burned shut. Doctors made a hole through which to insert a straw for nourishment, but it was doubtful, at first, that the young pilot would survive. He had sustained severe burns to one side of his face, ear, neck and leg. The ear was nearly gone, the eyelashes and eyelids also gone.

Meanwhile, back at home, family members waited. They had learned of the crash, but it was another three weeks before the Red Cross was able to tell them that Douglas Thompson was still alive.

Then Thompson's long journey began. Six months after the crash, he was sent to a POW camp in Germany.

Without a plastic surgeon in the POW camp, Thompson had to rely on the general surgeon, himself a prisoner of war, who —through the intervention of the Red Cross—was given permission to receive articles that would instruct him how to do temporary operations on Thompson. After six months in the POW camp he was repatriated to England aboard the *Gripsholm*, via Norway.

Thompson arrived at East Grinstead where he—finally— received the ministrations of Dr. Tilley and staff. Dr. Tilley set about the enormous task of rebuilding Doug Thompson's face. Over twenty operations were performed in all (counting the temporary ones in Germany.) Thompson spoke highly of Dr. Tilley, his staff, and the people of East Grinstead, clearly aware of how they had helped him both physically and psychologically.

But as he had not seen a plastic surgeon for such a long time prior to his tenure in Ward III, he had much scar tissue and remained badly scarred for life.

He returned to Canada in the fall of 1945, had more work done at the Christie Street Hospital, and married Frances in June of 1946. That same year he returned to OAC in Guelph to complete his degree course in Agronomy. After this he became a Maltster and worked both for Dominion Malting Co. and with Canada Malting Co. until his retirement in 1985. The Thompsons had three children.

Although Douglas Thompson went on to have a successful career, he found dealing with the public difficult all his life. The strength he acquired in The Sty enabled him to meet this daily challenge, but the burden of his pain and disfigurement was always present. He was also plagued with ill health, much of which was the result of his burns. Douglas Thompson died in August of 1989 of pulmonary fibrosis which doctors stated was due to the scarring of his lungs during the fire. It is a reminder of the very high price the war exacted from the men and their families.

Obviously, even in the cases of burn victims there was better and worse luck. Getting out of the plane with less severe burns; getting to East Grinstead quickly—these were the elements that made the difference.

Les Caddel

A "lucky" Guinea Pig was Les Caddel. He was a tail gunner in a Wellington bomber and in April 1943 was the sole survivor of the crash that took his crew. Les was flying with the RAF, with a few of the boys he had known from back in his Edmonton school days. They had been on a mission over Germany and had been shot up quite severely, but they were on their way back to the base. Over England, the plane hit some electrical wires. The Wellington crashed and burned, breaking in half. The front end crew died instantly. Les Caddel, in the rear, was found alive but badly burned.

Caddel survived when all others died. He had not removed his gloves so his hands were undamaged. He was "lucky." But there was the face to deal with. His burns were so severe he felt little pain initially. The most painful injury, at the beginning, was his broken ankle. This, of course, would change.

It was off to East Grinstead where Dr. Tilley went to work on Caddel's eyes, nose, ears and jaw. While enjoying the hospitality of The Sty, Caddel took in the saline bath and the friendly atmosphere. He always had high praise for all the medical staff, especially Dr. Tilley and Nurse Marge Jackson.

Les Caddel would go on to have more operations at the Christie Street Hospital under Dr. Tilley's knife. An early marriage in England ended sometime later in Canada, and Caddel then married Lois and had three children. Les Caddel held several government jobs and enjoyed the company of family and friends. He died in 1984.

Like Doug Thompson, the war followed Les Caddel in certain ways. It was difficult for him to come to terms with being the only survivor of the crash. Intellectually, it could be understood given his placement in the plane. But emotionally he questioned it forever.

It is to the credit of the staff at East Grinstead, and to Les Caddel himself, that he was able to go on.

John Maxwell

John Maxwell was skipper of a Hampden which went down in fog in 1943. Two men survived the crash: Maxwell and Jack Allaway of Great Britain. Both were taken to the RAF hospital at Ely after which they were sent to East Grinstead. Maxwell, a quiet man who never married, came home to Canada after the war and returned to his job at the Aluminum Company of Canada. Maxwell is deceased.

Les A. Wainwright

"Les" Wainwright was finishing up a tour with 419 (Moose) Squadron when he received his next posting—to Dishforth, where what would become the 425 (Alouette) Squadron was being formed.

Wainwright was just settling into his new squadron when, in April 1943, he developed a severe pain in his left lower jaw. The Station Dental Officer diagnosed an impacted wisdom tooth growing horizontally below a molar. The first thing to do was pull the molar, which was done. However, when the dental officer tried to remove the wisdom tooth, Wainwright's jaw snapped.

This specific injury necessitated the best dental work available, and that, of course, was at East Grinstead. The next day he was off to the Sty, where Dr. Parfitt, under the direction of Dr. Tilley, set about repairing the damage. Wainwright was put out. When he came to, he was told that the gum had been cut away and the tooth removed. His jaw was also wired shut. As with other jaw cases Wainwright would have to endure six weeks with the wired jaw on a diet of liquid food. He had a chance to observe the patients and the dedicated medical staff, and he has nothing but praise for both. Of the Guinea Pig Club, he says:

They are a wonderful group of people who, like the staff at East Grinstead, deserve all the credit in the world.

Les Wainwright went on to complete his second tour of duty, receiving a DFC for his efforts. After the war he married his longtime sweetheart, Ethel, and they had three children. Following a career in marketing, Wainwright retired, and he and his wife continued "to live happily ever after" until his death in June 2000.

Wainwright's story is an example of the advanced care that was available to maxillo-facial cases.

A Trio of Guinea Pigs (Harry Anderson, John Kerr and George Wilson)

While many crashes resulted in all but one crew member dead, or one burned and the others unscathed, it occasionally happened that more than one member of a given crew had the opportunity to join the Guinea Pig Club.

This occurred in April of 1943 when Harry Anderson, George "Curly" Wilson and John "Johnny" Kerr crashed in their Wellington 10.

Harry D. Anderson

Harry D. Anderson, from Burnaby, British Columbia, trained as a navigator in Chatham, New Brunswick in August, 1942, and was posted in November of that year to 427 Squadron. As was the case with several other members of the Guinea Pig Club, Anderson was on a training mission when his crash occurred. The weather was bad, leading to the crash. According to Anderson:

As a result of the crash my pilot and wireless operator were killed, while my bomb-aimer and air gunner suffered third degree burns to face and hands. I thank the good Lord for my escape from this crash suffering

Left to right:
George Wilson, Harry Anderson and John Kerr

some second and third degree burns to my face, and third degree to my hands. These were somewhat minor considering those of my comrades.

What Anderson modestly omits is his altruistic rescue of fellow crew member George "Curly" Wilson. It was Anderson who reached through the flames to get to Wilson.

Anderson was flown to East Grinstead for treatment and remained there from April to August 1943 under the care of Dr. Tilley and his staff. Despite the seriousness of his injuries, Anderson was back on flying duties, this time with 420 Squadron, by January 1944. August of 1944 saw him completing a tour of ops. He was discharged from the RCAF in October 1945.

Harry Anderson married Joan and lives in Surrey, British Columbia. He is an active member of the Guinea Pig Club.

George A. Wilson

George "Curly" Wilson, of Ottawa, was in the plane with Harry Anderson. Wilson, the bomb-aimer, had trained as an observer but in late 1942 was converted to bomb-aimer.

Wilson is a man with a prodigious memory and a fine eye for detail. He is also a man who understands the ironies of life. It is he who noted that in a description of his crash, he, Anderson and Kerr are listed as dead and RAF rather than alive and RCAF.

George Wilson

Wilson describes the crash like this:

The first explosion, and probably the one reported, occurred when the starboard undercarriage struck a Nissan hut. It appeared that the oleo legs pierced the starboard nacelle tank and started a fire which spread quickly. The wind was gusting at about thirty knots at an angle to the runway. The aircraft remained airborne for a few hundred yards with the starboard engine still running though probably not delivering much power until we crashed and burned on the edge of the bomb dump.

Of the three or four other aircraft sent up with them on this training exercise, their charred Wellington was the only one on the field the following morning. According to Wilson, strong headwinds on the return trip had exhausted the fuel reserves of the other aircraft, and they were over the Channel when they fell. Wilson continues the story:

> When I regained consciousness I made some ineffective attempts to get out and had begun to feel a sort of impotent rage over turning into a cinder, when tough and resilient Harry Anderson opened the bulkhead door behind me, found me enveloped in flames and struggling to escape, lifted me onto the nose of the machine, and followed me. The fire was worse on the starboard side so I dropped off the port side and found myself in a triangular alcove with the nose on one side, a wing with ruptured fuel tanks on the second, and a high barbed wire entanglement on the third. I ran through the barbed wire and was soon joined by Harry inside the bomb dump. While Harry and I were in the squadron clinic receiving first aid John Kerr who had escaped from his turret was brought in by the crew of a second ambulance. Soon after that we were transferred to Darlington Memorial Hospital.

At the Darlington hospital, George Wilson received standard burn treatment—standard for those who had not read the directives issued by the burn unit at the Queen Victoria Hospital, East Grinstead.

> My face was covered in tripple dye and my hands were put in bunyan bags.

Nine days after arriving, Wilson, Anderson and Kerr had a visit from Dr. Tilley. He and Dr. McIndoe wished to determine whether the men were seriously enough burned to qualify for entry into the Sty. Dr. Tilley examined the men, and was annoyed to see that the East Grinstead advice on treatment of burns was not being followed. He was more than annoyed to learn that George Wilson was slated for a double amputation of his hands the following morning!

Dr. Tilley worked fast, arranging for a Bristol Bombay at Middleton-St. George to move the men to Three Bridges airfield, the location of Gatwick Airport. From there they took the uncomfortable seven-mile ambulance ride to the Queen Victoria Hospital and the Guinea Pig Club. Wilson expands:

> Harry, Johnny and I gradually learned that this was a different sort of hospital. Physically, it consisted of a brick and masonry central unit with several huts adjacent. Three of the huts which were typical large military barrack buildings were hospital wards. One ward housed mainly army and navy casualties, another was occupied by female patients and children sent by the Department of Health. A lot of them were air raid casualties. The third, Ward III, was almost entirely airmen. Several other smaller but similar buildings were used for a kitchen, a dental clinic, and laboratories and workshops for the manufacture of some of the prostheses required for the treatment of patients. Two other similar buildings housed a recreation room for patients and a lounge for staff. There were also two other permanent masonry buildings for physio- and occupational therapy clinics and a morgue. But the atmosphere! No hospital blues, no rank separating the men, a beer when you wanted one, and a routine that could best be defined as "organized chaos."

One was never to underestimate the order in that organized chaos. In May 1943 nurse Olwyn Thomas spotted a problem with Wilson's right eye. Contracting scar tissue was causing drying of the eye and a change in the shape of the eyeball. Nurse Thomas inspected the eye, called in Head Nurse Marge Jackson, who called in Dr. Tilley and anaesthetist Dr. Norm Park. In turn they called in Dr. Ridley, a specialist from London. All of this took place in less than an hour, including the arrival of Ridley, who was on call at the hospital. Ridley operated that afternoon and, typically for Ward III, it was a somewhat unusual operation. [see "The Science"]. The operation probably saved Wilson's eye. As he summarizes:

> I had been rescued from a doctor who would have amputated my hands and who told some of my squadron friends in a scornful way that if I did live I would be blind. I was promptly moved to the foremost burn centre of our time.

George Wilson was discharged in August 1945. As a young civilian, he pondered his future settling on engineering and geology courses at Queen's University. There he met with some adversity. It seemed that while his efforts were applauded, there was no real belief that he would or could succeed, given his condition. Wilson, a bonafide Guinea Pig, would of course prove them wrong. His work was of sufficient high quality that the Geological Survey of Canada employed him several times over the summer months while he was a student. Wilson remained at Queen's University until 1949, graduating with a B.Sc. in geology and mineralogy. In the meantime, he wed Mary, the beginning of a long and happy marriage. He went on to an M.Sc. in geology in 1951, and from there to a distinguished career as a geologist. He was the first geologist to examine the Granduc copper property northwest of Stewart, British Columbia, in 1952. And later, in 1960, while working in the Arctic, he recognized and staked the Polaris Group of mineral claims on Little Cornwallis Island. The Arvik lead-zinc mine, owned by COMINCO, is a result of that discovery. He also recognized some oil and gas bearing structures while on survey.

George Wilson is also a talented wood-worker and an accomplished sailor. He has served on the Canadian Wing's executive. Wilson clearly has not let the events of April 6, 1943, slow him down in any way. But it would be wrong to say that the time at East Grinstead did not change his life. Wilson explains:

> I suppose that if I have to summarize my East Grinstead career in some way, I would say that until my marriage in 1950, the time I spent in East Grinstead was the happiest, fullest part of my life— but I would not want to qualify for it again. Perhaps the enjoyment we had was because everything that is nearly lost seems better than before, and that is particularly true of life.

John J. Kerr

The third survivor of the crash was gunner John J. "Johnny" Kerr. The Guelph native had joined up in 1941 and was already married to Ruth when he went overseas in the fall of 1941. He arrived in England on November 6, and by January 1943 he was posted to RCAF 427 (Lion) Squadron.

The crash, which both Harry Anderson and Johnny Kerr remembered as involving their aircraft hitting some trees, sent Sergeant Kerr to East Grinstead along with Anderson and Wilson.

Meanwhile, back at home a young wife awaited word. Ruth Kerr remembers:

> I was a basket case when I received that telegram from the RCAF Casualties Officer advising me that Johnny had been dangerously injured on active service overseas, sustaining burns to face and hands. Other telegrams followed. I learned later how badly burned he was around the eyes. He wasn't able to write to me with pressure bandages on his hands, but the padre and others at the hospital wrote to me and I did receive the telegrams. All messages were censored so I still didn't know which hospital he was in until one day a telegram arrived with East Grinstead on it (someone slipped up). Then I realized he was in Queen Victoria Hospital which I had heard about.

One can appreciate what this must have been like for a young wife back on the homefront.

Like George Wilson, Johnny Kerr would spend a long time in Ward III. Between operations he liked to stay with "Mum and Pop Moore" in Dartford, Kent. He was treated as a son, and the friendship remained intact through the subsequent decades.

Johnny Kerr survived his injuries. He left the Queen Victoria Hospital in April 1944. Back in Canada he had one more operation in St. Thomas in March 1945. He was ready for civilian life. This Guinea Pig became a quality control technician and raised a

Left to right: John Kerr and Dr. Ross Tilley

family, a peaceful conclusion to a harrowing brush with death. Kerr was an active participant in the Guinea Pig Club until his death, attending reunions and catching up with his fellow crew members, Anderson and Wilson, as well as the rest of the Guinea Pigs. Ruth Kerr summarizes it like this:

> The reunions were occasions to compare notes about each other's well-being. Dr. Tilley also checked on his boys at each reunion he attended. He told me how badly injured Johnny was when he first saw him, and I was so pleased to be able to thank him in person for sending Johnny back to me.

At the beginning of March 1943 the Battle of the Rühr was being fought. Bomber Command had focused on the heavily-defended industrial stronghold of cities like Essen, home of the Krupp arms factory, and Duisburg. To effectively bomb a city in the *Rührgebeit* the bomber stream had to be large. But large bomber streams over areas of heavy flak made evasive action extremely difficult. Tight knots of aircraft meant little room to manoeuvre, and with everything but the kitchen sink being thrown up at them, casualties mounted.

As we have seen, these casualties occurred both in training and on ops. And crews were being pressed to the limit.

Leonard Tremblay

One young Quebec airman, Leonard "Len" Tremblay, found out first-hand how rapidly one's active service career could come to an end.

Having received his wings at St. Hubert, Quebec, (No. 13 SFTS) in December 1942, Tremblay enjoyed his two-week embarkation leave before heading to the United Kingdom where he was assigned to training with the RAF. His flying career would come to a fiery end only months later.

On May 26, 1943, Leonard Tremblay crashed in a night flying accident. The plane hit the ground in a blaze. Tremblay was terribly injured, with severe burns to his face, hands and legs. He was taken to a nearby emergency hospital and five days later flown to the Queen Victoria Hospital, to Archie and Ross and the Guinea Pigs.

Tremblay's burns were very bad. Treatment was not able to stop gangrene from setting in in his right leg. The leg would have to be amputated.

This must have been a very low day on Ward III. Amputations were rarely done. It was said that Archibald McIndoe considered them a failure on his part regardless of the circumstances. Tremblay describes his ordeal this way:

> [The leg was amputated]...at the upper third part of the femur; this was done June 15, 1943, a date I shall never forget should I live to be 110 years old! ...Later on, the staff at the hospital continued treatment to the rest of my sore body, mainly by applying patches of skin on the raw areas of my entire remaining leg, and my hands. By then the slight superficial burns on my face had healed completely.

Seven months later he returned to Canada where he was a patient, for a time, at the Christie Street Hospital. There his right thigh was re-amputated and he was fitted for an above-knee prosthesis. Yet despite this difficult adjustment, Tremblay has nothing but praise for everyone in Ward III:

> The Head Surgeon, Sir Archibald McIndoe, had proceeded with the amputation whilst the tedious "job" of applying skin grafts to my remaining leg, stump and hands was performed by Wing Commander Ross Tilley....I cannot find the appropriate words to describe Dr. Tilley's skill and dedication, and to him I owe an immeasurable debt! Shortly after each operation he had performed on my aching body, he would soon appear at the foot of my bed, comforting me with the kindest words. Just to see his smiling, reassuring face did more than any medication to restore my morale and boost my desire to pull out of it all! And I can say as much about the devoted and efficient staff who took care of me during this difficult period of my life. When you think about it, a twenty-two-year-old lad going through these torments has a tremendous need for this kind of encouragement, and I was fortunate to be offered such support.

Once "on his feet again," Tremblay worked for a year in Ottawa at the National Film Board. He returned to his home town of Quebec City to work for the Department of Veterans Affairs [now Veterans Affairs Canada]. In 1948 Tremblay married Pierette and they eventually had three sons.

Leonard Tremblay also spent part of his career at the Department of Indian and Northern Affairs remaining there until his retirement. Now a widower, Tremblay passes the time pursuing his many interests, including singing and listening to opera. He has become an active member of the cyberspace generation, spending a lot of time on the internet. He also remains actively associated with the RCAF Benevolent Fund, with which he has served for over thirty years. And, of course, he is a proud member of the Guinea Pig Club. Of the staff at East Grinstead, he has not praise but a prayer:

God bless...all who so fervently cared for me.

Tremblay represents yet another Guinea Pig who felt "fortunate" to have had his bad luck countered with the experience of Archie, Ross, Ward III and the town of East Grinstead.

Cyril F. Hicks

Cyril Hicks, a Saskatchewan native, joined the RCAF in Regina in 1941. He took his elementary training at Virden, Manitoba, and his service flying training in Saskatoon. He graduated with his pilot's wings in 1942. Hicks was sent to Charlottetown for coastal command training, and from there he was sent overseas in late 1942. After a short stay in Bournemouth he was sent to Northern Ireland for advanced flying training on Wellingtons and familiarization with anti-submarine reconnaissance. Further training on reconnaissance and torpedo training on Wellingtons took place in Scotland, and then it was a posting to Wales for yet more coastal command training, after which Hicks was posted to North Africa to join the 458 Australian Squadron on Wellington torpedo bombers. This was during the Sicily campaign, and the squadron was flying out of Tunis.

It was July, 1943, and Hicks was on his fifth operation. He was on anti-submarine patrol near Sicily. The routine was shattered by anti-aircraft fire which managed to hit and knock out one of his plane's engines. Hicks and crew hobbled back to Tunis but crash landed upon arrival.

Hicks was in a coma for five days. When he awoke it was to the news that he was badly injured, with facial lacerations and a badly burned right arm and shoulder. As well, both hands, expecially the right hand, were severely burned. He was sent to an RAF Hospital in Tunis. He would not get back to England until late 1943, and it would be 1944 before he would become a guest at East Grinstead.

At the Queen Victoria Hospital Hicks was operated on by Dr. Tilley. He found a friend in Guinea Pig Howard "Tex" Phillips. And he recovered enough to be released and sent home to Canada in late 1944.

Hicks returned to flying duty in Dafoe, Saskatchewan, as a staff pilot flying Ansons and Bolingbrokes. After training ceased at his base, Hicks entered the RCAF hospital in St. Thomas for treatment, primarily the removal of keloid tissue. He was released from service in 1945, joined the RCAF Reserve, and took a course in farming. He married Mildred and they had four children.

Cyril Hicks built a respectable career as a grain farmer. Although he now farms little, he still lives on the family homestead with his wife, "with plenty of windows to view the surrounding farm." Cyril and Mildred Hicks now plan to focus on fishing. He is grateful for all of the excellent medical care he received, not only at East Grinstead but also in North Africa.

Cecil Cooper

Cecil Cooper served in North Africa. He entered Ward III in the Spring of 1943 with severe burns. Guinea Pig Hank Ernst remembered his arrival, and the badly burned and malnourished frame of the man. Cooper had crashed in the desert sometime earlier but like many Guinea Pigs did not go directly to the Queen Victoria Hospital. Cooper would remain at the hospital until July 1943. He returned to Canada after the war.

Town Tragedy

This town that was a solace and a proving ground for these young men was also an English town in the middle of a war. And on July 9, 1943, tragedy struck. The Whitehall cinema in downtown East Grinstead was bombed by a single German raider. There were very high casualties: 108 dead, many of them schoolchildren; 235 injured. Some fifty-seven of the injured were treated at the Queen Victoria Hospital. The hospital staff worked diligently on the civilians, but it was a huge devastation for such a small town. Everybody was related to someone, or knew someone, who had become a casualty.

It is hard to understand the strain on, and the stamina of, the British people who endured personal loss almost daily, who saw their cities, art and architecture destroyed and their children broken. These were the same people who bought a young airman a brew in the pub, seeing in the flier's face a mirror of their own world. There was an empathy between them that was wordless.

Expansion and the Pea-Nut Club

The hospital, therefore, played a big part in the lives of the townspeople. In September 1943 a proposal was brought forward by Lord Kindersley, who had donated the land for the site of the present hospital, that the name "Cottage" be dropped from the  original "Queen Victoria Cottage Hospital" as it no longer pertained [a cottage hospital being one with few beds, run on the largesse of those involved]. One of the primary reasons for this change was that plans for the building of a Canadian Wing were taking shape. Land was procured, "Pea-Nut" land, on site and facing a southerly direction. By August 1943, plans for the 270 foot/fifty bed wing had been drawn up, and by October a crew of Royal Canadian Engineers was at work, financed by the Canadian government to the tune, at the time, of £20,000.

"Pea-Nut" land denotes the Pea-Nut Club, and it deserves a word as it was a unique phenomenon that displayed the charity and the spirit of the people. In the 1930s, a hospital was being built, the Kent and Sussex, in nearby Tunbridge Wells. The local newspaper, *The Courier*, asked its journalists to come up with an idea for a feature in aid of the hospital. A writer named Kitty "Kay" French (later Mrs. Gordon Clemetson) was a bit peeved at having to write this kind of copy, so she dashed off a fake letter, signed "Aunt Agatha," in which she promised a bag of peanuts to any child who could take to a bank a shillings-worth of "Bun" pennies [new 1931 pennies that displayed the image of Queen Victoria with her hair in a bun]. It was a joke, and Ms. French promptly forgot all about the incident. Until the bank called. What was the manager supposed to do with a little girl named Dorothy Jolley who had collected her bag of bun pennies?

The reporter was forced to see her stunt through. And so the Pea-Nut Club was born. Members were sent a little blue badge with a golden peanut emblem. And while all this sounds like a lark, something about it took off like wildfire. Everyone wanted to be a Pea-Nut. There were Golden Pea-Nut Awards; celebrities got on board, including the Archbishop of Canterbury, the actress Shirley Temple, and the pilot Sir Alan Cobham. The 250-member crew of a Royal Navy battle cruiser enrolled. There were Pea-Nut soldiers, sailors and airmen. Money was being collected everywhere; pennies adding up to real money. And through it all, Kitty French, now Mrs. Clemetson, was "Aunt Agatha." She took the salute when the crew of the *H.M.S. Revenge* showed up demanding to see Aunt Agatha, marching and shouting "We want our Auntie! We want our Auntie!" through the streets of Tunbridge Wells. Needless to say, she and the *Courier* cat Midge (the mascot) were highly visible members of the Club. There were fund-raising parties, concerts, and plays. There were Pea-Nut pantomimes, including two written by the dramatist Christopher Fry who lived in Tunbridge Wells.

When the Tunbridge Wells hospital was built, the Pea-Nut Club furnished a large part of the hospital's children's ward, and Midge the cat was the mascot in charge of raising money for the toy cupboard. So when the Queen Victoria Hospital was being transformed, in 1943, there were also plans to build a new children's wing to replace the existing emergency huts. Dr. McIndoe had heard of the good work of the Pea-Nut Club and went to Tunbridge Wells to speak with Mrs. Clemetson. The Club's decision to help would have a far-reaching impact.

The Pea-Nuts immediately set a target of £10,000, but its worldwide members eventually raised £24,000. This would take until 1948, and by then the hospitals would have been nationalized by the National Health Service. It was said that the £24,000 pounds would be appropriated as well, which began a battle that saw Aunt Agatha and Archie taking on the National Health Service. McIndoe, as always, understood how to use the media, and together with the journalist Aunt Agatha, they convinced not only the East Grinstead Trades Council, but Fleet Street, to back them. "Aunt Agatha" Clemetson offered to go to jail rather than turn over the money. The standoff ended when Aunt Agatha and Archie had the guarantee that a children's ward would be built with the money. Following the opening of the children's wing in 1955, the Club went on to raise funds for a burns unit, a day room for the Canadian Wing, a swimming pool and sun lounge, a children's garden, a schoolroom for child patients, a children's recovery room and rooms for parents to stay while visiting.

The Club would eventually boast over a million members worldwide. It was a remarkable example of vision, humour and fortitude. The Club exists to this day, in reduced form, and it still supports the Children's Ward of the Queen Victoria Hospital.

Ray Edward Leupp

Ray Leupp

Not long after the July 9 tragedy in downtown East Grinstead another Guinea Pig checked in. Ray Edward Leupp was an American from Columbus, Ohio, a former locomotive fireman who had travelled north to Toronto in October 1941, to join the RCAF. He got his wings in Canada and was sent to an RAF OTU in Scotland in 1942. There he flew Hurricanes without major incident until July 10, 1943, when his plane crashed near Carlisle. Leupp suffered severe injuries to the head, losing an eye and sustaining extensive jaw damage. After a few days in a Manchester hospital Leupp headed to Ward III, the Sty, for fixing up. His jaw, which was fractured, was in splints, and he suffered through the usual soft-food diet.

Despite the recent town tragedy and the daily schedule of operations in the ward, Ray Leupp was well taken care of. Between slabbings he was sent to Marchwood Park for rehabilitation. There he announced that he preferred to work with animals rather than doing woodwork or metalwork. So, daily, he was sent out to farms to work with the animals. The place would have an influence on the rest of his life.

Ray Leupp eventually recovered, and in July 1944 he was repatriated home to Columbus, where he studied and became a veterinarian. Leupp remembered his time at East Grinstead with great fondness despite his injuries:

> My stay in Britain during those war years was unforgettable, and I enjoyed every moment of it. I'll never forget [the] kindness and hospitality, [the] calm reserve and, above all, [the] deep and abiding respect

for a man as an individual....It was great, too, to be in the company of such a fine bunch as those fellows at the Hospital; I'm sure proud to be a member of the Guinea Pig Club.

Here we see the perfect marriage of all the factors: the townspeople/ the Hospital/ the "bunch of fellows" known as the Guinea Pigs. Were one not to know the circumstances of Leupp's quote, one might assume it was someone summarizing a leisurely stay with friends.

Dr. Ray Leupp, DVM, married Marilyn and had a very successful practice in Columbus, Ohio. He was the president of the local Humane Society, and he was made a distinguished alumnus by his university for his services to the community and in particular for animal welfare. And his attachment to Marchwood Park? The Leupp family farm was called Marchwood Farm, and his clinic was called "Marchwood Animal Clinic." Ray Leupp died in August 1986, following a visit to East Grinstead.

The fact that Ray Leupp was an American with the RCAF underlines once again the mutability of the service during the war. A Canadian might be serving with the RAF, or an American with the RCAF might later transfer to an American unit. And, of course, allies from France, Poland, Czechoslovakia, Australia and elsewhere might end up anywhere.

This is one of the reasons why there is no definitive list of Canadian Guinea Pigs. Men like Gerry Dufort, who live in England, belong to the parent club while an Australian like Harry Stannus, who now makes his home in Canada, is a current member of the Canadian Club. War is a time of great mutability. It is only natural that words bend to accommodate the various meanings they are given.

Paul S. Warren

Paul "Sid" Warren was a wireless air-gunner flight lieutenent in a crew stationed at Graveley, in RAF Squadron 35 Pathfinder Force. They flew Halifax bombers out of Graveley, and on the night of October 4, 1943, they were on a mission to Frankfurt when they got coned. Searchlights pinned them where they flew making them easy targets for heavy flak.

The terror of being coned in searchlights is almost impossible to convey. The black night sky suddenly becomes as bright as day, and there is only one target—you, your plane.

They were hit. Two engines failed and another was losing power. They were on their way home, though, so perhaps they could hold out. The third engine sputtered out over the English Channel. Limping home on one good engine, they had just cleared the cliffs of southeast England when they crashed.

Warren and the navigator suffered burns to the face and hands. They managed to get to a farm house where a doctor and an ambulance were called. Warren had the good fortune to be sent to East Grinstead the following day. At the Queen Victoria Hospital, Wingco Dr. Ross Tilley and Dr. Norman Park, the anaesthetist, took him in and began to care for him:

> Both of these gentlemen were more than skilled doctors in their fields. They were instrumental in giving hope and purpose to all their patients. The nurses also were all a special breed. I liked one of them so much that we married in May 1944. She was from Ireland, a woman named Paddy Brennan.

After the war, Paul Warren became an air-traffic controller in Montreal. The Warrens have enjoyed a long marriage which has been blessed with children, grandchildren and great-grandchildren. He has been an active member of the Club, serving on the executive.

Nurse Brennan is remembered fondly by many Guinea Pigs. And it is in this story that we see the Guinea Pig spirit fully manifested. Not only did Paul Warren recover from his wounds, he made the most of his hospital stay by marrying one of the nurses! The story also illustrates the true empathy that existed between the young airmen and the staff. Who better than one's nurse to understand the daily challenges of an injured young man?

Of the many marriages that occurred between staff and patients, the majority of them proved successful, a tribute to the true recovery of these men.

One must remember that not all Guinea Pigs met their entrance requirements in the sky, or with fire. James Hicks found another way to join the Club.

James L. Hicks

Jim Hicks became a Guinea Pig in an unusual manner. The Winnipeg native was a mid-upper gunner enjoying his leave in Nottingham in October 1943. That enjoyment, and that leave, were curtailed dramatically when he was hit by a drunk driver.

Hicks was a "mashed" variety of Guinea Pig, his head taking the brunt of the accident. He had a skull fracture, cuts and abrasions. He also had a left eye that was hanging out of his head.

Hicks was taken to Rauceby and later was sent to East Grinstead where he was introduced to the Sty and to the skills of Drs. McIndoe and Tilley. Hicks arrived by limousine, at the behest of General Montague of London Army Headquarters. His stay in Ward III allowed him to observe the condition of some of the other patients. He saw men with no eyelids who lay in bed with eyes constantly open. He saw men with no noses and men with no ears. Men with finger stumps that were useless until Dr. Tilley slit their hands past the knuckles and gave them new "fingers."

Hicks was restless and wanted to help out, so he got two jobs. One was helping in the OR. Dr. Norman Park had arranged this. The other was doing outpatient work making airplane instruments at one of the plants.

He was also well enough to participate in sports. For this he often relied on Dr. Tilley. Tilley, a more than proficient athlete, often challenged young Jim Hicks to badminton matches and regularly prevailed. Dr. Tilley also accompanied the men to the pub where he proved himself as fit as the rest of the young crew.

Hicks remembers the black humour of these men waiting to be "slabbed", waiting to go to the "chop" the next morning, humour designed to keep a guy from feeling sorry for himself. Tilley would partake in this, Hicks remembers, "carving the Christmas turkey with cap and gown and scalpels."

Like all Guinea Pigs, Hicks was more than encouraged to watch the operations on his fellow Pigs. This alleviated fear and prepared a Pig for his own turn. He remembers the relative absence of mirrors on site and how there was always someone new coming in with a worse injury, a more complicated challenge to the expertise and the imaginations of Archie McIndoe and Ross Tilley.

Jim Hicks remained in the Queen Victoria Hospital long enough to have experienced the aftermath of the bombing of the town cinema and, later, the V-1 "buzz-bomb" attacks.

He returned home to Winnipeg where he had a family. He helped found a company, Hicks-Baker Ltd., a wholesale business, and he also worked in the motel and construction industries. He is a proud member of the Guinea Pig Club.

Robert T. Lloyd

Bob Lloyd

Robert "Bob" Lloyd was at No. 23 OTU Satellite, Atherston, Stratford-on-Avon, Warwickshire. He was managing very well there until April 18, 1943, when, while going downhill on a *bicycle* he spotted some airmen coming up. Lloyd dutifully rang his bell to warn the men. For some inexplicable reason they tried to cut across his path, and Lloyd crashed head first into one of the men.

Lloyd was definitely what the Guinea Pigs called "mashed." His face and jaw needed work, so after a stay in a hospital at Halton, in Buckinghamshire, where he was told that all the teeth on the right side of his face, as well as his right eye, would have to be removed, he opted instead to journey to the medical and dental surgeons at the Queen Victoria Hospital. Here Ross Tilley and staff fixed him up, repairing the eye and working on bone and facial structure, proving again that the staff at East Grinstead excelled not only in burn therapy but in dental, facial, and jaw work.

This brief but harrowing mishap didn't deter Flt. Sgt. Lloyd. He left the hospital on June 8, 1943, and returned to OTU, to complete his Wellington Mk.3 and Mk.10s training on June 23, 1943. From there it was a stint at Heavy Conversion Unit, Croft Spa., Yorkshire, for training on Halifaxes until, on August 8, the entire 408 Squadron was transferred to Linton on Ouse and converted to Lancaster 2s.

There he would have other close shaves while flying to targets like Stuttgart, Hannover, Leipzig, Düsseldorf, Berlin and Frankfurt. One night, November 26, heading for target, the starboard outer engine choked, and the plane began to lose altitude. Still, Lloyd and his crew pressed on to target, bombing Berlin, at which point their engine kicked in again. But just as the Lancaster was regaining altitude, they were hit by flak. As if this weren't enough, a Junker 88 night fighter had latched onto them. Lloyd managed to shake the fighter and headed over the North Sea to Lincolnshire. They must surely have wondered when their luck would run out, and over Lincoln the troublesome engine kicked out for good. The escape hatch wouldn't open so there was no bailing out. Lloyd called "Mayday" and frantically checked out his options. He saw what turned out to be a sewage disposal plant, in Lincolnshire. He managed to "belly-land" the damaged Lancaster only feet from the actual plant. All of the crew survived.

Bob Lloyd, Guinea Pig, survived his years of service. He would go on to marry Dorothy, have a very successful career at the Rothmans of Pall Mall Canada, Ltd., and become one of the key architects in the formation of the Canadian Guinea Pig Club, serving on its executive. Widowed, Lloyd has since remarried.

Were it not for the excellence of repairs Lloyd received, he would not have been able to continue his tour. The crew at East Grinstead allowed Lloyd to return to his own crew, where he served on dangerous operations. The hospital had done its job in preparing Lloyd to return to active service.

William E. Tanner

P/O William Ezra "Bill" Tanner joined the RCAF on May 16, 1941, with Dave Christie. They were two young men from Cardston, Alberta, the first two to enlist in the air force. Tanner graduated at a wing ceremony at No. 7 SFTS at Fort MacLeod, Alberta, on January 15, 1942, as a sergeant pilot. He was sent overseas with Christie in March of 1942, where they were posted separately. (Christie was later killed in action). Tanner became a pilot for the reconnaissance division, seeing coastal command service from bases in England. He was flying Lockheed Hudsons. After nine months he flew his Hudson to North Africa, following the scene of activity in the Middle East to Gibraltar, as part of a four-man crew one of only four such Canadian crews working with the RAF in the North African Campaign. His duties there included night-flying recon-naissance missions as he describes in an interview in a Cardston newspaper:

Bill Tanner

We were attacking subs, and light shipping vessels at night. That's

81

when the U-boats came up to the top. At night they surfaced to charge their batteries.[4]

Then it was on to Sicily and then into Italy. He finished his first tour of ops in November 1943. After returning to North Africa for a week, he was back in Italy, this time at an OTU instructing new pilots. On December 7, 1943, while training a pilot near Salerno, Tanner experienced disaster:

We had just got off the ground when one engine quit and the plane swung around.

The wing of the unstable plane hit a stone silo and broke off, and the plane crashed into a haystack where it burst into flames. Fortunately there were American officers nearby. They pulled Tanner from the burning plane. The two pilots in training did not survive.

Tanner was in bad shape with a concussion, paralysis, and broken ankle, nose, shoulder, thumb, and chin. He was also missing six teeth. As well, there were burns to the hand, lacerations of the eye and brow, the hands, arms, cheek and chin, and a smashed lower lip. He was taken to an American hospital where he remained unconscious for the first two and a half days. He remained in the American hospital for two weeks and then was sent to an English military hospital where he was operated on numerous times. It was determined that he would be moved across Italy from Naples to a hospital in Bari. This was a 250-mile journey that took two days. The terrain was mountainous, and the ride was rough. While he was en route, the harbour at Bari was hit so that by the time he got there the hospitals were full. He had to go back to Naples.

Finally, in the spring of 1944, he was sent to East Grinstead. He was one of the airmen who entered the Canadian Wing in mid-summer of 1944. Among his operations was a flap graft to his face.

Tanner was known as an engaging man with a fine sense of humour. He was also a man of principle. George Wilson remembers hearing that Tanner had been offered a commission while still on his tour of ops. When he discovered that the rest of the crew would not be getting a commission, he turned his down.

Bill Tanner eventually did receive his commission sometime in late 1944. The pilot officer was repatriated to Canada in late 1944 and returned to Cardston. He joined the RCAF Reserve after his discharge. He possessed "the only plane in town" and happily gave rides to the local population. He also dated and married Lajeanne. They would have five children.

Tanner bought a local garage. He eventually worked in the real estate industry in Edmonton, and in a trust company in Calgary. Both active members of the Mormon Church (Cardston is the headquarters of the Mormon Church in Canada), the Tanners attended some of the Guinea Pig reunions. They retired back to Cardston where Tanner summarized:

> I met a lot of people, travelled a lot, it was a good life.... But, I like this life too."

Bill Tanner died in 1990.

On December 11, 1943, the cornerstone of the Canadian Wing was laid by Air Marshall Harold "Gus" Edwards, Air Officer Commanding-in-Chief, RCAF Overseas.

The wing was sorely needed. With the increase in casualties due to the active bombing campaign, the Sty was overflowing with Guinea Pigs. Since the largest allied contingent in the ward was Canadian, the wing was not only logical but practical and inevitable.

Dr. Tilley had worked behind the scenes to make this wing a reality. As he headed into 1944, with the bodies of the singed, the fried, and the mashed still coming, he must have hoped the wing would be completed as soon as possible.

The Guinea Pigs, however, had their own version of the need for a new wing. The third verse of the Guinea Pig Anthem goes like this:

> We've had some mad Australians,
> Some French, some Czechs, some Poles.
> We've even had some Yankees,
> God bless their precious souls.
> While as for the Canadians—
> Ah! That's a different thing.
> They couldn't stand our accent
> And built a separate Wing.

Guinea Pigs (January–June 1944)

It was a wicked winter, the winter of 1943–44. The weather was far from an ally, throwing its elemental forces at aircrew as they planned their raids on Berlin and other targets.

Berlin was often the goal. "The Big City" was a logical hit, and a psychological focal point for Bomber Harris. It was a long trip into German airspace, to a well-defended fortress and a country teeming with night fighters [See Bob Lloyd's story]. The Battle of Berlin, which really got going in November of 1943, was to last through the spring of '44 culminating in the Nuremberg raid and exacting a very high price in crews and bombers.

Crews and bombers.

The war had been on for some time. Where were these crews coming from?

Two Guinea Pigs: Garnett Moore and Bob Tait

One of the pilots, Garnett "Tar" Moore, had started out his career as a cub reporter for the *Calgary Herald* newspaper. The Medicine Hat native then joined the army, serving with the Lord Strathcona Horse Royal Canadians from 1932–1936. After this he joined the Air Force in May 1937 as an AC2. Like many fitters and riggers, he was moved around. He lectured in fabricwork for a while. At No. 6 Repair Depot in Trenton he took a crew and started assembling Fairey Battles. He was later transferred to Calgary in January 1941, where he assembled Tiger Moths and Ansons. But like many ground crew he dreamed of flying, so in July 1942 he remustered to aircrew. He received his commission in April 1943.

This made Tar Moore somewhat older than most men in training. After all, he had already had a stint in the service. But June 1943 found him overseas. While he had trained for Coastal Command, he was transferred to Bomber Command, and attended OTU Honeybourne. Moore was almost through his training, but the commanding officer determined that he needed just two more hours of "circuits and bumps." It was Saturday, February 12, 1944. There was a skeleton crew in the Whitley. Mid-upper gunner Bob Tait was in the seat next to Moore (Tait had traded duties with another air gunner that night.) Dick Hoffman, the bomb-aimer, had wanted to take the gunner's turret, so Tait sat with Moore.

(Although two gunners were required on ops, there was only one gunner's turret in the training aircraft). Wireless operator Michael Grady was also on board.

The first circuit and landing was a piece of cake. On the second circuit the weather turned on them. Here is Moore's account of what happened. Moore was about to become a Guinea Pig:

> I heard the tower telling other pilots to "continue with the exercise, continue with the exercise." On our second approach, we were shot off with Very lights and had to do an overshoot. I remember doing that overshoot and going around once and missing the funnel, so I had to go around again. I found the funnel and came down and was about fifty feet off the deck when all red broke loose again, with the Very lights and the red flashing lights so I had to do another overshoot. And I remember, it's funny the things you remember, taking off my gloves because my hands were so hot, and shoving the gloves in the front of my battledress.
>
> I went around again, found the funnel, but I remember the Drem lights were hard to see. I came on down for a normal landing in the green. Touched down. All I remember is for a second seeing...a white light and then—crash—and we were into it.

What Moore hit was another plane. He had been given the green light but the runway wasn't clear. Moore speculated as to what the other kite was doing there:

> The crew ahead of me [in the plane ahead] had an instructor-pilot, and as it was Saturday night, I guess he had a date, so instead of going up to the end of the runway and around the perimeter track he'd stopped and done a 180 degree turn on the flare path and was coming back....And we rolled, I rolled along and hit him head on just like two cars on the highway. There was an immediate flash and Bob Tait, also a Guinea Pig, had to reach to the top hatch to open it up to help me taxi because I couldn't see my starboard wing. When we crashed he smashed his face on some armour plating that was just ahead of him and was thrown flat on his back in the navigator's compartment. I

remember his big black boots, and that's all I could see when I glanced around.

All of this must have occurred in a couple of seconds for the next thing that happened, Moore's props cut into the other plane's petrol tanks and the other plane's props cut into his and there was a huge flare:

> Until the props stopped—I kicked the switches off—it was throwing flaming petrol. First load took out the perspex and my face stopped most of the rest. I had to turn around to scream at Bob; he was dazed, but he was out of the road of the flaming petrol. I remember screaming at him and hitting his toe with my hand and pointing to the top hatch, and he stepped on my knee and was out the hatch. He burned his right hand as he was getting out because the top hatch was burning from the flaming petrol. I followed him out closely, and I could glance down and see that I was burning from the flying boots up. I guess my Boy Scout training came into use because I dropped off the wing and onto the tarmac and was rolling over onto the wet grass with my hands shoved above my head: rolling, and rolling and rolling myself out.

Miraculously, the crew of this plane survived. The wireless operator had escaped. The bomb-aimer, who had been in the gunner's turret, also escaped, stepping out onto the wing through the broken fuselage. It had, luckily for bomb-aimer Hoffman, broken apart right at the gunner's turret. As Moore later observed, "I guess we didn't hit right head on."

The "sprog" crew in the other aircraft escaped unharmed, but their instructor, the screened pilot, was not as fortunate. His feet were mangled in Moore's props, and he didn't get out. Moore's burns were serious. He believed his woollen underwear probably saved him from worse burns to the body, because his main burns were to the face and hands.

He was taken to an RAF hospital at Cosford. His eyes were closed those first ten days. Archie McIndoe came to see the men and moved Moore as soon as possible to East Grinstead. Moore remembered an ambulance, a shot of morphine, and then all was a blur for the next two or three months.

Moore arrived in the Sty around the beginning of March 1944. He later referred to the Sty as "that wonderful ward." He had fond memories of Dr. McIndoe, Dr. Tilley, Dr. Park and the nurses—Marge Jackson, Fran Oakes, and Sister Mealy. He spoke of the town, the Whitehall pub, and, of course, the Sty itself:

> There was a wonderful attitude in Ward III. I'll never forget it. It's not too many people can say that some of the most pleasurable parts of their lives were spent in pain and in hospital, but I can say that. I have fond memories, although, between you and me, I'd rather die than go through that first two, three months again. It was murder. However, we survived and we're the lucky ones.

Moore was repatriated to Canada in August 1944 and went to the Christie Street Hospital for more operations. As many Guinea Pigs felt, things weren't quite right at Christie Street until Dr. Tilley returned in the fall of 1945.

Moore would leave the RCAF in 1948 as a 100 percent pensioned burn victim. He was also married to Jacqueline and had two children (eventually three). The Moores travelled to Edmonton, where Tar found a job with the Federal Taxation Department. From there it would be a promotion and a move to Nova Scotia. By 1952 he was in need of further repairs. Dr. Tilley was again his surgeon. Further employment opportunities took the Moores to Fort Smith, (Northern Affairs), and Ottawa (Indian Affairs and Northern Resources). Following his retirement in 1970, which seems to have lasted five months, Moore took a job as "Fire Look-Out" on Goat Peak Mountain, for the B.C. Forestry Service. He would keep this job for another twelve years. Garnett "Tar" Moore died in January 1986, leaving his wife, children and grandchildren. As a last deed, Moore donated his eyes to an eye bank. Garnett "Tar" Moore lived life to the fullest despite, or probably because of, his serious brush with death.

Robert Tait

Meanwhile, what was happening to Bob Tait? Robert "Bob" Tait of Winnipeg had seen the green light go on. The landing was clear. As Moore had stated, Tait was standing right behind the pilot when they crashed. His face smashed into the armour plating behind the pilot's seat. He had just become a "mashed" variety of Guinea Pig. His front teeth were gone and his lips were ripped open. He also had burns to his eyelids and the right side of his face. His hands were burned even though he was wearing gloves.

Bob Tait

He does remember Moore shouting at him, but because of the force of the collision he was initially stunned. He admits, "If Tar had not said 'Out the top hatch!', I might not have made it."

The Cosford hospital where they were taken did have a burn unit that included saline bath treatment. Archibald McIndoe paid another visit to Cosford, and Bob Tait followed Tar Moore a few months later.

Tait would become an early resident of the new Canadian Wing. He was impressed:

> Other than what we had to pay to be there, it was very much like living in a hotel.

There Dr. Tilley operated on his left hand:

> Dr. Tilley said I was one of those (un)fortunate types who weren't burned very badly but who had developed this keloid scar tissue all over the back of my left hand, my right hand and the side of my face. So the first operation had him take all this keloid scar tissue off the back of my left hand and put on a beautiful graft. It took really well, and I'm very grateful to Dr. Tilley for what he did there. In the next operation I had my mouth straightened out from where I had hit the armour plating, had scars removed and new teeth put in. I also had a skin graft to my right hand and a graft on the side of my face where I had the keloid scar tissue. Grateful to the Wingco and all his staff—nurses like Sally McLellan and Sister Pat and Frankie and Marj Peacock and of course Marge Jackson, the head nurse, and Frankie Anderson. And this goes for all the other doctors and all the orderlies, too. We certainly were treated well.

After the war Bob Tait married Gudy and became a machinist for Canadian Pacific Railway. Although he would many years later refer to the crash as an "aircraft barbeque," Bob Tait also knows luck when it hits him. The gunner he switched shifts with? He flew another mission and was killed.

Reginald Harrison

Reginald "Reg" Harrison is a Guinea Pig familiar with the ironies of fate. A gregarious, energetic man, Harrison knows all too well how much luck, fate, or grace plays in an airman's life. Reg Harrison's military career has been summarized as "When a Tour Equals 19 Trips."[5]

Reginald Harrison

Harrison, a Saskatchewan native, did his training in Regina and Virden, Manitoba, as well as No. 11 SFTS Yorkton, Saskatchewan. On July 1, 1943, he arrived in England, did advanced training, OTU and heavy conversion, and by March 12, 1944, was posted to 431 (Iroquois) Squadron based at Croft, Yorkshire, flying Halifax bombers.

Harrison describes the events leading up to his entry into the Guinea Pig Club:

> My introduction to the Guinea Pig Club came about as a result of being in the immediate vicinity of a 500 lb. bomb when it exploded. It was my very first day, March 15, 1944, on an operational squadron.

Harrison was scheduled to fly "second dickie" that night, with a P/O Thirsk. But Thirsk had a friend who had just arrived on the station and who was also scheduled for a second dickie flight that evening. Would Harrison mind switching planes so the friends could fly together? Harrison agreed to the change and promptly saved his life. The plane piloted by P/O Thirsk never returned. Meanwhile, Harrison was crewed with F/O Philbin in a Halifax Mark 5. They went on ops to bomb a marshalling field in Amiens. All went well until they returned. A 500 lb. bomb had hung up in the wing rack. It was jarred loose upon landing, and exploded when they hit the runway.

The crew in back were immediately killed. The three survivors at the front of the plane (the only part that remained following the explosion) were the pilot, Harrison as second dickie, and the bomb-aimer. Harrison *should* have been at a crash station position behind the main spar, but he had asked to remain up front to witness the landing. Again, he had cheated death.

Harrison received a flash burn on his left forearm as he was blasted from the aircraft. Given the fates of the other members, he was shaken up but grateful to have survived.

On leave for a few days, Harrison stayed with relatives in Hull. It was his uncle, upon examining his arm, who decided he needed medical attention. So Harrison journeyed to the nearest military establishment, an RAF anti-aircraft unit. He was examined there by the doctor on duty and told to return to his base without delay.

Bandaged, and aboard a train back to the base, Harrison was the object of stares and discreet sniffing as the odour from the fish oil dressing on his burn slowly permeated the air in the small compartment.

Back on base, the medical staff pondered what to do. Harrison was sent to an army hospital at Basingstoke and from there to East Grinstead. At the Queen Victoria Hospital Harrison was introduced to Ward III:

> The entire staff were friendly and showed a great deal of compassion towards the patients. They seemed to sense the difficult adjustment that many of the patients would face when they left the Sty and did their best to prepare them for the long uphill battles that they would have to fight.

Here, Harrison also had pause to consider his own luck:

> When I saw the severity of the burns on most of the patients, I soon realized how fortunate I was to have survived the bomb explosion with a mere burn on my left forearm.

He also recalled the bustling activity surrounding the Canadian Wing, which would open within months. As with most of the Canadians, he was fortunate to have Dr. Tilley work on him:

Dr. Tilley decided that a pinch graft would likely be the answer to my burn problem.... The operation was 100 percent successful, and I well remember Dr. Tilley proudly showing his handiwork to one of his colleagues. Dr. Tilley removed fifty-eight pinches from the upper portion of my left leg and did such a neat job that it now looks like a cribbage board. I should perhaps point out that every single pinch of the fifty-eight removed from my leg took hold when transferred to the burn area, and that was what pleased the Wingco.

Harrison was back on active flying duty by mid-May 1944. He would manage to cheat death several more times, in other prangs. On July 5, 1944, his plane lost an engine on take-off with a full load of bombs and petrol and crashed. They lost the bomb-aimer in that crash. Then on August 9, due to a diversion, they ran out of fuel over the Lake District and were forced to ditch their plane and parachute, immediately gaining entrance into the Caterpillar Club. Everyone survived that incident, although most were suffering from frayed nerves by this point. Taking this into consideration, Headquarters screened the crew, and Pilot Harrison was given the same option. He chose to continue flying and was given a makeshift crew. He would now be flying a Lancaster.

On November 30, 1944, Harrison was on ops over Duisburg. Again, fate would play with Harrison's life. While on the bombing run they were fired upon by a sprog crew from 6 Group, their comrades in arms. One of the engines burst into flames, and the hydraulics were shot out. The fire was extinguished, the bomb run completed, and Harrison aimed the craft home.

Approaching the airfield at Croft, Harrison lowered the undercarriage. Only one wheel came down. It is difficult to imagine a more frightening scenario. Both Harrison and the Tower knew how dicey it was trying to land on the short runway at Croft, so he was diverted to the crash airfield at Carnaby. Harrison managed to land the plane even though the landing gear had snapped off. The plane did two ground loops and stopped.

Harrison survived all these misfortunes, none of which were due to pilot error. He looks back on his military career with a mixture of pride, awe and frustration. Whether it was the series of extraordinary circumstances that plagued his tour of ops, or the DFC he was commended for but never received, he occasionally wishes certain things could have been different. Yet his memories of the Guinea Pig Club are all good ones:

> To be a Guinea Pig is a unique experience as this is a very exclusive club, of which membership to the club does not come by the easy route. Severely burned patients with very disabled abilities have proven that such disabilities can be overcome with sheer determination and courage. This was due in no small part to the encouragement and support received from the doctors, nurses, and all support staff at East Grinstead—a very unique place and a special one to all Guinea Pigs who gained strength, comfort and support from fellow Guinea Pigs who were going through similar trauma.

The post-war years have been interesting ones for Harrison as well. In November 1945 he began working for the federal government in Veterans Land Administration. Here his farming background came to good use as he worked to help in the resettlement and rehabilitation of veterans who wished to return to farming. He stayed with the VLA in different positions, settling in Saskatoon. He furthered his education with courses on property management at the University of Saskatchewan and worked as VLA Supervisor of Property Management for Saskatchewan, Manitoba, and northwestern Ontario. He married Jean in 1946, and they had three daughters. He has remained active in the Legion, in his church, and with such activities as horticulture, curling, golfing, photography and travel.

While Harrison's injuries were sustained on flying operations, his phosphorous burns were of a type more often associated with tank burns. Yet at East Grinstead they were equipped to treat all types of burns, lacerations, and bone and jaw fractures.

Kenneth Branston

Kenneth "Ken" Branston was one such "jaw" case. Branston was an RCAF mid-upper gunner with 419 Squadron out of Middleton-St. George. After he suffered double fracture of the jaw in a non-military accident, it was determined that he be sent to East Grinstead as they had the facilities and the training to deal with this type of injury.

He arrived at the Sty on March 21 and was bunked down next to none other than George "Curly" Wilson. As Branston had not yet begun flying ops he was impressed with Wilson's stories of the number of operations in which he'd taken part. Branston was surprised to learn that the 'ops' his friend was referring to were medical operations, on the slab at East Grinstead!

Branston was learning the language of the Sty. In fact, he uses his own descriptive language in outlining what it was like when his colleagues ate their meals:

> There were eight jaw cases, and at meal time it sounded like pigs feeding, for our jaws were wired shut and we had to suck the gruel through spaces in our teeth. The highlight was being issued with two pints of Guiness daily, which we saved for weekend partying.

Branston was also learning the recreations of the Sty.

And while he would eventually go back to his squadron and complete thirty-three ops, he did not forget the sights, and sounds, of Ward III. As he says:

> I was impressed with the fortitude and courage of the horribly burned patients I encountered as I walked through the wards. The doctors and nurses were not only competent but also caring and compassionate.

Kenneth Branston went home and got a university education, married Pat and had a family. He had a career in the aircraft industry. He lives in King City, Ontario, where he enjoys a comfortable life.

As the bombing campaign continued, plans for the invasion were underway. Bomber crews were kept busy as eyes, and targets, were set on France.

Douglas McCallum Stephen

Douglas "Doug" Stephen was the navigator of a Lancaster CJ3. A North Bay, Ontario, native, Doug had been serving, since the 27th of February, 1944, with RAF 550 Squadron, 1 Bomber Command, having been seconded from the RCAF in 1942.

On the night of May 3–4, 1944, he was on his thirteenth mission (mission "12A" to the crew), a raid of 346 Lancasters. The destination was Mailly-le-Camp, a Panzer Division training base some eighty miles east of Paris. The plan was to assemble nineteen miles north of target and orbit there until called in to bomb the target markers.

Inevitably, they encountered night fighters. To add to this, they arrived at the assembly point early, and the target markers went down late. Then the R/T transmissions from the Main Force Comptroller were overpowered by a ground station broadcast. The bombers were forced to orbit for a further fifteen minutes, ample time for the night fighters to pick off crew after crew. As Doug Stephen recalled, "It was a shooting gallery, and it certainly wasn't pleasant being one of the ducks."

They bombed their target and were heading home at 12,000 feet when they were hit by flak. The rear gunner was hurt and left his turret, entering the fuselage. The wireless operator, Sgt. Reg Moore, was about to replace the rear gunner when a night fighter shot up the turret. The fighter then moved along the craft, targeting the front end. He fired and the fuselage erupted in flames. Doug Stephen was burned in the face and severely burned on his hands.

One can hardly imagine the panic in the craft. The pilot, Sgt. T.A. Lloyd, was trying to hold the plane steady despite a useless inner port engine and damaged hydraulic lines. The aircraft went into a dive. Pilot Lloyd ordered the crew to jump. The bomb-aimer escaped through the nose hatch; Sgt. Moore, at the rear fuselage door, helped the gunner jump, and jumped himself.

At this point, the plane evened out. The dive had actually put out some of the flames. Lloyd continued piloting, with Doug Stephen navigating despite his burns, while the wireless operator and the flight engineer tried putting out the fire with extinguishers, leftover coffee from their flasks, and their hands and feet.

In this fashion they managed to get back to England, crash-landing at Ford, a satellite of Tangmere. The pilot, the wireless operator and the engineer were awarded immediate DFOs. Doug Stephen, instead, was awarded a trip to East Grinstead and membership in the Guinea Pig Club.

As Stephen said:

I got burned on the infamous Mailly-le-Camp raid where we lost forty-nine kites out of about 300, one of the worst losses Bomber Command ever suffered.

Official count has the losses at forty-two planes out of 346, but admits that the casualty rate was "very heavy...particularly for a French target."

Interestingly, so light did they see the risk that prior to this raid, Bomber Command had stipulated that a French target would only count for one-third of a mission (out of a thirty-mission tour of ops). Following the Mailly-le-Camp raid, a French target tallied as a full mission.

Doug Stephen spent time in the Sty, returning to active duty on the 24th of June, 1944. Most of the remainder of his ops were daylight raids, and often he was a formation leader.

Following the war, Doug Stephen married Maye, and they had a daughter. He had an active life and was a member of the Kiwanis Club, the 406 Squadron Association, RCAF, the Air Crew Association of Great Britain, The Nipissing Masonic Lodge No. 420 A.F. & A.M., and the North Bay Curling Club, where he served as president. Douglas Stephen died in July 1999.

This story illustrates the number of possible outcomes to any one crew's op. A seven-man crew climbed into a plane. Happily, in this instance, all seven survived. But three were awarded medals, and one was passed over while suffering severe burns. As for the three who jumped? Two were taken prisoner of war and the third became an evader, escaping through France, the Pyrenees, Spain, Gibralter, and back to England.

Two Guinea Pigs: Owen Jones and Jacob Redekopp

Owen J. Jones

Owen Jones was born in Belleville on June 30, 1924. With a family background of military service (father and brother in the Army), Jones was eager to do his part. He joined up on October 7, 1943, shortly after his eighteenth birthday. Jones chose the air force and was trained as a gunner, graduating from Mont Joli, Quebec. In September 1943, he was sent over on the *Queen Mary*.

Jones was rear gunner, Lancaster 898, RAF Station 50 Squadron at Skellingthorpe, Lincolnshire. His operations log for May 1944 shows the crew bombing ammo dumps at Lovaille, the Lanveoo South Plane Station in Brest, the marshalling yards in Lille, the military camp at Bourg Leopold and the marshalling yards at Tours.

These ops occurred night after night from May 6–7 to the attack on Tours on May 19–20. It was this operation that would prove the undoing of their Lancaster. Because no sortie report was ever handed in from Lancaster 898, Jones has utilized the squadron log from another crew to reconstruct that night:

> Attacked from 6,000 ft. 8/10th thin cloud. Visibility moderate, slight. Target identified by three spot fires. Bombs were seen to burst on the railway lines. It was a concentrated attack.

Jones remembers that night. There had been moderate flak, which they had managed for the most part to avoid. (Jones recollects that if the flak exploded with a brownish colour, they did not worry. If it was a bright flash it was too close.)

The crew had bombed their target and were heading home. They were so close when fate intervened:

> We were diverted to Benson because of fog at our home base, Skellingthorpe. Our aircraft was in the funnel [approach to runway] and was seen passing a church steeple with a red light on it, then there was a big flash—we were down!

At this point, Jones lost consciousness. He was pulled from the burning Lancaster, still unconscious:

> It is believed we had hit a small building prior to bouncing/sliding into the Barn on Crow Marsh Battle farm. Our aircraft destroyed 2/3 of the Barn, parts of the Barn dating back a thousand years—to 1066 and William of Normandy. [For history buffs, this Barn is mentioned in the Domesday Book].

Fortunately for Owen Jones, he was able to get in contact with people who helped him reconstruct his story at this point. One such person recalled seeing an airman on a stretcher in the hall of the farmhouse nearby, and an army doctor coming in to pronounce the man dead.

Jones's pilot, Jack Irving, the navigator, Doug Jewell, and the bomb-aimer, F.I. Drever, were killed on site. It is not known what happened to flight engineer "Paddy" Lawn.

Meanwhile, the mid-upper gunner, Jake "Red" Redekopp, who would himself become a Guinea Pig, had smashed/axed the doors away from the rear turret and dragged Jones out by the parachute harness across a field. Shouts of "Stand still!" followed them. Apparently, the area was a mine field. The two men did not budge until extricated by army personnel who knew the area.

Ambulances arrived to take the survivors to the appropriate hospitals. Jones was sent to St. Hughs/College Hospital in Oxford. (St. Hughs was specializing in head injuries during the war). Jones remembers that his head was swathed in bandages, and his jaw was immobilized. Jones stayed in this holding pattern while at St. Hughs, recalling a scene that occurred during his stay which must have been heartening to all patients at the hospital:

> An early day in June, 1944. There was an eruption of noise that must have awoken the whole area of Oxford. The shattering sound of Pratt/Whitney engines on the Dakotas (DC 3s) towing equivalent numbers of Horsa Gliders, with regiments of paratroopers aboard, to help establish the Beachhead on Normandy. We all stood outside the doors of this hospital to watch. It seemed like hours, between the darkness of night and an early dawn, as staggering numbers of aircraft and gliders passed overhead. Millions around the world must have shared my emotions on that historic day and believed this to be the Beginning of the End— D-Day, June 6, 1944.

In late June Owen Jones met Drs. McIndoe and Tilley. After examination it was determined that further maxillo-facial surgery might improve Jones's situation. He was "Styed" in Ward III awaiting surgery. As he waited he was kept busy, sent to Marchwood Park for R & W (Rest and Work). There he entered the carpentry shop and made parts for Sunderland Flying Boats.

Jones would have the distinction of being one of the transition patients, beginning his stay at the Queen Victoria Hospital in Ward III and moving, with a handful of Canadians, to the new Canadian Wing, sometime around July 20, 1944. There he was treated with nose, lip and lower jaw surgery as well as internal jaw redefining. He also had teeth replaced on the right side of his jaw.

On July 30 Jones turned twenty. The mail he received that day was his first since the crash, and it included a letter from his mother containing the grim news that his brother, Murray, had been killed in the battle for Caen. When Dr. Tilley learned of this:

> ...he came to my bed and asked me if I would go out with him to the Whitehall Pub in the local area. He spent hours with me and talked me through my grief. For his compassion, in those hours, I am forever grateful.

As with most Guinea Pigs, Owen Jones is philosophical about his stay at East Grinstead and his tenancy at the Queen Victoria Hospital:

> We were expected to be as you are, try not to get into too much trouble, try to be an adult and like-minded. (How does this happen to an immature boy of nineteen—heaven only knows, and a rear gunner at that!) It happens as more and more you see that your own injuries (perceived to be "medical problems") are only a blemish compared to the others, a closely knit group around you—the Guinea Pigs. It takes years and years afterward to realize that your being "a part of" was achieved by the non-apparent giving by the likes of the McIndoes and Tilleys that were with you all the time when at the Queen Victoria Hospital, and the future "Pig" Reunions. This is part of the making of "The Guinea Pigs."

Owen Jones was discharged in February 1945, and he had one month with his mother before she died of grief over her lost son, Murray. Jones went back to school and received a diploma in business administration from the University of Toronto. He accepted a position with the Powell River Company, in British Columbia, where he has lived since 1946. Jones has been twice married, and has children, step-children and grandchildren. He enjoys taking life as it comes and calls his home "a virtual paradise."

Jacob Redekopp

Jacob "Jake" Redekopp was born and raised in Kelstern, Saskatchewan, in a family of five brothers. Redekopp joined the RCAF in January 1943, in Moose Jaw, Saskatchewan. He did his ITU and gunnery school in Manitoba and further air gunner training at Mont Joli, Quebec, graduating in the summer of 1943.

Redekopp was posted overseas to an RAF OTU where he crewed up with Pilot Officer Jack Irving as his pilot. Redekopp was mid-upper gunner in a crew that included tail gunner Owen Jones. After OTU they went to a Lancaster bomber conversion unit and were posted to 50 RAF Lancaster Squadron at Skellingthorpe Lincoln.

Following the crash described by Owen Jones, Redekopp, who was still conscious, extricated himself from his mid-upper turret. He was able to remove Jones as well, dragging him to safety. He and Jones and the wireless operator, Jim Philips, were the only ones who survived.

Redekopp was badly burned. He eventually arrived at the Queen Victoria Hospital for treatment of burns to his hands, face, back and arms. The most severe burns were to his hands, and Redekopp was grateful to Dr. Tilley for his excellent treatment. He would be a year at East Grinstead before being able to return home where he needed further rehabilitation at a hospital in Calgary.

When Redekopp left hospital, he returned to Kelstern, Saskatchewan, for a visit and then went to work in Kelowna, British Columbia, in the lumber business. He also worked in Calgary as a welder and then in Toronto in the prefabricated housing industry. Jacob Redekopp eventually moved to Shaunee, Oklahoma, where he has retired with his wife of twenty-six years, Shirley.

Henri J.A. Marcotte

Henri "Hank" Marcotte was a pilot with RCAF Bomber Squadrons 103 and 425. Marcotte's distinguished military career included two tours of operations during which time he was awarded the DFC and CD. He also became a member of the Guinea Pig Club.

After the war Marcotte married Jeanette. He joined the Canadian Department of Transport's Air Division and worked there until his retirement as an air carrier inspector. Henri Marcotte,

DFC, died in 1989. His widow, Jeanette, has established the Henri Marcotte Memorial Scholarship which is awarded annually to a promising economics student at the Université de Moncton.

Frank Hubbard

Frank Hubbard was a young pilot who went overseas in September 1941. Hubbard would have an exciting career flying with four different squadrons, the last one being 401 Spitfire Squadron. Guinea Pig Lorne Cameron was the CO there. Little did Hubbard know he would soon join the Guinea Pig fraternity.

Listening to Hubbard describe his exploits, one is reminded of the youth, energy, language and superstitions that the air force embodied:

> The Air Force had its superstitions. The RFC types believed that having your picture taken was a sure harbinger of cashing in, buying the farm, etc. [In] my generation in the cast system in England that... distinguished between "officers and other ranks" types, [there was] a large number of aircrew of NCO rank. After a certain length of time, depending on the whim of fate, an NCO would be commissioned. Enter WWII aircrew superstition: getting your commission was almost certain to lead to "buying it" or becoming a POW.

After two and a half years in England, Hubbard had been granted his commission. He wryly noted that a friend of his who had received his commission two weeks previously was wandering around France, having been shot down as if on cue. Hubbard describes his situation at the time:

> We were at Tangmere, under canvas of course, and were to do a show from Hawkinge, which of course entailed a trip. The idea was to fly low to Hawkinge, land, have tea and refuel, take off and fly over to "Stomer." Unfortunately I don't remember the object of the exercise. We were carrying 45 gallon drop tanks and flying on the deck in order not to alert Jerry. About halfway to Hawkinge I thought of checking my "jet tank," so-called because we could jettison them when necessary, but being busy keeping station I decided

against it! We landed in Hawkinge and in my new status, I could have tea in the Officer's Mess. Tea over, we went out to do the main part of the trip.

Hubbard readied himself for the flight:

> It was May 28, and for England a very hot day. The three aircraft which were supposed to be the CO's red section could not get started. My YOY started beautifully so I teamed up as his number two. We took off. The drill was to climb to 2000 feet, form up, drop down to the deck and proceed to France. At 1,500 feet I selected my "jet tank" and the next thing was looking at a very still prop. The Spit 9 had a sink rate of 2,000 ft./min. so I had little time to do much, but found a field and landed there. I use the term loosely.

Hubbard's crash had just qualified him for entry into the Guinea Pig Club, but first there was the trip to Canterbury where for some reason he was placed in various plaster casts from head to toe. From there it was the famous ambulance drive to East Grinstead. Hubbard was soon initiated into life in the ward:

> My first experience in the brine bath was definitely interesting. While it was great when they removed my casts, it was not nearly so pleasant when they trimmed the ends of my fingers! The Wingco had a great laugh at my casts since they covered my head, arms and legs, and he was not quite sure what to expect. Whenever we met after the war he would have another laugh.

The casts had, however, spared him doses of gentian violet, which he had experienced following a previous crash.

Hubbard was soon making the rounds in a wheelchair, taking part in the ward parties. He spied a pretty redhead in a Canadian (WD) uniform and promptly told her he would marry her. Such was the spirit of Guinea Piggery.

Frank Hubbard had the privilege of moving into the Canadian Wing before it was officially open, enjoying the brand new facilities. He would also have the privilege of witnessing the runaway doodlebug and the 20 mm. slug that shot down "Fergie's" bed [See Everett Ferguson in "The Canadian Wing"].

The positive "medicine" that was life at the hospital worked its wonders on Frank Hubbard. In August 1944 after a weekend out on the town with fellow Guinea Pigs and Canadian female staff members, Hubbard again uttered words to the attractive redhead named Shirley, and on September 2, at East Grinstead's St. Swithun's Church, Shirley became Shirley Hubbard and Frank became a married man. His only complaint about the service was all the kneeling in church which was hard on his burned knees. The reception at the hospital, put on by Nurse Marge Jackson and staff, was a resounding success.

Frank and Shirley Hubbard were sent back to Canada, where their first child was born. Frank Hubbard went into Rehab and then on to the University of Toronto where he took a degree in aeronautical engineering. He went to work for A.V. Roe where his speciality was engines, working on the Iroquois which would have powered the ill-fated Avro Arrow. He later worked for the Defense Research Board.

By 1968 he was eager to fly again, so he took a refresher course and gained a Commercial Licence Instructor's Rating. He purchased an aircraft maintenance shop in Prince George, British Columbia, in 1973. He later worked as an aeronautical engineer with the Canadian Department of Transport on the coast.

As with several other Guinea Pigs, retirement was merely a theory. Accordingly, when he "retired" he became a Design Approval Representative and bought a hobby farm. He also joined the Abbotsford Flying Club and maintains his flying licence.

Frank Hubbard was and is an active member of the Club. He was instrumental in organizing the early reunions and was a key player in the formation of the Canadian Wing.

D-Day. A date that would be remembered by anyone serving his country; a date that many would not live to remember. Every plane that was airworthy was up there on June 5–6, the Canadians contributing an impressive show of strength to Bomber Command. Throughout the invasion, crews would do sortie after sortie. Many of these crews had been on ops for some time and were finally seeing the tangible result of their labours. As well, newer crews were being prepared for the push.

James Martin

Flight Lieutenant James "Jim" Martin was in one of those crews. A Fort Erie, Ontario, native, pilot Martin was crewed with a collection of fellows from all across Canada: the navigator was from Victoria; the bomb-aimer from Vancouver; the rear gunner and the engineer from Alberta; the wireless operator from Trois Rivières; and the mid-upper gunner from Antigonish, Nova Scotia.

During a training flight on the morning of June 6, W/O Bourdages picked up the information that the allies had landed in France. This was good news to Martin and crew. They would soon be on ops.

Accordingly, they were posted to 428 (Ghost) Squadron at Middleton-St. George in Yorkshire. There they met the flight commander and the CO and were told to prepare for a training mission the following day. The entire 428 Squadron was in the process of converting to "Lancs," but the crew would be flying a Halifax V for the purposes of the training flight. Martin notes:

> I believe most new crews got the older aircraft. I guess they figured if you were going to "prang" it might as well be in an old kite.

They took off the evening of June 10. The plan was to fly north to Scotland, west to the sea and then south to a point west of their base. They would then drop some practice bombs on a range in Yorkshire. Martin describes that happened:

> Our ceiling was down to 3,000 feet and we made our runs at that height. On the third or fourth bombing run—just as we were coming up on target—the port engine caught fire! It was more than a fire—the engine was vibrating and appeared to be breaking up. In moments, the vibration was so severe that metal from the cowling around the engine was tearing away in strips. This metal would stand up in the airflow for some time before breaking off. Each time this happened the drag would pull the aircraft sharply to the left. We lost altitude with each of these swings. The aircraft was extremely difficult to control, and it was all I could do to keep it level.

Martin was later to learn that two blades of the propeller had broken off, and the remaining two blades set up the vibration that tore the assembly apart. One blade cut into the wing and severed control of the engine.

Martin alerted the crew to stand by and went through the drill to feather the prop and put out the fire, to no avail. Martin then ordered the crew to prepare to abandon, which meant they would be gathering in the nose of the craft. Martin gave the "Abandon" order, aware of the low height and the raging fire. There was confusion due to a dislodged intercom plug and valuable seconds were lost:

> [The navigator] "Doc" Savage told me that they had removed the hatch and thrown it out of the opening. The wind (air stream) caught it and jammed it in the opening. Thus the delay and the reason for the plug being disconnected from the intercom. I guess it was a real problem getting it free.

But the men jumped clear. Then just as Martin was preparing to leave the cockpit he made a discovery:

> I took off my gloves and helmet and swung over the step to go below. For some reason I took a last look down the fuselage and saw the mid-upper gunner, Neil McDougal. He apparently had trouble getting out of his turret because of the behaviour of the aircraft and had struck his head and become confused. He thought he was alone. I motioned to him to get out as I climbed back into the cockpit. I got the aircraft straightened out again, and he jumped.

McDougal was very low. He just had time to open his chute before he hit the ground. He landed in front of a pub with a sign that read "Wines, Spirits and Ales." Martin was later told that McDougal thought he was in heaven. (Neil McDougal would later be killed in action). Meanwhile, Martin had to contend with the fact that his chance to jump had passed:

> I don't recall what our altitude was, but I knew that we were very low. It was the middle of the night. There were no lights, of course. No stars. Nothing. My last

conscious move was to grab the hand grip between the two windscreens with my right hand. Then everything went quiet.

Martin came to about 100 yards from the aircraft which was enthusiastically burning, the air gunner's ammunition exploding like fireworks. Martin could make out a man standing nearby. Afraid that the man hadn't seen him, Martin tugged at his leg. The man assured him that an ambulance had been called, then demanded his own assurance that there were no bombs on board. Martin was taken to York Military Hospital:

> It appeared that I had landed in an open field, and the crew told me afterward that the aircraft had exploded when it hit the ground. I must have been blown through the starboard side of the aircraft. The fact that I had not put my helmet or my safety harness back on when I got back into the cockpit probably saved my life. The fact that the aircraft blew up probably saved my life or at least minimized the burns I received.

Martin was on the critical list for two weeks. He had suffered first, second and third degree burns to his right hand, left leg, the left side of his face and his scalp. His hair had been burned off. He also had four fractured vertebrae and a fractured right ankle.

During the month spent at York Hospital Martin celebrated his twenty-third birthday. He was then sent to an RAF Hospital at Northallerton and from there to the Canadian Army Hospital at Basingstoke. At Basingstoke Martin was able to see the cost of the invasion as scores of casualties flowed in from France. The burn ward was crowded, the doctors and nurses overworked. Martin and the one other mobile patient in the ward assisted where they could. Here Martin was also to see the types of burns soldiers generally received. While an airman's burns were often the result of fire in the aircraft, "flash" burns of brief exposure but intense heat, a tank corp member's burns, for example, were more often of the chemical, phosphorous variety. [Which made the phosphorous burn of Guinea Pig Reg Harrison somewhat of an exception].

After a month at Basingstoke Martin was finally sent to East Grinstead, which, due to the time frame, made him one of the early patients in the new Canadian Wing. At the Queen Victoria Hospital, Dr. Tilley got busy repairing Martin. By early October he was on the road to recovery:

> My burns had healed. Some plastic surgery was scheduled to build up my ear. The hair had grown around the burn on my scalp and had grown long enough to cover part of the scar. Having to walk home from the "Whitehall" [pub] after the last bus had gone was great therapy for my ankle. And, I started thinking of what was to happen next.

Dr. Tilley informed him that he would have the work done on his ear and then be sent back to Canada. Martin pushed for a return to active duty, and, after a medical, Dr. Tilley approved his return to the squadron.

Jim Martin did return, this time to 429 (Bison) Squadron and flew ops until VE Day.

Possibly because Martin had been moved from hospital to hospital and had seen both the casualties and the conditions, he was able to summarize his experience so succinctly and eloquently:

> It was at Northallerton that I realized that the hair in the centre of my scalp would not grown back; it was at Basingstoke that I realized I had lost part of an ear; but it was at East Grinstead that I realized how fortunate I had been.

James Martin returned to Canada, married and had a family. He was an active member of the Guinea Pig Club serving on the executive. He died in 1999.

Funny things happen in the service. Coincidences. One meets a fellow on the boat over and ends up on station with him years later. One asks a buddy to console his best girl if anything happens to him, and that buddy ends up marrying the bereaved girl. And then there are the people who "ghost" one another around from place to place.

John Everett

John Everett

John Everett must have shaken his head a couple of times over the number of occasions he ran into Jim Martin. Everett joined the RCAF in 1940, training as a bomb-aimer. He graduated in 1942 with results so impressive that he was pressed into service as an instructor which delayed his own overseas service. Everett was instructing at No. 6 ITS in Toronto in 1942 when young Jim Martin arrived, a new student pilot.

Eventually both men got overseas and were posted to their respective squadrons. Everett was with a Liberator Squadron as a bomb-aimer. He was on many ops until an accident left him with a fractured skull and a broken jaw.

Little did Everett and Martin know that they would crash at approximately the same time, be taken to Basingstoke hospital at the same time, and be transported to East Grinstead not only at the same time but in the same ambulance, only to find themselves side by side in the Canadian Wing!

That ambulance must have been full as it was carrying two other Canadian Guinea Pigs, Frank Hanton and Frank Hubbard.

John Everett survived the war, and following his retirement from long careers in the military and in the insurance business, he emigrated to Ireland and then to England where he remained until his death.

John Everett is a good example of the fluid movement of Guinea Pigs across the planet.

Paul Branch

Paul Branch, a young Torontonian, was finishing off high school when he noticed the depleting ranks of school chums in his classrooms, even as the ranks of servicemen on the streets increased. Accordingly, he took himself down to the recruiting centre and in the summer of 1941 was called up, making his way to Manning Depot.

Like many a new recruit, his first choice was to train for pilot duties, so he signed up for

Paul Branch

pilot or observer. He was sent to No. 6 ITU in Belleville. This was a new unit, so new that these first-course participants had the opportunity to help build the Pistol Range and the Drill Hall!

Following this exercise they were sent to Cap de la Madeleine to do Elementary Flying, then on down to Moncton to No. 8 Service Flying School. Washing out prior to the Wings Parade, Branch quickly remustered to wireless operator/air gunner and was sent to a new OTU in Nova Scotia, "Greenwood," which was involved with Coastal Command. Branch was screened there as an instructor for a while, at a time when Coastal Command relied heavily on OTU support for U-Boat detection, convoy duties, and the like. Before Paul Branch knew it, his first tour of duty was over. He had yet to leave the country.

He was sent to Dorval for a couple of months. Here the crew would familiarize themselves with Lochheed Hudsons and with flying the Atlantic: Gander to Goose Bay to Iceland to Prestwick. It was after this that they made the trip across the pond.

Upon arrival in Bournemouth, the crew was split up, Branch going on to an OTU near Liverpool. He was still on coastal ops but was eventually reassigned to Bomber Group and proceeded to OTU No. 23. Then it was on to Topcliffe to a conversion unit where he converted to Halifaxes and was attached to 429 Squadron. At this point, Branch made a decision that would change his life. He volunteered to join a Pathfinder Squadron in North Africa that was in the process of re-forming. This meant more course work, at Huntington, where Branch finished the Pathfinder course.

Now the young airman was ready to see the world. He was shipped to French Morocco, flew across North Africa at Algiers and Tunis. He joined his squadron, 614 Pathfinder Squadron (RAF) in the Sudan. The squadron was still flying Wellingtons, awaiting their new Halifaxes in preparation for the invasion of Italy. From their base they led bombing raids on German soldiers retreating into Italy, as well as taking part in longer range missions to Munich, Hungary, Bulgaria and Yugoslavia. Following the invasion the squadron moved onto the Lombardi plain were it was based with the American 456 Bomber Group.

It was June 10. Branch and crew got the go ahead:

We were taking off for Yugoslavia and dodging two fresh bomb craters on our runway that had been put there the day before and had not yet been filled in. As luck would have it, halfway down the runway...my skipper turned to his bomb-aimer and invited him to hold forward the throttles while he locked the boost throttles up. He [got] no response from the substitute bomb-aimer who was flying with us that night. This came as a great surprise to the skipper.

In the confusion over timing and response the plane started to veer off the runway:

Now it's bad enough when this happens, but with nine tons of target indicators on board it becomes a bit hairy.

They were headed toward an American Fortress in dispersal:

The fuselage of our aircraft went forward with no resistance while the wings were clipped off.

Branch reacted, opening the astrodome and heading down on the starboard main-plane:

Just as I got out to run, the tanks went up. It was warm. And in the position I assumed to run out of the flames, I could see my hands in front of me just, sort of, melting away. I don't know what gave me the encouragement to run out of the flames other than I saw my tail gunner fumble out of his turret, and in the light of the explosion I saw him "disappear" into the dust. I ran in the same direction, encountered him and implored him to help me. I was, needless to say, on fire.

It was ultimately the pilot of the plane taking off after Branch's own who rescued him, leaving his craft and grabbing Branch and rolling him in the dust until the flames died:

The next thing I knew, I was on the examination table in the American hospital on the aerodrome. I suppose I went through fits and starts of consciousness and unconsciousness while lying on that table, because I can remember a good deal of what happened. I can recall I lifted my head to see the rest of my body and saw that my legs seemed to have swelled up and split wide open in a number of places, like a barbecued pig.

And in the middle of this trauma, the voices:

> I remember an American doctor or orderly saying, "Oh, give him up, he won't last more than an hour." I can remember my tail gunner, Douggie Heath, saying, "Paul, it looks like your watch has had it." I also remember a doctor coming to me, looking at me upside down and saying, "Where's your home, son?" I told him Toronto was my home and he said, "Isn't that wonderful? I'm from Buffalo!"

Thus began Branch's sojourn. He would be taken to an army hospital in Italy and tended:

> ...to the best of their ability and knowledge, their knowledge of burns, of course, being very limited and so they, for weeks, left me in my original bandages on my legs and body. They did, however, dress my hands three or four times a day. It was obvious that they knew nothing about saline bath treatment. There was no bath in evidence at the hospital.

This did not bode well for Branch. Undressed burns could be anything from uncomfortable to completely debilitating to fatal. But Branch's luck was about to change for the better:

> One day I heard a bellow obviously intended for me, and the bellow went, "Who in the hell smells like that?" and as I looked to my right through the one eye I could see out of, a huge Group Captain doctor stood in the ward. He was a red-headed giant with a huge walrus mustache, and he said to me, "That's you that smells like that." I said, "'Fraid so, sir." He said, "Well, we'll remedy that very quickly." In a few short minutes he had what seemed to me to be the entire medical staff circled around my bed, and he was bawling them out, explaining to them the proper treatment for burns. He had just left England, and fortunately for me I was on the operating table under his knife, and he gave me my first grafts, my healing grafts.

Paul Branch was soon moved again, this time to an aerodrome to be transported to the Naples General Hospital where he received his first saline treatments:

> I sat in the saline tub for endless hours waiting for the warm saline solution to soak the bandages off my legs. This did not happen, and the matron came into the saline room to find that she had to give me needles and rip the bandages off. It was uncomfortable, to say the least.

Not long after this he was on his way to Britain, landing at Hearns and taken to hospital for a week. From then, at long last, he was escorted, as he remembers, "by a beautiful WAAF," to East Grinstead. He must have made an impression upon arrival:

> I was dressed in service cap, South African khaki battle dress, a pair of yellow shammy gloves, and a pair of red canvas rope-soled shoes. All of this was Red Cross issue in Italy.

That very day Ross Tilley happened to be interviewing and examining for potential surgeries. Paul Branch got immediate attention. Waiting for his first surgery, he was sent to Marchwood Park for industrial therapy, where he could perform useful duties. Branch realized that the other reason for sending him there was so that he could meet some of the most seriously injured Guinea Pigs who were between operations. These men would inspire him and give him pause to consider his own fate. The first operation, it was decided, would be on his nose:

> I was to have my nose done, and it turned out to be the best nose...a dermatome nose.

Paul Branch was by now a full-fledged member of the Guinea Pig Club. Proof of this was the manner in which he used his time. By Christmas 1944, while enjoying the Christmas and New Year's parties, he met Phyllis who would some four or five months later become Mrs. Paul Branch.

Another proof of his Guinea Pig status comes in his appreciation of Dr. Tilley. Addressing Dr. Tilley on audiotape several decades after their experiences at East Grinstead, Branch celebrated his surgeon and friend:

Certainly, Ross, you were...totally responsible for the high-toned atmosphere, the amiability, the comradeship and the ultimate respect of all of your patients, bar none, and also your staff—not only the medical staff but the kitchen staff, the administrative staff—it was obvious to us all that they had been hand-picked and certainly by your hand. Like all of your Guinea Pigs I am deeply grateful to you for all you have done for us.

As with many of the Guinea Pigs who would require further surgery, Paul Branch headed home to await the end of the war and the return of Dr. Tilley to the Christie Street Hospital.

Paul Branch furthered his education, then went into industry, and eventually back into education, becoming a teacher. He had two children, and also grandchildren. Later married to Pam, Paul Branch was an active member of the Guinea Pig Club, serving on the executive. Paul Branch died in July 2000.

Kenneth C. Smyth

Kenneth "Ken" Smyth a St. Catharines, Ontario, native received his wings with the RCAF and was sent overseas in November 1941. His OTU training was done with the RAF in northern England until March 1942. Ken Smyth was a fighter pilot, and, although always flying as RCAF, he flew with six different air forces during the war. Smyth explains:

After being in transit in some west African countries I

Ken Smyth

started flying Hurricanes in Egypt (29 June 1942) with the RAF. At Gaza, Palestine, I flew with the Composite Operational Unit (COU) with a Greek squadron that had just escaped from Greece (August 1942). Then I was sent to fly with the RAAF (Australians) for several months in various airports around Palestine. Then, RAF again in Tehran, and Abadan near the Persian Gulf, flying Hurricanes, defending the oil refinery (1942– 1943). Our Squadron then joined the Desert Rats at Tobruk and along the North Africa coast with duties to escort merchant navy and warship convoys through the Mediterranean. I was then sent to the South African Air Force for convoy escorts (July 1943). Back to the RAF and defense of the Suez Canal and the Nile Delta (early 1944).

Smyth remembered more details:

I had switched to Spitfires in the summer of 1943 and changed RAF squadrons. I was sent to the western desert again, and then in the spring of 1944 I went to Corsica where I did many behind-enemy-lines strafing sorties, and then was attached to the USAAF (Americans) where I fighter-escorted U.S. bombers over Italy.

Clearly, Smyth was seeing much of the air war first-hand and from the points of view of various allied forces. But Smyth's luck was about to turn. On his 88th operational sortie on June 11, 1944, a strafing run over Italy, Smyth was shot down in flames. The plane was rapidly losing height. He jumped at an altitude of only forty-five metres, very low. Smyth recalled:

Before I got out of the flaming Spit to use the parachute I was somewhat singed, so that in the few minutes after landing I knew I was about to be blind. My hands and legs were also burned.

His eyelids were gone. Given his condition, Smyth gave himself up as a POW, "not expecting to be taken alive because I'd been strafing in that area a few months."

The SS saw that a medical officer looked at Smyth, but in the few minutes of interrogation, he became totally blind. The blindness would last two months, coinciding with the time Smyth had to spend in solitary:

The German medical staff looked after me very well, but I lost about sixty pounds during those two months. After that I started to walk again and over the following months my eyes came back to normal sight—but with no eyelids or eyebrows to protect them.

The Germans then moved him around to POW camps in Italy and Germany. Near Nuremberg he was issued Red Cross boxes and began to regain a little weight. Smyth recalled:

> I ended up in a POW camp (Stalag Luft 1) near the Baltic Sea—from which I was exchanged (repatriated) through Switzerland as a wounded POW, and at Marseilles, France, I was destined to return to Canada via the U.S.A.. But I arranged in Marseilles to go to England because I had heard about the plastic surgeons there.

(Smyth also had a girlfriend in England whom he would marry overseas). So, by the labyrinthine route described, Smyth made his way to East Grinstead:

> My memory of East Grinstead—February '45 plus a few months—is now very hazy, but of the Queen Victoria Hospital I have nothing but pleasant memories of the overall conditions for me. As a tea-totaller (but not one completely) I didn't go to any taverns, but I attended and danced at a couple of dances, and experienced the way that the local girls in East Grinstead mixed with the Guinea Pigs. Very good! The medical support team and others at the Queen Victoria hospital were always the best possible, and the Guinea Pig patients always mixed pleasantly—both among themselves and with the medical support team and others.

Dr. Tilley performed several operations on Ken Smyth's eyes. Smyth was sent back to Canada in July 1945 where he waited, like many Guinea Pigs, for the safe return of Group Captain E. Ross Tilley, the beloved "Wingco" [Guinea Pigs continued affectionately to refer to Dr. Tilley as "Wingco" despite his promotion].

At the Christie Street hospital, Smyth underwent several follow-up operations and was finally discharged from hospital a little over two years after he was burned.

Smyth's story continued to be interesting. He formed a small country dance band and also purchased an auto service station in his hometown of Shawville, Quebec. Five years later he would leave Shawville, his marriage over and a young son in his custody. (The son would one day join the air force like his father).

Smyth went into sales work, and he even re-entered the active air force when fighter pilots were being recruited during the Cold War. When it became clear that he would actually end up as a SNIP (Staff Navigation Instructor Pilot), Smyth took another honourable discharge. He went to work for the federal government as a special inquiries officer with the Immigration Department and stayed there until his retirement. He also remarried, a long and happy marriage to wife Debbie, and was blessed with children and grandchildren.

A lifelong sports enthusiast, Smyth kept himself active, roller-blading well into his 84th year. Ken Smyth died in October 1999 after a peacetime life that was every bit as successful as his wartime service.

His final words on the Guinea Pig Club were words of praise for the efforts of the members who have kept the Club going, and for the value of receiving regular newsletters (from the Canadian Wing) and *The Guinea Pig* (from the parent Club), both of which he always read cover to cover.

Edgar G. Cecile

Edgar "Ed" Cecile was a young pilot who arrived in Bournemouth in June 1943. He did advanced flying at Oxford and then was posted to OTU at Market Harbour. During this time he captained three different crews in a Wellington bomber.

Cecile tells of the moment he became a member of the Guinea Pig Club:

> On July 1, 1944, while on a training mission, the port engine caught fire, and we crashed. There were six of us on the plane, and the tail gunner was killed. This happened about 2:00 p.m. I had the choice of attempting to land through some trees or through a hedgerow—I chose the trees because often the hedgerows concealed a stone wall—the starboard wing was clipped off by the trees, and we ended in an oat field, and everyone but the tail gunner escaped. I was burned climbing out of the pilot's escape hatch—the one time I wasn't wearing my gloves. So my hands were severely burned and my face and the back of my neck.

The ammunition was firing off in all directions which inhibited the efforts of a local farmer who had come on the scene to help. It would be a day later that they would find the gunner's body in his turret, burned to death.

But at the point the plane was going in, the tower saw it and sent an ambulance. Cecile continues:

> We were taken to the Royal Leicester Infirmary which was about eight miles away. This was where the minister told me about the tail gunner. At this infirmary they operated on my hands, removing the burned skin, and then I was sent to a military hospital in the Midlands. I was there for three weeks, and then Dr. Tilley requested that I (since I was a Canadian) be sent to East Grinstead.

Arriving in the new Canadian Wing, Cecile was greeted by the Guinea Pigs. He realized right away the unique quality of the place:

> One of the best things that happened to me at East Grinstead was that on arrival I was put into a bed next to Everett Ferguson (Fergie). What a wonderful person he was. His injuries were more serious than mine, but he always had a joke or a story to tell.

Cecile would go on to spend three months at East Grinstead and still marvels at the place:

> It was unlike any other hospital I had been in. The doctors, especially Dr. Tilley, the nursing sisters and medical staff were all caring people. They did their best to help these young burn victims overcome their injuries. The patients, once they were ambulatory, were allowed to leave the hospital and go into the town just as long as we let them know where we were going and when we would return. I remember one time in particular, two of us were going to the pub in town and mentioned it to two Yanks whose feet were burned and of course [they] couldn't walk—they said they really wished they could go with us—so we talked to Dr. Tilley, and he allowed us to take the station wagon so we could put the back gate down, and we loaded them into the station wagon and off we all went into

town. When we arrived at the pub, we carried them in and set them in chairs—they had a great time and enjoyed themselves completely, and if it had not been for Dr. Tilley, this could never have happened.

Ed Cecile and his wife Patricia have been close to the Guinea Pig Club ever since:

> The Guinea Pigs are a wonderful group of people. My wife and I have made many good friends since we received the first letter inviting us to a reunion in Toronto. Even though we just met every three years at first, and lately every two, whenever we see these good friends it's as if we had been together just yesterday and having a good time, as usual.

Robert C. McCallum

Robert "Bob" McCallum was an airman from Scotland. After his war service and his entry into the Guinea Pig Club he attended Glasgow University where he graduated with an honours degree in chemistry. He worked for I.C.I. until he emigrated to Canada in 1952 to work for Canadian Industries, Ltd., as a chemist. He married Katherine in 1956 and they had two daughters.

Robert McCallum

In later years Robert McCallum suffered from a long and debilitating disease. He died in December 1988.

Robert McCallum is another Guinea Pig who chose Canada after the war. He was, of course, a welcome member of the Canadian Wing of the Guinea Pig Club.

E.A. Doyle

E. Arthur "Art" Doyle joined up on May 23, 1941. He was sent overseas that November. His first postings were as office clerk with the following squadrons: 408 RCAF Squadron at RAF

Balderton, a satellite of RAF Syerston; 418 RCAF at RAF Ford; and 414 RCAF Squadron, Army Co-op.

Doyle then remustered to aircrew, receiving his A/G (air gunner) Wing in 1943. He trained at ITS St. John's Wood, London, and at AGS in Stormy Downs, South Wales. While he was at No. 22 OTU, he was approaching a flight on his motorbike when he met with an accident. His right heel slid into the rear wheel of the motorbike. The leg was quite badly damaged.

Doyle was sent to Hospital Stratford-on-Avon. There the doctors applied a free graft with skin taken from his stomach. The graft was not successful, and it was cut off. Doyle was then sent to RAF Cosford where an attempt was made to clean up the job, and from there it was on to East Grinstead. The Canadian Wing was still being finalized when Doyle arrived. Dr. Tilley took a look at Doyle's leg and decided to perform a cross-leg flap.

Doyle stayed a while at the hospital and had the opportunity to witness the "baptism by fire" buzz-bomb attack on the Canadian Wing [see Everett Ferguson's story].

By January 1945, Doyle was back at No. 22 OTU, and from there he went on to a Halifax Conversion Unit. By June 1945, he was shipped home where plans were being made for a Tiger Force to fight in the far east. This necessity did not come to pass, however, and Doyle was discharged from the service in December 1945.

Art Doyle has held an executive position within the Guinea Pig Club. He and his wife Helen live in Gravenhurst, Ontario.

Harold Stannus

Harold "Harry" Stannus, a young Australian, had enlisted in the RAAF on February 1, 1942. Like so many, Stannus was trained in Canada under the British Commonwealth Air Training Plan. This meant a long journey from Port Melbourne to Los Angeles and then to Vancouver. He eventually arrived at an Embarkation Depot in Edmonton.

He had been selected for Navigator training, and he was categorized as a Navigator B (navigator/bomb-aimer) with his first posting to the Bombing and Gunnery School in Mountain View, Ontario. Stannus explains:

> Up to that time I had never been aloft in an aircraft, so it was with some trepidation that I put on a flying suit and accepted a parachute from the stores department prior to climbing into an Anson for my

first flight for practice bombing. I found it exhilarating as we rolled down the runway and finally became airborne. At that moment I knew I had made a good choice in enlisting in the air force.

Later he flew in Bolingbrokes as he completed his bombing and gunnery course. By April 2, 1943, he had completed his Navigation course. He had the pleasure of taking that course in Ancienne Lorette, Quebec in winter and remembers, most of all, the weather:

I had never, before coming to Canada, seen snow or experienced temperatures of thirty–forty degrees below zero, and I found the clothing with which the RAAF had provided me was less than adequate for such conditions. But with some additions and modifications my fellow Australians and I survived the rigours of the Quebec winter....

Stannus went on to Paulson, Manitoba, to the high-level bombing program and ship recognition course. He arrived in England in May 1943 and was variously posted to Jurby, Isle of Man, and Skaebrae in the Orkneys. He trained on Wellingtons but went on to four-engined Stirlings. He was soon posted to 149 Squadron, 3 Group, Bomber Command, RAF.

By April 1944, Stannus and crew were laying mines off the coast of Belgium and Holland and supply-dropping to the Maquis, one of the mandates of his squadron. These "Special Operations" missions involved dropping containers filled with machine guns, ammunition, boots, work clothing, and the like. Also in the drop was usually a burlap wrapped, padded radio unit. The material was stored in the bomb racks.

These drops were carefully staged and coded. This was precision flying of a different sort, and it is interesting to hear the detailed preparations. Stannus explains:

The preparations for a drop operation were begun by a coded radio message from a Maquis operator picked up by a BBC facility and relayed to a Special Air Services operations centre. The message would detail the equipment and supplies that were needed by the group with whom the message originated, identify the location of the intended drop site, the time recipients would be there and, an essential item in the procedure, a morse code letter that would be flashed from below to confirm their location and identity. A second, alternative, letter would be used if a backup crew had turned out in the event the first group had been prevented from getting to the scene for some reason.

The briefings would then begin:

> [The first would be by] a Special Services officer who had been stationed at the target site (these officers were attached to Maquis units, being landed there by night and picked up after their tours of duty had ended by short take off and landing Lysander aircraft). The officer would have a detailed knowledge of the site, its topography, geographical and other features that would be identifiable from the air at low level on a bright moonlit night. These drop operations were always carried out when the moon was full and the sky clear. As our altitude on the approach to the drop area was 400 ft or so, we needed to know of any hazardous features along our track, such as power pylons, tall radio antennas standing on high ground, etc.. Our briefing would conclude with a small field or a little wooded patch being described by the officer and pinpointed precisely on one of our topographical navigation maps.

The drop generally meant crossing the French coastline at 3,500 feet. As Stannus has said, the drop itself would take place at about 400 feet. This meant that they would quickly be flying below the level at which their navigation equipment would be effective. So, working with the navigator's dead reckoning plot, lying on his stomach in the nose compartment of the plane, checking his maps and the visual path below him, Stannus directed the pilot along the track. Once they had received the signal from below, Stannus went into action:

> I would open the bomb doors and instruct the mid-upper gunner to lift the underside escape hatch cover and prepare to push the radio out with his feet while I had the bomb release toggle in my hand ready to press the button to release our cargo supplies. Those

tasks done, the bomb doors and the escape hatch would be closed, and we could turn for home.

This was exactly what *should* have happened on the evening of July 5–6. They were flying over the Savoy District of France. They were waiting for their signal, circling the designated area, but they could not spot it. In what must surely have been some frustration, they turned for home. They flew back up to 3,500 feet to take advantage of the electronic navigation aids and were heading back when they were engaged by ground fire.

Although no one was initially injured, the shells had damaged the plane. The two port engines were rendered useless:

> The outboard engine failed completely while the inboard engine revs dropped from the normal 1800 to about 1100, to the point that it was causing drag rather than providing propulsion. The pilot was able to feather the airscrews of both engines, but the aircraft began to bank to port and the nose to drop as the two starboard engines were now the only source of power. The pilot directed us to prepare to bail out, but before he had to give the order to do so he had to manage with considerable difficulty to partially stabilize the aircraft.

Stannus returned to his seat beside the pilot and the two of them:

> ...applied hard right rudder and with the control column hard over to starboard the aircraft resumed more or less level flight but in a crab-like attitude.

But there were other problems to contend with:

> We now became aware that a large quantity of gasoline had entered the fuselage; the fuel had escaped from a wing tank of about eighty-five-gallon capacity through a gaping hole beside the wireless operator's position. A shell had come up through the underside of the wing, ripped through the fuselage wall and passed, just inches from our W/O, out through the upper surface. Efforts to chop holes in the aircraft floor using on-board fire axes to let gasoline drain out were

fruitless as the back-eddy of air from outside blocked its exit.

They were approaching the English Channel. Lightheaded from the petrol fumes, they nonetheless maintained their course. Stannus jettisoned the undropped supplies to lighten their load and help them stabilize. They were almost to the coast. Stannus got on the radio and gave the coded signal, *Shipmast M mother*:

Mayday, mayday, mayday, Shipmast M mother, in dire emergency, please clear us for landing.

They received a response from a nearby airfield, a Coastal Command station at Thorney Island:

It had been under the usual complete blackout, but its runway glim lights were immediately turned on. When I attempted to lower our undercarriage for an attempted landing nothing happened. The electrical circuit or hydraulic system on which the function of the undercarriage depended had been disarmed, and we had no time to try the many turns of a handle required to manually lower the wheels. We would have to make a crash landing.

Remembering that crash landings usually left a distorted airframe and jammed equipment, Stannus released the disposable section of the plexiglass canopy above the pilot's head.

They were coming in for a landing, unaligned with the runway. Stannus remembers covering his eyes with his arm. They were coming in at 120 knots, instead of the usual 90, because the wing flaps could not be lowered due to malfunction. The pilot put the plane down at an angle on the grass surrounding the runway. In what must have momentarily appeared miraculous:

...there was only a light bump and we slid easily along the turf. I gave the pilot a congratulatory "thumbs up" on his skilful touchdown; prematurely as it turned out.

What happened next was swift and terrible. The plane skidded *onto* the runway. Stannus describes it like this:

[I heard] the noise of tortured metal screeching against the abrasive surface. Everything came to a stop suddenly except the gasoline which had not been evacuated from the interior of the fuselage. It was sloshing about inside, and then was ignited by the sparks struck from the airframe by the runway surface. Our aircraft was on fire.

Everyone tried to leave the craft. When Stannus's turn came he found his left side exposed to the flames:

[I] sustained burns, some of them third degree burns, to my legs, left arm and hand, and my face.

Interestingly, Harry Stannus had always had a particular trepidation about being burned, having read as a youth the accounts of burnings at the stake. But when it happened to him he discovered:

...it was my experience that it was not really painful to sustain my burns but the healing process was at times excruciatingly painful. The explanation, I suppose, is that the nerve ends which transmit main messages to the brain are destroyed with the skin tissue which is being destroyed at the same time. It is only when those nerve ends are restoring themselves in healing raw flesh that they are again able to sense the pain caused by contact with the covering bandages or other dressings and to convey messages of pain to the nerve centre.

Stannus was taken by ambulance to the Station Infirmary, then to a hospital in Chichester and then "on the most uncomfortable journey I have ever taken" to the Queen Victoria Hospital.

As an Australian flying with the RAF, Stannus was under the care of Dr. McIndoe and Squadron Leader Gerry Moore. He remembers especially Sister Ramsay and her care. He has fond memories of both the Maestro and of Gerry Moore, who took a graft from one of Stannus's thighs and successfully attached it to the back of his hand. The many grafts they made to the hands and face took, and continue to function to this day. Stannus moved to Vancouver in 1947 and lives there with his wife Fay and family. He continues to be a loyal member of the Canadian Wing of the Guinea Pig Club.

Throughout this period the spirit of the Guinea Pig Club was growing so that in the first Guinea Pig Newsletter (there would eventually be a magazine), Archibald McIndoe wrote the following in a open letter to the Pigs:

> I strongly believe that the same spirit which brought this Club into being three years ago is still operative today and that it will grow and flower with the passage of time.

He could not have known just how much they would take these words to heart.

The Canadian Wing

The long-awaited Canadian Wing opened its doors, at least a crack, on July 12 admitting nine patients. Most people consider the "official" opening to have occurred on or around the middle of July. What is certain is that by the beginning of August all of the beds were occupied.

One can only imagine the extra boon it must have been to arrive on site and enter "a little bit of Canada." Dr. Tilley's hand-picked staff was Canadian, the support staff was Canadian, everyone including the kitchen staff was Canadian! The Wing's design, by the staffs of the RCAF Overseas Headquarters and the Royal Canadian Engineers CMHQ working in conjunction with F. Gordon Troup, FRIBA, was brought into being by the Royal Canadian Engineers.

It was a one-storey, T-shaped structure with three dining rooms (for "pigs", "scientists" and staff), a large kitchen facility, a comfortable patients' lounge complete with leather furniture, stationery-filled writing tables, artwork on the walls and even in a piano, in case anyone felt like playing.

Then there were the sterilizing rooms and operating theatres, the offices, several private rooms, the all-important saline baths, and the ward itself which was bright with lots of windows and a view of pasture land in the foreground and the town beyond. The colour scheme was cream with blue-green accents and dark green blackout shades. The beds numbered fifty, the staff around fifty to fifty-five. Dr. Norman Park was the anaesthetist and Dr. John Hiltz was the operating theatre doctor. There was an adjutant, twelve nurses, orderlies and general duties staff. The dieticians and kitchen staff worked with civilian rations, as the wing was part of a civilian hospital.

Dr. E. Ross Tilley

The Canadian Wing was headed, of course, by Dr. E. Ross Tilley, OBE (for by the end of July 1944 Dr. Tilley had received the Order of the British Empire and was also named Group Captain). Dr. Tilley was extremely proud of the wing, understanding its practical purpose:

The opening of the Royal Canadian Air Force Wing in July 1944 was a very happy occasion. It was the fruition of a long period of planning, starting in 1941 when Archie and I first met. It was also the beginning of our opportunity to return some of the kindnesses which had been given to us at East Grinstead over the previous two and a half years.

Dr. Tilley was obviously aware, as well, of the symbolic presence of the Canadian Wing. There had been plans for an elaborate official opening but fate curtailed them:

An opening ceremony had been planned, but it was cancelled because by that time there were too many flying objects, V-1s, overhead.

Dr. Tilley had a right to be proud of his spanking new wing. It was a completely modern facility run by a top-notch staff. Into their hands would be entrusted the Canadian airmen who had yet to be "fried, mashed, or hash-browned," as well as those Guinea Pigs who would transfer over from Ward III. Any lull in Canadian casualties would be made up for by taking in injured men from other allied services. Over the next fourteen months this would translate into seventy-six RCAF patients, thirty-two RAF patients, and eighty patients from other allied services comprising five nationalities.

So who were these medically-trained Canadian men and women who were to become part of the phenomenon known as the Guinea Pig Club? Many had been transferred from other assignments, East Grinstead being merely another posting. Others were sent to East Grinstead as their first overseas posting. But all of them saw their time in East Grinstead as unique. Unfortunately, many of their stories are lost to time. What follows is by no means inclusive, but it is representative of the group of dedicated medical personnel who served at the Queen Victoria Hospital.

Dr. Norman Park

The anaesthetist, Dr. Norman Park, or "Norm" to the men, was one of those quiet and serene individuals capable of putting a person at ease. This was surely an advantage for a "Sandman." He faced a patient about to go "under the knife for a bit of slabbing," reassured him, and sent him off to oblivion for a few hours; his face was the last thing a patient saw and, usually, the first upon reawakening.

Norman Park came to East Grinstead in the fall of 1942 and thus made the transition to the Canadian Wing with ease and confidence. Dr. Tilley relied on Dr. Park implicitly, and the two would pick up their ties in Canada after the war, working together to the benefit of their patients. (Norman Park would become the Medical Liaison officer for the Club's Canadian branch when it was formed in Canada years after the war).

Dr. Norm Park

With Dr. Park at the gasworks, Dr. Tilley had a right-hand man with whom he was comfortable. Their joint experience in Ward III allowed them to hit the ground running when the Canadian Wing opened.

Dr. Park joined the staff of the Sick Children's Hospital in Toronto after the war. He married Betty and they had two children. Dr. Norman Park continued as Medical Liaison Officer with the Canadian Guinea Pig Club until his death in August 1977.

Dr. John Hiltz

Operating theatre doctor John Wesley Hiltz was another member of Dr. Tilley's team. Dr. Hiltz was known as the "Flying Medical Man," and specialized at East Grinstead in orthopaedic surgery although he was a general surgeon as well. He also fashioned and manufactured many of the specialized casts that were worn by healing Guinea Pigs. In his post-war career, Dr. Hiltz would go on to specialize in ophthalmology, writing a textbook that has been used in medical schools worldwide. Dr. Hiltz's career flourished, and he eventually was to became Chief of Ophthalmology at North York General Hospital in Toronto. Dr. Hiltz died in February 1992.

Dr. Al Gardiner

Dr. Al Gardiner was one of the dental surgeons whose skill helped rebuild the smashed faces and destroyed jaws of the young fliers. From May 1944 until the transfer of the Canadian Wing, Dr. Gardiner fashioned devices specific to each patient's need, and his innovation was crucial to the functional, and aesthetic, repair of those damaged faces.

Dr. Gardiner married Mary after the war and they had a daughter. He died in 1994.

The Nursing Sisters – "Angels of Mercy"

What does one say about the part played by the nurses in this phenomenon? Not only were they able to alleviate discomfort, but their female presence, their interest and concern in a patient, validated his ego and assisted his recovery. To truly appreciate the accomplishments of the nurses it is best to listen to the men who were in their care. Several of the nurses in this group have been personally credited as "saving my life." A life—the life we are talking about at East Grinstead, at least—is a fragile thing. The young and fit men who came into this Wing had suffered brief but horrendous assaults on their bodies. The healing would take some time. But the healing of their spirits, as envisioned by Dr. Tilley and Dr. McIndoe, was at least as critical. This healing was aided immeasurably by the compassion and the care of the nursing sisters.

As with all staff at East Grinstead, they were chosen not only for their abilities but also for their empathy, their sense of humour, and, in this case, their looks. Their role was clearly larger than that of medical support for they were also to assist in rebuilding the confidence of these damaged men.

Frances M. Oakes

"Fran" Oakes began her career as a graduate of the Kitchener-Waterloo School of Nursing. She went on to post-graduate studies in surgical techniques at the Montreal General Hospital after which she was appointed operating room supervisor at the Kitchener-Waterloo hospital.

Fran Oakes joined up in October 1940, enlisting in the RCAF medical service as a pilot officer. Up until this time the RCAMC (army) had provided army nurses to the RCAF. However, it became obvious that the RCAF would need its own medical branch, so in September 1940 the medical branch was established by Order-in-Council. On November 28, 1940, the RCAF Nursing Service was authorized.

Fran Oakes' first posting was to the Technical Training School in St. Thomas, Ontario, a large facility where she was assigned, primarily, to the operating room. By April 1942 she was posted overseas along with N/S Leonora Loyst. They were the first RCAF nurses sent over, both to East Grinstead where Dr. Tilley was in the process of organizing an RCAF surgical unit within a civilian hospital. The original unit consisted of one surgeon, one anaesthetist, one dental surgeon, two experienced surgical nurses, one nurse for ward duty, and two medical assistants for the saline baths.

Fran Oakes fit in well there, where the innovative, experimental surgery combined with the extraordinary atmosphere. This was prior to the opening of the Canadian Wing, and nurse Oakes remembers the extra efforts everyone made to make the boys feel at home:

> These aircrew were far away from home, injured in a different country, and the physical problems were prevalent. We tried to help create a Canadian atmosphere.

Among her memories of the "extras" was that of a medical secretary in Victoria, British Columbia, who collected zippers and

Fran Oakes

sent them to a tailor in East Grinstead who then fitted them into the trousers and jackets of burned men. One forgets, in this age of Velcro, how much the then-recent invention of the zipper aided men with burned fingers. The precious zippers would be used, and when the patient's hands healed, removed and sewn into a new patient's clothing. It is no wonder the men felt that these "scientists" were looking after them. The nurses cheerfully wheeled men down to the Whitehall for a beer, took them to theatre parties in London, went to dinner and dances with them in East Grinstead. They co-ordinated the visits of a number of female visitors from the women's division in London. These women, including Bea Jackson, Olga Lavalee, Shirley Hubbard and Sue Cawston, came weekly to see the boys, to chat, play cards or write letters for the patients.

Fran Oakes is justifiably proud of the hospital's history—in five years it was never necessary to send one man to an institution. Most of the men went back on flying duties, and the majority of the men went on to live successful, happy lives.

Nurse Oakes would see to the boys during the building of the Canadian Wing, but upon its completion she and Nurse Loyst were posted back to Canada.

Fran Oakes went on to have a distinguished career in the service, retiring in 1958 as a squadron leader and principal matron of the RCAF Nursing Service. She lives in Guelph, Ontario.

Marjorie Jackson

Head nurse, Matron Marjorie "Marge" Jackson, was someone upon whom Dr. Tilley depended. And she was, simply, beloved by her patients for her caring, altruistic ways. Few Guinea Pigs speak of their treatment in the Wing without mentioning Marge.

Flight Lieutenant Marjorie Jackson began her career as a graduate of Brandon General Hospital School of Nursing. At the outbreak of the war she was nursing in Peekskill, New York. She felt there was something she could do for the war effort, so in 1942 she became an RCAF nursing sister.

This meant heading to No. 12 Flying School back in Brandon. By August 1942, she was posted to East Grinstead, to the Burns and Plastic Surgery Unit. Nurse Jackson was part of the transition into the newly built Canadian Wing where she became head nurse. Matron Jackson spoke of her time at East Grinstead, of what it meant to be a nurse under these circumstances:

Marjorie Jackson

Plastic surgery wasn't really big before the war, certainly not for hands and faces, but so many pilots came in who were burned terribly in their hands and faces, we had to do something. We treated their burns and because of loss of skin they had to be grafted, and that's where plastic surgery came in. They called themselves guinea pigs because it was all so new, and we were really only experimenting. We didn't know how to do all these things to begin with.

But Jackson, who was instrumental in organizing a social life for the men in her ward, also remembered the other side of their healing:

> We were all young nurses, and we went out socially with them and got them out as soon as we could, going down to the pub, going into town. We worked very hard on the psychological aspects.

Marge Jackson remained at East Grinstead until the end of 1945. After the war she took courses in hospital administration at McGill University in Montreal. She continued a career in nursing for many years. Beloved nurse Marjorie Jackson died in July 1998.

Leonora Loyst Mardall

Leonora Mardall was another of the very early RCAF nurses to serve overseas. Like Fran Oakes, Nurse Mardall spent much of her time working with Guinea Pigs at the Queen Victoria Hospital. After the war she married and raised two sons while working with Dr. Tilley in his private office in Toronto. She retired in 1973 and died in 1998. She is fondly remembered by members of the Club.

Margaret Watt (Peacock) Paterson

Nursing Sister Margaret Peacock began her career after graduating from the Neepawa Hospital in 1934. She did post-graduate work in Regina, earning her post-graduate certificate in surgery. She joined the RCAF in 1941 and was later sent to East Grinstead where she was a welcome addition to the staff.

After the war she married and returned to Manitoba to farm. Margaret (Peacock) Paterson died in 1980.

Marion J.R. (Patterson) Ferguson

Marion Patterson graduated from the St. Boniface Hospital School of Nursing, St. Boniface, Manitoba, in 1932, following up with post-graduate work in 1933 at the Mental Health Centre in Brandon, and at St. Mary's Hospital in Rochester, New York. Flying Officer Patterson was one of the first nineteen nurses to enlist in the RCAF. Her first posting was to set up a hospital at RAF training base Carberry in Manitoba. The cases they saw there were primarily due to accidents by inexperienced pilots flying outdated aircraft. This gave Nurse Patterson experience she later would rely on when she worked in the Canadian Wing of the Queen Victoria Hospital, where she was affectionately known as "Sister Pat."

Sister Pat went on to a post-war teaching career at the Brandon General Hospital and the Brandon Mental Health Centre. Marion "Sister Pat" Ferguson died in May 1993.

Dorothy Irene Mulholland

Flying Officer Dorothy "Molly" Mulholland graduated from St. Joseph's Hospital School of Nursing in Guelph. She joined

Dorothy Mulholland

the service in 1941, serving at No. 1 Technical Training School in St. Thomas, Ontario. She also served in Gander, Newfoundland and in Grantham, England. "Molly" Mulholland had the distinction of being the first nurse of the allied forces to arrive in France during the war. The day was June 19, 1944, thirteen days after D-Day, and she was a nursing sister serving with 52 (RCAF) Mobile Field Hospital.

After eight months of service at the field hospital, F/O Mulholland was sent to East Grinstead to work in the Canadian Wing.

Nurse Mulholland was recognized for her devotion to duty, being awarded the Royal Red Cross, First Class, which she received personally from King George VI at Buckingham Palace in January 1945.

Elaine Matheson

Flying Officer Elaine Matheson was trained at the Victoria Hospital School of Nursing in London, Ontario. Following her graduation in 1940 she joined the RCAF, the youngest nurse in this branch of the service at the time.

Nursing Sister Matheson was sent overseas in 1943 and assigned to 6 Bomber Group at Linton, Yorkshire. She remembered the days leading up to D-Day, the sky black with planes. She remembered also the reticence of the crews that returned from D-Day operations, and the awful silence left by those who did not.

Elaine Matheson went on to East Grinstead in the latter part of 1944 to serve in the Canadian Wing. She remained at the Queen Victoria Hospital until she returned home to Canada in October 1945. Nurse Matheson saw her service in the RCAF as a highlight of her career and, like many, retains significant memories of her time at East Grinstead.

Elaine Matheson

Enid (Faulkner) Matheson

Flying Officer Enid Faulkner graduated from the Toronto Western Hospital School of Nursing in 1940. There she had had the opportunity to observe the work of Dr. Fulton Risdon, the eminent plastic surgeon who had been Dr. Tilley's colleague and teacher. Enid Faulkner was offered a position in the operating room of the Toronto Western General Hospital where she would remain until joining the RCAF in the fall of 1942.

She was posted around Canada and then overseas where she first went to the operating rooms at No. 1 Neurological and Plastic Surgery Hospital at Basingstoke. This was supposed to be a two-week posting; it lasted six months. Nurse Faulkner was the sole RCAF nurse in the company of one hundred army nurses.

In the fall of 1944 she was posted to East Grinstead to take over nursing in the OR, replacing nurse Curly Vernon who left for the continent.

Enid (Faulkner) Matheson remem-bers the Wing vividly and the young men she met there whom she has seen over the years at reunions. She

Enid (Faulkner) Matheson

remembers the three young English boys who stayed in the Wing following the bombing of the Cinema. (She herself, as with all the nurses, boarded in private homes and were driven to the hospital daily by Motor Transport).

Enid Faulkner returned to Canada in August 1945 preparing to go to the Far East. With the war over, she was sent to Trenton where she was reunited with some of the Guinea Pigs who were arriving to have further surgeries performed. In December, Enid

Faulkner married an RCAF type, Squadron Leader Ken Matheson, a Pathfinder pilot with DFC and Bar. She attends Guinea Pig reunions and says that she "always enjoys seeing the boys again and how well they have done."

Hilda Emke Moore

Nursing Sister Hilda Moore worked on the medical team. She was a good nurse to her patients, supporting them while not coddling them. Evidence of this is contained in an interview Moore gave to Charles Barber[6]. She was remembering her first encounters with Guinea Pigs when she arrived on the ward:

> I told myself I'd keep cool, no matter what. Then I saw my first patient. He was horribly burned, only one lip, no nose at all. I talked to him awhile and then turned to leave. He pinched me! I was in shock anyway, and so I turned to him and very angry and without thinking said that I would punch him in the nose if he did that again. "Hahaha," he laughed, "Go ahead. I don't have a nose."
> "I'll wait," Nurse Moore replied.

Nurse Moore also remembered the people of East Grinstead:

> East Grinstead was so good. I remember once being in the pub and the owner was asked by two healthy young men from out of town how he could stand to serve all these burned guys. "I can stand them, all right," he says, "I can't stand you. Get out." And he threw their money at them.

Hilda Moore attended Guinea Pig reunions in the post-war years and was welcomed at every one.

Mabel Kathryn (Gardner) Remigio

Nurse Mabel "Mabs" (Gardner) Remigio was a native of Welland, Ontario. She studied at St. Michael's Hospital School of Nursing in Toronto and graduated as a registered nurse. She worked at St. Michael's until enlisting in the Royal Canadian Air Force, first seeing service in Labrador and then transferring to

East Grinstead where she worked with Dr. Tilley. She is remembered for her humour and her goodwill.

After the war, Mabs married and had three children. Nursing Sister Mabel Remigio died in June 1998.

Marjorie Olive Nancy Stapleford

Nurse Marjorie Olive Nancy "Mons" Stapleford (the acronym is named for Mons, France, where her father was serving in the First War when she was born) served at St. Thomas Technical Training School with Mabel (Gardner) Remigio and also at RAF Bombing and Gunnery School in Picton, Ontario. She eventually made her way to East Grinstead where, among her other duties, she was the "star" of a film documenting the burn treatment unit. From East Grinstead she was posted to 5 Group in the North. Nursing Sister Mons Stapleford continued nursing after the war.

Sara (McLellan) Flynn

Nurse Sara "Sally" McLellan served at No. 34 OTU Pennfield Ridge and was later transferred to the Canadian Wing at East Grinstead. She is remembered for her caring bedside manner.

Some RCAF Nurses

Other Nurses

Other nursing sisters who served at East Grinstead include Nurses Midge Phillps and Bee Philips, Nurse Olwen (Gregory) Parratt, Nurse Frances "Frankie" Anderson, Nurse Maggie Kaines, Nurse Ina (Bishop) Jewsbury, Nurse Helen Brown, Nurse Soper, Nurse Bernie Arnett, Nurse Lillian "Holly" Hall, Nurse "Curly" Vernon McLellan, and Nurse Eileen Angly.

Technician – Murray S. Boyce

Murray Boyce was born in Virden, Manitoba. He was raised and educated in Neudorf, Saskatchewan. He graduated with a bachelor of science degree from the University of Manitoba in 1939, began some medical courses at the University of Manitoba (Winnipeg), and then enlisted in the RCAF Medical Branch at No. 2 ITS in Regina as a medical orderly. Then it was on to No. 4 ITS Saskatoon followed by a posting to Halifax.

Murray Boyce went overseas on the *Letitia* on July 19, 1942. Stationed first at Hastings, and then at the RAF airdrome at Digby, he was posted on March 23, 1944, to RCAF Headquarters at Lincoln-in-Field, where he was promoted to sergeant.

Sergeant Boyce arrived at East Grinstead on December 11, 1944, in time to take part in the general Christmas festivities. He would remain at East Grinstead until VE Day working as a dental technician, after which he would be posted to Torquay and then to Southhampton. He returned home in September 1945 and was officially discharged in November as sergeant-wardmaster.

Murray Boyce enrolled in the faculty of dentistry at the University of Alberta, despite a late November start. He notes that half the members of his class were World War II veterans. Boyce also took time from his studies to marry Dorethy. By spring 1949, Murray Boyce, now the father of a daughter, became Dr. Murray S. Boyce, DDS. Dr. Boyce would practice in Rocky Mountain House and later in Red Deer and Lacombe, all in Alberta. By then he would have three children. In 1975 he moved to Calgary to practice at the Colonel Belcher Hospital under the Federal Department of Veterans Affairs and became Chief of Service. Dr. Boyce retired and currently enjoys dancing, gardening and pursuing his family genealogy.

Orderly - William Rhode

LAC William Rhode joined the RCAF in 1942 in Vancouver. He was sent to the medical school in Trenton where he trained to be a medical orderly. He served at No. 2 Wireless School in Calgary before being sent, in 1944, to the Canadian Wing at East Grinstead.

At the time of Rhode's arrival, these staff members were also serving: F/L C.L.B. Bateman, Tilley's deputy; F/L Matron Marge Jackson; Sgt. John Ingram; Sgt. Murray Boyce; Sgt. Lillian "Holly" Hall; LACs Leo and Ethel Lacroix (a happy marriage of two orderlies in the Canadian Wing—Dr. Tilley gave the bride away; Rhode was best man).

William Rhode loved his work in the Canadian Wing, due in a large part to the Guinea Pigs themselves. As hospital staff, he lived in town, in a room above a pub on High Street. He fondly remembers weekends in town:

> Some of the happiest times were on the weekends when staff, patients and locals would gather at one of the pubs (mainly the Whitehall) for wonderful evenings of friendship, fun and camaraderie. Another pub we visited was the one in the Dorset Arms Hotel.

Rhode goes on to recall the difficulty when the Canadian Wing was handed over to Britain after the war; the staff was then posted to different locations, breaking up a cohesive group of people.

William Rhode

Rhode remained in the service, was posted to England, and sent home to Canada. Posted to Sea Island, Vancouver, a plum location, William Rhode found himself in love with Nursing Sister Marg Hartt; however, the difference in their ranks caused a problem, and they were separated by as much of Canada as the service could arrange. Nurse Hartt went to Goose Bay and Corporal Rhode to Victoria. They managed to overcome this particularly Canadian handicap and were married in 1952. They had three children. Rhode continued in the RCAF until taking his discharge in 1968 after which he spent further years in hospital work, retiring for good in 1985.

William Rhode speaks of the unique time spent at East Grinstead in words that echo the experience of so many:

> War has a way of making acquaintances into buddies, buddies into friends, and friends into brothers.

Orderly - Bruce "Dutchy" Miller

Bruce "Dutchy" Miller was another orderly in the Canadian Wing. He was known for his kindness and sense of humour. Born in Russia, he emigrated to Canada in 1927. After the war he returned home to Victoria where he was a strong supporter of his church, Hope Lutheran. He married Lydia and they had two daughters. "Dutchy" Miller died in September 1983 at the age of seventy-five.

Of course, the good work at the hospital was aided, to a great extent, by the tireless volunteers who visited the men weekly, writing letters for them, playing cards, reading to them, laughing with them. Many WDs would come visiting on the weekends, among them Olga Lavalee, Sue Cawston, Bea Jackson, and Shirley, who would become Mrs. Shirley Hubbard, wife of Guinea Pig Frank Hubbard.

The Science

Ever since Sir Harold Gillies performed grafts, including the pedicle graft, on the young men injured in the First World War, the science of plastic surgery had moved forward, although between the wars the advancement had slowed due to a lack of patients.

In the Second World War, Doctors McIndoe and Tilley at the Queen Victoria Hospital were in a unique position both to help the patients and, in turn, to advance the science of plastic surgery. As mentioned, one of the significant accomplishments of this period was the eventual phasing out of the use of tannic acid and gentian violet (escharotics) for the general treatment of burns. These methods had been employed until the war and were still being used in units other than the Queen Victoria Hospital. It would be the experience at the hospital which would convince medical personnel that the use of escharotics only served to constrict and render non-functional limbs that could possibly have been saved. As well, there was the matter of the aesthetic benefit of turning away from escharotics: properly grafted skin that "took" was more visually presentable than leathery features and keloid scars.

A patient entering Ward III or the Canadian Wing could expect long soaks in the saline bath. This treatment was popularized at the hospital. At the very least it provided comfort to the patient and aided in the removal of bandages and burned flesh, and at most it prevented infection and kept the burn area fresh for grafting. Sulfa drugs and, later, penicillin, also sped up recovery time.

Patients were also consulted about their treatment. In fact, the patient was encouraged to view operations ("chops" or "slabbings") particularly those of the type that they too would be undergoing. When a fellow Guinea Pig was going in for a bit of slabbing on his hands, for example, another Pig scheduled for the same treatment would watch his buddy's operation, asking questions and generally familiarizing himself with the procedure. When he was comfortable with the idea, he would undergo his own operation.

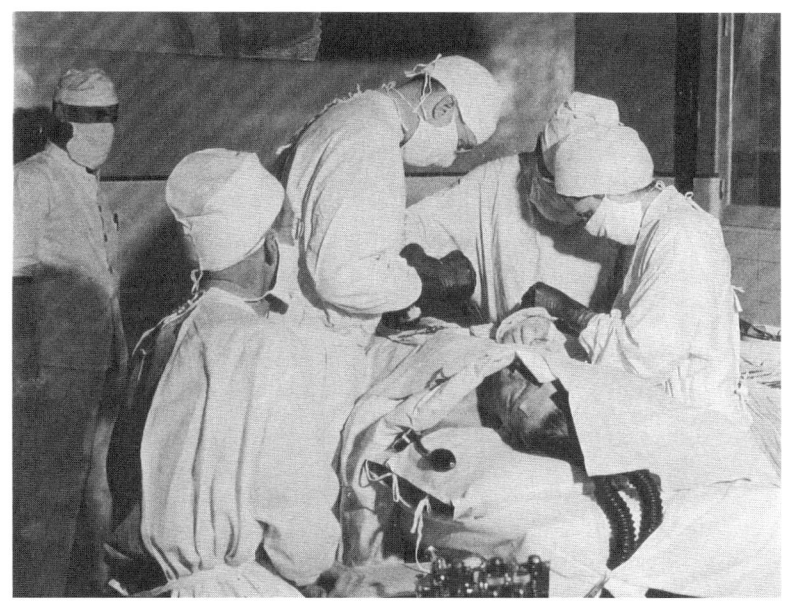

An Operation

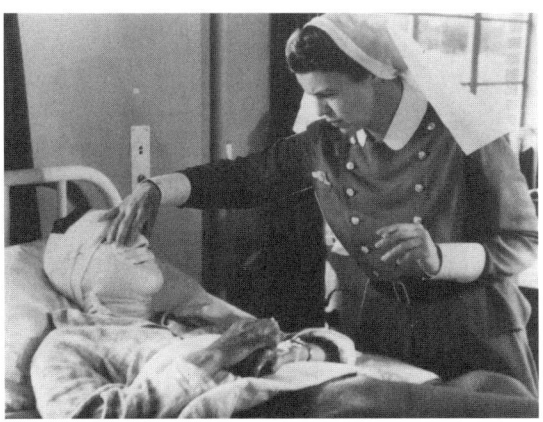

Marge Jackson and Patient

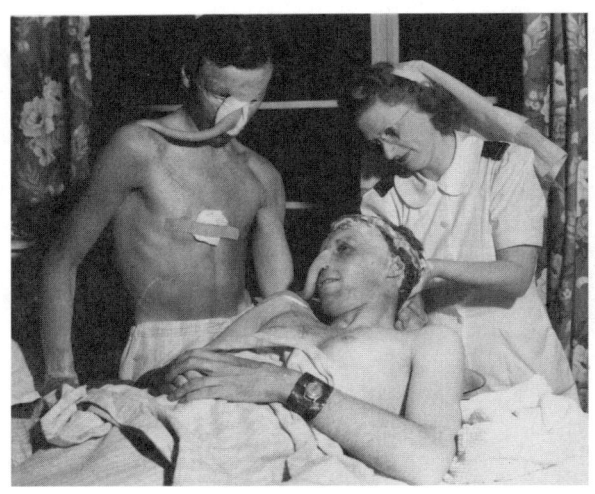

Pedicle Grafts

Rotation Flap Graft

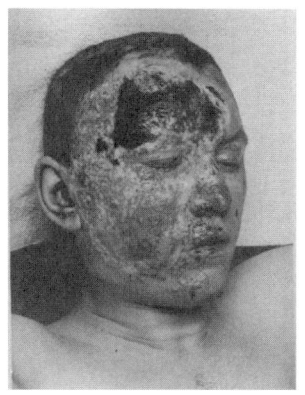 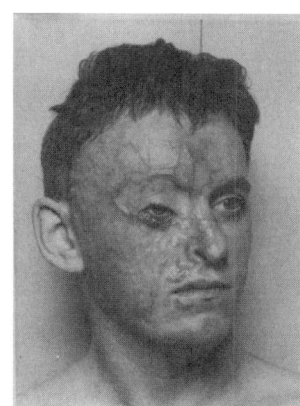

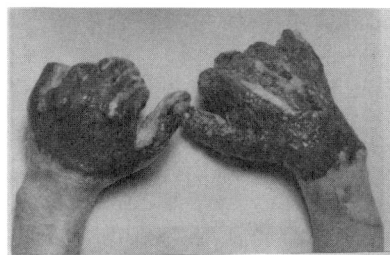 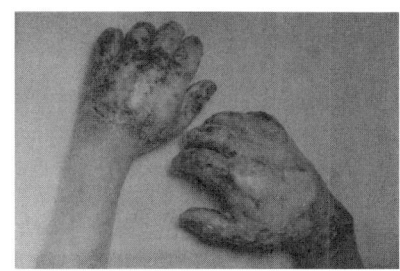

Reconstruction of an airman's face and hands

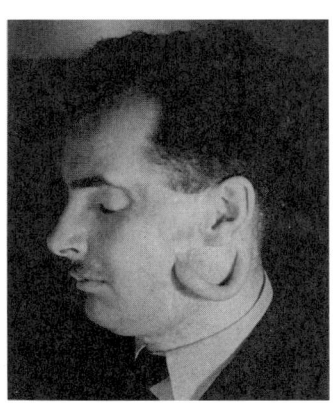 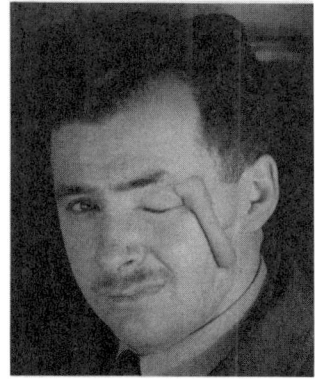

Pedicle Grafts

Likewise, when a patient had been repaired to the point where he was comfortable with himself, where another operation would be refinement upon refinement, it was he who could decide: "No, that's okay. I can live with this."

Both Dr. Tilley and Dr. McIndoe were proponents of this policy and had little cause to regret it. To this day, many Guinea Pigs talk calmly and dispassionately about their many operations, with a clinical detachment that would have made their doctors proud. And when they talk, they speak of:

Stamp Graft – tiny, stamp-sized pieces of flesh removed from a healthy area and placed one by one over a large burned area.
Pinch Graft – similar to stamp grafts; small pinches of skin placed on a burned area.
Flap Graft – a piece of skin raised and 'flapped' onto an injured surface, (for example, a cross-leg flap.)

Some of the more medically-inclined Guinea Pigs will speak of Thiersch Grafts, Dermatome Grafts, Wolfe Grafts and Pedicle Grafts, and would be speaking of the following:

Thiersch or Ollier-Thiersch Graft – These grafts were "free grafts," thin pieces of skin cut freehand and placed on an exposed area primarily to help it heal.
Dermatome Graft – Dermatome grafts were somewhat thicker. They were also free grafts. A special dermatome tool invented in the 1930s by Earl C. Padgett, an American, was used to cut within a layer of regenerative tissue, leaving some on the donor area and some on the transplant site.
Wolfe or Wolfe-Krause Graft – These were small, full-thickness free grafts.
Pedicle Graft – Also a full-thickness graft, these were used for larger areas, where a piece of healthy skin was lifted and turned in on itself to form a tube. The tube ("sausage" in Sty parlance) then grew and was eventually attached to the affected area, the theory being that a piece of skin that had always been attached to the human body, receiving its blood supply and thriving, would make a better graft.

The fact that a patient could freely converse about such matters with his surgeon, his anaesthetist, his therapist and nurses, allowed that patient to "own" his situation. Giving authority to the patient also returned dignity and responsibility to that patient, a fact of which Doctors McIndoe and Tilley were aware.

George "Curly" Wilson, in remembering the operation that saved his eye, was able to describe the procedure in detail. As has been mentioned, the sharp observation of Nurse Olwen Thomas had alerted Dr. Tilley to a problem with Wilson's eye. Specialist Dr. Ridley was called in from London. Wilson notes:

> He [Ridley] explained what he wanted to install an artificial cover over my eyeball to prevent further deterioration. To do this he had to have a cast of my eye from which would be made an acrylic mould which would be given a thin layer of wax and fastened to me so that it rested on my eye as a temporary replacement for eyelids. Its function was to reverse the effects of drying and to polish the cornea as I rotated my eyes in normal use.
>
> The only way to fasten the substitute for eyelids to my skull would be to take an impression of my upper jaw and from it make a metal mould which was cemented in place. The inside of the mould was to be an exact copy of my upper jaw and teeth so that it would fit snugly. The outside was to be an exact cast so that it would mesh with my lower jaw and teeth. On the front of the falsies there was to be soldered a drilled and tapped plate to which the acrylic-wax part could be rigidly fastened by two small machine screws.
>
> His explanation was complete but brief. After he finished, he informed me that the program, not having been tried before, was experimental and might be uncomfortable. He noted further that he would not predict how long I would wear it. He then enquired whether I was willing to let him try it. It did not take me long to reply. I knew that I was about to lose my eye. Besides that, I had learned that when one eye was lost frequently infection, and I had lots of strep-laden cooked flesh nearby, so damaged the optic system that sight was lost in the other eye. His notation that there might be discomfort was of no concern—I had plenty of that already. Some more or some less did not matter. I invited him to proceed.

By mid-afternoon the device was installed...I wore the device until June 6, [1943] when Dr. Tilley judged that the area was clean enough to permit a skin graft and successfully made a transplant from the inside of my upper right arm to my upper eyelid.

In this one example we see the level of innovation, and the level of cooperation, at work at the Queen Victoria Hospital. All options possible were available to the patient. The Guinea Pigs trusted their scientists while the scientists respected their Guinea Pigs. The result, as in this case, was often the development of a new technique [later written up in the British Medical Journal].

Whether it was Ross Tilley examining you in the ward or in the pub, or one of the nurses offering her own meal as your second helping; whether it was "Sandman" Norman Park putting you to sleep and then smiling at you as you opened your eyes, or Dr. Gardiner fashioning a new dental device to aid the reconstruction of your jaw, you knew you were in good hands.

The Guinea Pigs from Ward III had known this comfort, and the new boys, who would be crash-landing in the Canadian Wing, would come to know it too.

Dr. A. Ross Tilley

The Canadian Wing, Queen Victoria Hospital

Entrance to the Canadian Wing

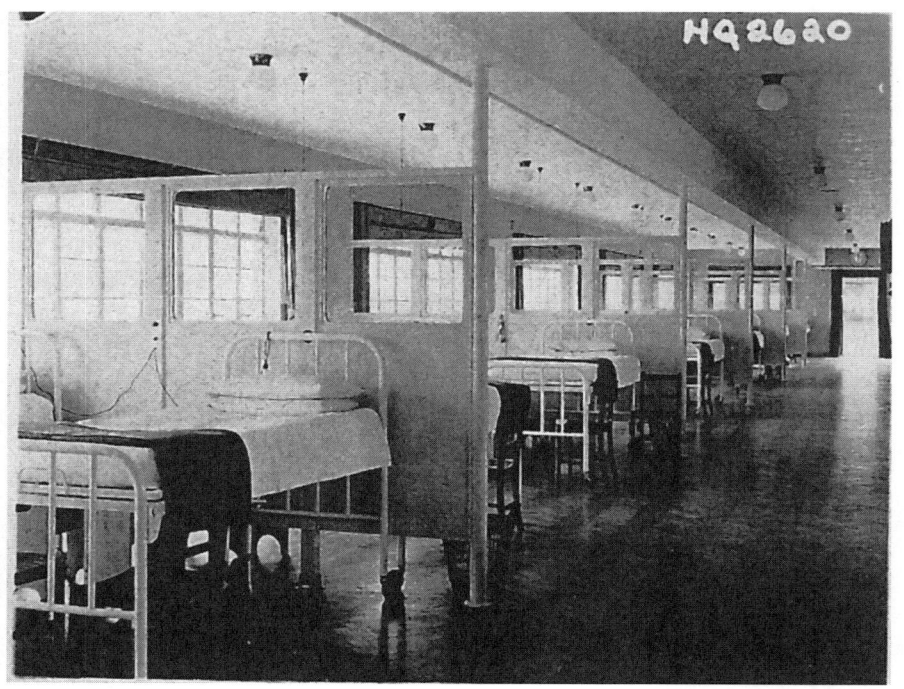

Ward

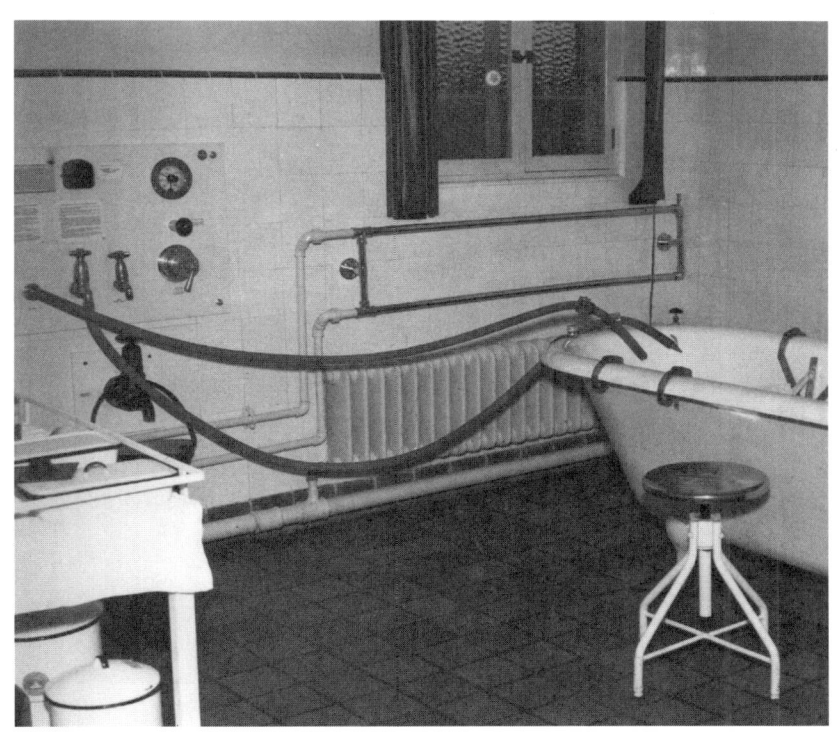

Saline Bath Treatment

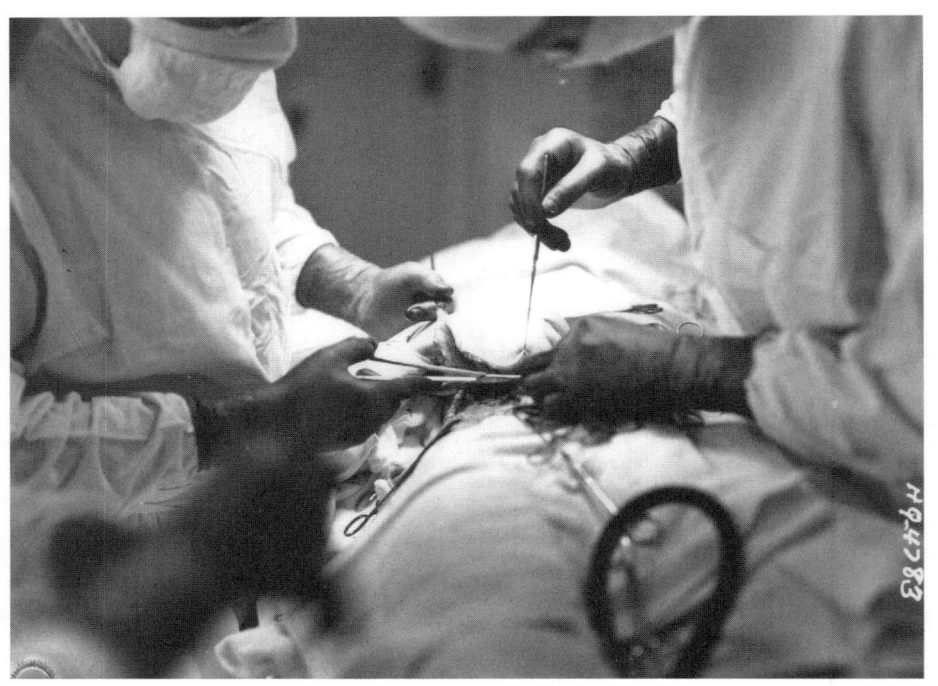

An Operation

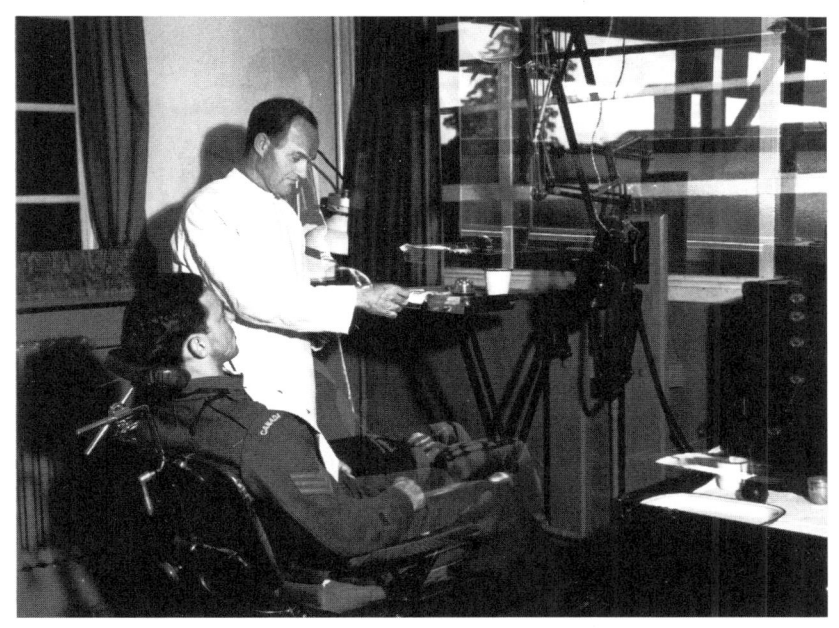

An Examination

Nurses in Canadian Wing

Back row left to right:
F/O Ina (Bishop) Jewsbury; F/O N/S Helen Brown; F/O N/S Soper;
F/O N/S Bernie Arnett; Matron Marjorie Jackson

Front row left to right:
F/O N/S Mons Stapleford; F/O N/S Enid (Faulkner) Matheson;
F/O N/S Marion (Patterson) Ferguson; F/O N/S Hilda (Emke) Moore;
F/O N/S Frankie Anderson; F/O N/S Elaine Matheson; F/O N/S Maggie Kaines

Guinea Pigs (July–December 1944)

Kenneth Allison

Kenneth "Ken" or "Kenny" Allison was a pilot who had the honour of being the first to be operated on in the new Canadian Wing. Ken Allison, a Typhoon pilot, was hit by flak over Normandy. He lost consciousness due to lack of blood and crashed his kite into several parked aircraft.

He is remembered as a character. He is also remembered as a man of great fortitude. Dave Lunney, another Guinea Pig, was on a trip to Ireland with Allison and remembered seeing the extent of the burns Allison had suffered. But like so many Guinea Pigs, Allison was not one to complain.

After the war Allison was an accountant in the income tax department. He eventually became vice-president of a trust company in Montreal. Ken Allison was an active member of the Guinea Pig Club until his death.

Two Guinea Pigs (Stanley G. Reynolds and George Fawcett)

Stanley "Stan" Reynolds came from a flying family. His father had flown with the Royal Flying Corps in the First War; his older

Stanley Reynolds

brother was in the RCAF, as was his younger brother. It was inevitable that Reynolds would take to the air, and in early 1942 he entered the recruiting office in Wetaskiwin.

On April 15, 1942, he found himself at RCAF No. 3 Manning Depot in Edmonton, where the young AC2 settled into life on the base. When he received passes he would leap aboard his 1928 Harley Davidson motorcycle and race back to Wetaskiwin where he was building a Model T Ford race car. For this was Reynolds' other passion—antique vehicles. It would come to play a large role in his post-war life.

July 19, 1942, saw Reynolds at No. 7 ITS in Saskatoon. Following this course, at which Reynolds excelled, he was selected for pilot training and promoted to LAC (leading aircraftsman). By the end of October he was posted to EFTS, course No. 67 where he would fly twenty-nine different Tiger Moths. In January 1943 he was sent to No. 4 SFTS at Saskatoon, course No. 72. There he flew Cessna Cranes.

Every pilot remembers Wings Parade, the day he received his pilot's wings. For Stan Reynolds that day occurred in the base hospital where, recovering from an appendectomy, he had his pilot's wings pinned to his pyjamas! The location and the circumstances did not lessen the moment, however, and the newly minted sergeant looked forward to recovery and to action.

On June 21 at No. 1 "Y" Depot in Halifax, he waited for his trip over. His mode of conveyance was to be the *Louis Pasteur*. On July 1, he was sent to No. 3 Personnel Receiving Centre in Bournemouth, and by August he was at Empire Central Flying School at Hullavington doing airspeed tests in a Miles Master and an Airspeed Oxford.

From there it was on to further training. Objective: night fighter. Location: No. 12 AFU Grantham, Lincolnshire, Course No. 17. They were flying twin-engine Bristol Blenheim Mark V's, or, to the British, "Bisleys." Ground school classes consisted of Morse code, wireless, navigation, meteorology, aircraft recognition, armament and engines. On October 30, Stan Reynolds was promoted to flight sergeant.

February 29, 1944, saw Stan Reynolds in No. 51 OTU at Cranfield, Buckinghamshire. It was here that he learned to fly the twin-engined Bristol Beaufighters, planes with a top air speed of over 300 mph. There was no dual instruction in these one-seaters. Training was done on the ground until the instructor was satisfied the pilot was ready. Then he was sent up in the Beaufighter. Reynolds made his first solo flight on 19 March.

It was now April 1, April Fool's Day, and Reynolds experienced an example of what luck was like in the service. He was flying near London when German planes came over, dropping bombs. Reynolds could see the planes, but because he was on a training flight, he had no ammunition for the guns. To add to the confusion, his normal ground communication was being jammed by the enemy. He had no instruction, could not be vectored back to base, and could not find it on his own as the lights on the airfields had been shut off. So there he sat, treading air until the raid was over and the radio frequencies unjammed. He was lucky.

On May 1 he was posted to RAF Station Winfield on the east coast of Scotland, the only RCAF crew in "A" Flight. From there they would fly over the North Sea in Mark VI Beaufighters. On June 6, 1944, the supercharger in their starboard engine was found to be unserviceable, so they headed back to base after a short flight. They were not informed about the D-Day invasion until the next day.

Stan Reynolds crewed with George Fawcett and flew other Beaufighter ops. On June 21, he and radio-navigator Fawcett were posted to 410 Cougar Squadron where he flew Mosquitos, a plane Reynolds preferred to the Beaufighter.

It was during the night of July 9, 1944, that Reynolds and crew ran into bad luck. During the flight the starboard engine of the Mark XIII Mosquito caught fire. Reynolds shut the fuel line and switches to the damaged engine, feathered the prop and activated the fire extinguisher. The fire went out.

But his trial was not over. He was forced to fly back to base on a single engine, arriving there at about 0230. Reynolds describes what happened then:

> When a twin-engine airplane flying on one engine slows below a certain airspeed, there is not enough rudder control to keep the aircraft at a safe altitude if too much power is used on the operating engine. The increased pull from the operating engine causes the plane to become uncontrollable and crash. Consequently pilots are trained to approach the landing field at a greater height than is usual; if there is an overshoot or undershoot during landing, it is safer to hit the far fence at a slower speed than it is to hit the near fence at flying speed.
>
> When I was certain I would reach the landing field, I activated the flap and undercarriage controls. There is a hydraulic pump on each engine; as one engine was inoperative the hydraulic pump connected to that engine was not working. The hydraulic pressure from the single pump operated the flaps and undercarriage so slowly that they were only partially down, and I could not get the plane stopped before it ran out of landing space. As soon as I was aware that the plane was not slowing down fast enough, and the undercarriage was only part way down, I returned the landing gear control to the retract position, and the

plane skidded on his belly into a coulee adjacent to the landing field. The plane could not be stopped while it was skidding down the slope on the near side of the coulee; however, it came to a sudden stop when it went across a small creek and hit the bottom of the ascending slope on the other side.

Reynolds jerked forward, hitting his head on the instrument panel and receiving facial lacerations. George Fawcett's jaw was broken. Then, things got worse:

The port engine caught fire, and in order to save time, I disconnected my parachute and threw off my helmet with earphones and oxygen mask, rather than disconnect them.

His left foot was caught under the rudder bar. Reynolds succeeded in twisting his foot free, spraining his ankle:

By this time the fire was burning up the left side of the fuselage, singeing the left side of my clothing and the hair on the left side of my head. We crawled out a hole on the right side of the fuselage, and while we were crawling away on our hands and knees the port fuel tanks exploded. A few seconds later the ammunition also started exploding. After we had crawled about 100 yards away we sat on the ground getting our bearings and watching the burning plane. After another ten minutes we got up on our feet, I put one arm over George's shoulders to take some weight off my sprained ankle, and we walked about a quarter mile to a house.

They were eventually picked up by an ambulance-hearse and taken to the base hospital. Reynolds notes that:

Lacking any anaesthetic, the doctor stitched the lacerations in my face without benefit of painkillers.

They were taken by Oxford ambulance plane to Gatwick and from there to East Grinstead. Dr. Tilley visited Reynolds in the Canadian Wing, looked him over, ripped the scabs off his face, and discussed his case. It was then that Reynolds realized there were Guinea Pigs worse off than himself.

Stan Reynolds went back to active flying on August 11, flying a Mark XIII Mosquito. He would fly thirty-five day-and-night flights before being sent to the Repatriation Depot at Manchester. He was promoted to warrant officer, second class, on April 30. On October 14 he was awarded a wound stripe and on October 30 was promoted to WO I (warrant officer, first class.) He sailed home on the *Queen Elizabeth*.

Stan Reynolds was discharged in 1945. In January 1947 he was offered the option of flying with No. 2 Air Command RCAF Winnipeg in a Mosquito Squadron for overseas service as a flight lieutenant. But by then he had begun a successful career in the car sales business. He married Hallie and had a family. His successful business allowed him to further his passion for collecting vintage vehicles. This collection was to become the basis for the Reynolds Museum in Wetaskiwin. This would later become the foundation for the provincially-built, provincially-run Reynolds-Alberta Museum, the finest transportation museum in Canada. It would include, among other things, over $6 million dollars worth of vintage aircraft from Reynolds' personal collection. He is a founder of Canada's Aviation Hall of Fame, in Wetaskiwin, Alberta. Stan Reynolds received Alberta's Award of Excellence in October 1999, and in the Spring of 2000 he received the Order of Canada. Stan Reynolds continues to live in Wetaskiwin and recommends the museum and the Hall of Fame to anyone interested in transportation, aviation, and Canada's technological history.

George Fawcett

Sergeant George Fawcett, the radio navigator who crashed with Stan Reynolds, had originally been crewed with Sergeant Bob Walker. They had been on the same course at No. 51 OTU at Cranfield, Buckinghamshire. While Reynolds and his then-navigator Sergeant Don MacNichol were sent to RAF Winfield in "A" Flight, Fawcett and Walker were posted to Winfield in "B" Flight. As often occurs in the friendships struck on a base, Walker and MacNichol hit it off particularly well and wanted to crew together, so the switch was made and Fawcett flew with Reynolds. Following the crash both Reynolds and Fawcett were taken to East Grinstead, but Fawcett's broken jaw took longer to repair than did Reynolds' injuries.

After the war George Fawcett returned to Canada. He died in the early 1980s.

Canadian Entertainment

Shortly after the opening of the Canadian Wing, as if on cue, the hospital received a visit from a group of Canadian air force entertainers, the "All Clear" Troupe. They were the icing on the cake of this all-Canadian wing.

Elizabeth Hicks, née Stone, was a member of the troupe.

The "All Clear" Troupe
with patients

An Ottawa resident, the Toronto-born Stone was a student at the University of Toronto during the war. Like many of her generation she sought to become involved in the service in some way. So she joined up. Given her background in drama at the university, she eventually wanted to become involved in the entertainment sector, so she searched out a position. Hearing that a woman from the "All Clear" troupe was leaving, Corporal Elizabeth Stone donned her tap shoes for the cause.

The "All Clear" was a mixed (male/female) troupe. They entertained primarily in eastern Canada while "The Blackouts" covered the west. Elizabeth Hicks remembers entertaining in Newfoundland and keeps memorabilia of the period including Newfoundland postage stamps that show Newfoundland's pre-Canadian status.

The troupe performed for Canadians as well as Americans stationed in Canada, so by the time entertainment troupes were able to go overseas, the "All Clear" had a solid show. They were sent over to England in the summer of 1944, entertaining at Gloucester, York and elsewhere. Their shows were written up in the base news sheets with kudos such as: "Canada Can Produce Culture!"

And romance. For by September 1944, Corporal Stone would be married to her Navy husband, Douglas Hicks [no relation to Guinea Pig Douglas Hicks]. Elizabeth Hicks fondly recalls the forty-eight-hour leave she was allowed for her wedding and honeymoon. She did not retire from the troupe directly following her marriage, and she remembers calling her husband, who was stationed in London, to let him know when she would be coming home from a show. His romantic words were, "Don't forget your rations books!"

But the show at East Grinstead that summer is also one of her special memories. It was July 24, 1944, and they were entertaining at the Town Hall. The entire hospital—patients and staff—were invited, as were the townspeople of East Grinstead. As the first Canadian entertainment troupe to come through the area, they were warmly received. Hicks recalls: "We put our hearts into that show."

Afterwards, the patients at the Canadian Wing had a reception for the entertainers. Elizabeth Hicks speaks honestly of her first impression:

We were shy. How do you talk to...how do you avoid staring? Who is going to be embarrassed?

As it turned out, nobody. The men were so relaxed, "Very cheerful," they made the entertainers quickly feel at ease.

The trip to East Grinstead has remained a specific memory in the mind of someone who had put on many shows. In fact, Elizabeth Hicks possesses many fond memories of her wartime experience. Her troupe entertained scores of appreciative airmen; she enjoyed a long, happy marriage blessed with children. Upon reflection, she says, "I wouldn't have missed it."

Karl E. O'Connor

Karl O'Connor was a pilot serving with RCAF Ferry Command, flying between England and North Africa. It was sometime in 1944 that a plane he was ferrying exploded on the ground, and O'Connor became a visitor to East Grinstead—and a Guinea Pig.

The spirit of Guinea Piggery must have remained with the young pilot, for in his later years he would volunteer several days a week at the Credit Valley Hospital. Karl O'Connor and his wife Frances had two children. He died in 1997 at the age of 78.

Frank E. Hanton

Frank Hanton, of Kenora, Ontario, could not have known when he enlisted that he would have the active service career that transpired. His military career involved service with the RCAF in Fighter Command, Fighter Reconnaissance, PRU High and Low Altitude, and Night Intruder Operations from 1941-1946. Hanton would fly Hurricanes, all Spitfires from Mk.V to Mk. XIV,

P-51 Mustangs, Mosquitos, Typhoons and others. He would be awarded a DFC, perform as a top train-buster in the allied force, and gain membership in that exclusive organization— The Guinea Pig Club.

It happened on July 17, 1944. Hanton was stationed at Landing Strip B-8 Bayeux, Normandy. He was flying an Mk. XI Spitfire on a mission to photograph the Falaise area at 35,000 feet. Hanton was no stranger to danger having been wounded on two occasions by enemy anti-aircraft fire. After each injury he was able to return to action. On this particular op he was flying back to base with a badly-damaged Spitfire. Hanton explains:

> The critically damaged Spitfire lost all of its engine oil and coolant which sent all engine temperatures to the maximum, causing the engine to seize. The aircraft was flown dead-stick to Bayeux where an emergency landing was attempted. At 600 feet the engine exploded into a fireball with the fire coming back through the firewall into the cockpit, with a full blast into my face and upper body, setting on fire my battle dress, roll neck sweater, etc..
>
> Having previously prepared for a possible emergency exit from the aircraft, it was essential to get out of the aircraft as quickly as the situation now permitted. That was done—at 500 feet.
>
> Because of the low altitude, the parachute opened just above the trees, and the hard landing was made in a field full of boulders where the fifty to sixty mph wind smashed my shoulders, back and legs into the rocks lying in the field. The severe burns to my face quickly blinded me, and very little is remembered after that until partial consciousness returned for a short time in the field hospital. The only thing remembered is hearing voices saying: "What a mess. With all those burns, he'll never make it."

Fortunately, this was not the outcome. Hanton was picked up in a tank landing craft and dropped off at a Southhampton Hospital. His two kit bags containing his personal equipment went missing en route, and he arrived at Southhampton without a uniform, a change of clothes, or any personal gear. Blind.

He was taken from Southhampton to the Army Hospital at Basingstoke and from there, in August, to East Grinstead. The delay could not have been good for his burns, as he had had no remedial work done prior to his arrival, but by then partial sight (ability to distinguish light and dark) had returned to his left eye.

He was operated on by both Dr. McIndoe and Dr. Tilley, to considerable success:

> The great surgical and other work performed on me by the two great surgeons at the Queen Victoria, Sir Archibald McIndoe and W/C Ross Tilley, is in a class by itself, and I cannot speak too highly of them as well as the nurses and support staff. They are the people who got me back and serviceable once again so that I could carry on and finish the war with full ability to once again fly a fighter aircraft.

In order to be allowed to do this, Hanton took a trip to the Dunsfold RCAF base where he flew an Mk.1X Spitfire in the company of the CO in another Spitfire. Following this he had his interview at the hospital, and, respecting Hanton's wishes, the hospital cleared him for active flying duties. Hanton returned home to Canada on a thirty-day leave after which he returned and was posted to 402 Squadron and completed that tour at the Luftwaffe station at Fassenberg, beside the Belsen concentration camp. Hanton stayed on for one and a half years after the war, in Hamburg, as part of the first peacekeeping force.

Hanton maintains a fully valid pilot's licence to this day. His fascinating post-war activities have included flying duties with the Manitoba Government Air Service, guest speaking duties, and a period as chief aide-de-camp to the Lieutenant Governor of Saskatchewan.

Squadron Leader Frank Hanton, DFC, had an outstanding service career as a pilot and train-buster, and this, combined with his challenging post-war opportunities, has given him a personal history that would be hard to surpass. He has enjoyed a successful marriage to Joyce and is the father of several children.

July 1944 had been a busy month for 6 Group. There were the usual attacks on railyards and depots, as well as attacks on the sites that stockpiled buzz-bombs. There were raids on Caen, on the industrial sites of the *Rührgebeit*, on Kiel and on Stuttgart. The month ended with a heavy-loss raid on Hamburg.

But 6 Group was excelling despite its losses. Under direct orders from General Eisenhower, Supreme Commander, 6 Group was seen as a support force for the allied armies. This meant further ops like those already described plus operations against troop positions around Caen. Despite the fact that the coming month would see the heavy-loss August 14 raid on the Quesnay-Fontaine-le-Pin-Bons-Tassily area, 6 Group was a fully functional unit with close to 300 planes. The post-invasion period was successful, but it created a new supply of Guinea Pigs.

Duncan N. McTavish

A native of West Vancouver, Duncan Neil McTavish was born April 28, 1921. Unlike many Guinea Pigs, McTavish followed a different established career before (and after) the war, that of sports writer for *The Vancouver Sun*.

In 1941 McTavish enlisted in the RCAF and became a flying officer while taking time off the same year to marry Victoria. McTavish went overseas in 1944. Two months later, in August, his B-25 Mitchell bomber crashed during takeoff. McTavish was burned. He was sent down to East Grinstead where he accepted the hospitality of the Canadian Wing for seven months.

McTavish went home and after the war received the Defence Medal, the Canadian Volunteer Service Medal and the War Medal, 1939-1945 Star. Along with these and a fresh degree in business administration from the University of Western Ontario, he settled in Oakville in 1949 with his wife and one child. They were to add three more children to the McTavish family. Duncan McTavish enjoyed a long career with Ford Motor Company and kept up with 540 Air Force Association in various capacities including that of president. Like many other Guinea Pigs, he sought a new career in later years opening a travel agency with his son, Ross, in 1972. Duncan McTavish died in April 1999.

Stories like Duncan McTavish's remind us that for many, if not most Guinea Pigs, their RCAF or RAF service was confined to the wartime period. Many were so young when they enlisted that their air force experience was their very first job. Others, like McTavish, bracketed the war with a separate career.

Another Guinea Pig who did not remain in the service after the war was Ken Davies. But his experiences at East Grinstead were to have an impact on what, ultimately, would become his life's work.

Kenneth J. Davies

Kenneth "Ken" Davies, a young flier from Manitoba, joined up on November 17, 1942, and received his commissioned rank of pilot officer on October 29, 1943. He went overseas in February 1944.

Ken Davies

Davies became a Guinea Pig on August 3, 1944, when the plane he was flying struck a tree during low flying exercises at Maxwell Farm, Botolph-Layton, in Buckinghamshire. He was quite badly hurt, suffering a fractured left scapula, compound fractures of the skull and a lacerated scalp. He had just become a "mashed" variety of Guinea Pig. He was taken to the RAF Hospital in Halton, Buckinghamshire, listed as "dangerously ill." The family back home also received this news.

One has to be reminded, again, of the *language* of the air force, of the weight of words like "dangerously ill", and how only in such extreme cases could comfort have been found in hearing, some days later, that the man had been upgraded to "seriously ill."

Ken Davies would spend most of the month on those two lists. When he was finally out of danger, he was sent to East Grinstead for repairs. Davies returned to Canada at the end of March, 1945. He served with the air force until this discharge, whereupon he worked at various jobs while pursuing an interest in medicine that had germinated in the Canadian Wing at East Grinstead. He took time out from his studies to marry Lillian in 1948. They would have a long and happy marriage blessed with six children.

Ken Davies pursued medicine, becoming a physician in 1954, (Doctor of Medicine, University of Manitoba.) He continued his studies, significantly, in the field of psychiatry, studying at Stanford University where he became a Member of the American Society of

163

Clinical Hypnosis (1957). He followed this up with a Canadian certificate in psychiatry (1961).

An active man, Davies would balance the calm, caring precision of his calling with personal feats of physical endurance. He was an avid skier, and he also made regular use of his catamaran.

Ken Davies practiced psychiatry in Vancouver and Kelowna, British Columbia until his premature death from cancer in 1982. Even during his illness, his fortitude allowed him to attend the 1981 Guinea Pig Reunion. Known by his colleagues as a man "who saw the good in everybody," Dr. Ken Davies, M.D., F.R.C.P.(C), was a man who always remembered his time in the Canadian Wing. As his wife, Lillian recalled:

> He often related that his time in East Grinstead, and the opportunity to observe the work of the medical staff there, were what gave him the desire to become a doctor.

Edward Carlson

Edward Carlson served with the RCAF, both in Canada and in England, from 1940 until his discharge in 1945. Carlson was shot down over Germany in 1944 and was badly wounded in the face and the shoulder. He was taken prisoner of war and remained a POW until liberation at war's end at which time he was sent to East Grinstead where Dr. Tilley performed plastic surgery on his face.

Carlson was only at East Grinstead a short time before he was given the green light to go home. He settled in Vancouver where he and his wife Ilene had a daughter. Edward Carlson worked for a survey company as a photogrammetrist until his retirement. The Carlsons enjoyed travelling and saw much of the world. They also enjoyed the Guinea Pig reunions, and Edward Carlson counted himself a proud member of the Club. He died in 1992.

Donald Simpson

Donald Simpson was a young married man (to Betty) when he went overseas with the RCAF. His Guinea Pig injuries involved the nose area, primarily, and repairs were done on the bone structure of his face.

Simpson spent his post-war years working first in the Department of Education for the Ontario Government and later with Northern Affairs and Indian Affairs until his retirement. The Simpsons reside in Ottawa.

David M. Lunney

David "Dave" Lunney joined the RCAF in 1941 and received his observer's wing in 1942. His first overseas assignment was with 425 Squadron of 6 Group. He was later transferred to 405 Pathfinder Force as a flight lieutenant.

Lunney had occasion to avail himself of the services of the Queen Victoria Hospital, where Dr. Tilley worked at setting to right some scar deterioration. This involved fashioning a new lip. Lunney was mobile while at East Grinstead and got around the town. He remembers the Whitehall, where one time he encountered Douglas Bader in attendance. He recalls the ward fondly as well, how people referred to him by name, how the patients were given good food and good drink; how they were "treated politely."

Lunney remembers, especially, Drs. Tilley and Park, and the remarkable *esprit de corps* that was and is the Guinea Pig Club. Dave Lunney and his wife Barbara live in New Brunswick and still attend Guinea Pig reunions.

John Sydney Cummins

John Cummins was with 404 Beaufighter Squadron when he became a member of the Guinea Pig Club. Following the war, he married Margaret and had two children. In later years he was an active member of the Canadian Wartime Heritage Museum, and he played a significant part in the restoration and maintenance of the Lancaster on display at the museum. John Cummins died in 1997.

Two Guinea Pigs (George Allen and M.A. Platsko)

George Allen

George Willoughby Allen, known to his crew as "George" and to his family as "Bill," was a navigator with 422 Sunderland Squadron operating out of Lough Erne, Ireland. The flying boat squadron was stationed at RAF Castle Archdale.

August 12, 1944, was a warm summer day. It was just 1225 when F/L Pilot Cam Devine and M.A. Platsko, co-pilot, took the plane, T-422, up on an A/S patrol. George Allen was navigating, and the rest of the crew included F/O Roy Wilkinson, P/O John Forrest, Sergeant G.A. Colbourne and Roger Jael. They headed out to the Bay of Biscay, but before long they ran into engine trouble while climbing to their set course. Something was wrong with their starboard outer engine; it began backfiring and registering high temperature readings. Flying control received this report and told the crew to scrub the mission. They were instructed to fly to Donegal Bay to drop the DCs and to jettison the petrol on their return.

They proceeded toward the bay, Allen standing behind the pilot and co-pilot seats and keeping an eye on the temperature gauge. At this point they were flying at 1500 feet. Suddenly there was a roar and the outer starboard prop wound off and embedded itself in the right wing float. Captain Devine ordered the crew into ditching position. They were rapidly losing altitude and the plane kept turning starboard despite the captain's efforts.

They advised Flying Control that they were going to attempt a forced landing. Still trying to dump their bomb load, they found the racks sluggish to open. When the racks finally opened, they would not retract. Meanwhile, there was more fire in the engines.

They went down. The crash killed Captain Devine, F/O Wilkinson and P/O Forrest. All of the survivors were injured. George Allen and M.A. Platsko wound up in the Canadian Wing as two new members of the Club.

George Allen would eventually go back home to Alberta, where he owned a farm. He married Anne and had a family, remaining in Alberta until his death in 1997.

M.A. Platsko

M. A. "Al" Platsko, the co-pilot of the ill-fated Sunderland, recalled the August 12 engine troubles that began the harrowing flight. As the fire was raging and the pilot tried to hold the plane steady, Platsko intermittently jettisoned fuel, a dangerous job. As he notes:

[I soon] turned the petrol cocks off for fear of the engine fire causing an explosion and blowing us all to Hades.

It was clear to Platsko, as it was to everyone else, that there was nothing to be done. The plane was going down:

> ...the Captain and I were trying to keep the right wing up and the aircraft level as we descended rapidly to the ground and watched as we helplessly plowed into a small mound in a boggy area. I was sure that this would be the end of us. I had unsecured my seat belt before we developed engine trouble and never resecured it. As a result of this I was hurled through the windshield on impact....

Platsko estimates that he landed some twenty-five to thirty-five feet beyond the wreckage:

> I do not recall the impact, and I assume that I was unconscious only momentarily. I found myself lying in muck, dazed but in no pain. Everything around me appeared dark and hazy. I could hear and faintly see the roaring fire of the aircraft.

He spotted Roger Jael nearby and convinced him that they would have to move away from the plane:

> As we crawled away the ammunition was exploding, and we could see tracer bullets passing over our heads. I thought, man, that would be awful to be shot by our own bullets. We crawled into a nearby ditch and kept low, listening to the exploding ammunition and the burning wreckage.

They were aided by local farmers who risked their lives to remove the injured men from the wreckage site. The men were sent to Shield Hospital in Ballyshannon. Platsko remembers:

> I was bleeding from multiple head, face, neck and shoulder lacerations and had an injured knee.

George Allen, who had been lying on the deck behind the pilot's seat, had managed to find the emergency opening through the smoke before the fumes overcame him. He was suffering from extensive burns as well as lacerations to the head, a displaced fracture of the right leg, a dislocated left shoulder, an injured back and general bruising.

They were the lucky ones. As has been stated, all of the survivors were injured, but among the dead, P/O Wilkinson had been on his very first familiarization flight.

Platsko remembers his time at East Grinstead. Although it was relatively short, it would have a career-altering impact on him. Already quite healed from his time at the Shield Hospital, he arrived at the Queen Victoria Hospital on November 11, 1944:

> I was not prepared for what I saw. Every airman that was there was terribly disfigured as a result of extreme burns. It was an awful shock, and I was speechless. There were airmen with no noses or ears and badly scarred faces and others who were in various stages of reconstructive surgery. One had his right arm attached to a pedicle graft to his cheek (previously removed from his abdomen.)

Yet this was only half of the eye-opener:

> What amazed me most was the light-hearted atmosphere among the airmen. They were joking and kidding each other about their appearance and how many trips they made to the operating room while I was staring in disbelief. Many of these men were...having a surgical procedure every four to six weeks. They were completing a tour in the operating room.

The men were impressive, and then there was Dr. Tilley:

> Dr. Tilley and staff made it a point that everyone was upbeat no matter how bad their injuries were. It was like one big family with the parents taking care of their injured children.

And, of course, there was the community:

> The community of East Grinstead embraced all the servicemen and also treated them like they were their own children. It was a wonderful experience to be treated so caringly.

This spirit allowed Platsko to undergo his own plastic surgery to remove facial scars on November 14. While at East Grinstead he had the opportunity to watch two three-hour operations. He describes with fascination a rhinoplasty:

> The pedicle graft which was attached to the forearm and forehead was severed from the forearm and rotated to form the basis of a new nose. I was all eyes....

M.A. Platsko credits this exposure to the wonders of medicine with playing a role in his decision to return to school to further his own education.

But first there was checkout, November 22, two weeks leave and then back to active flying duty. He was transferred to 422 Squadron, Pembroke Dock, on December 9, 1944, and joined a new crew, going on to fly 19 ops excluding training flights. His last flight was May 27, 1945.

True to his promise to himself, Platsko did go back to school. M.A. Platsko received his medical degree in Winnipeg in 1953. Dr. Platsko was in family practice and then spent twenty-four years practising radiology until his retirement in 1983. Dr. Platsko lives in Pebble Beach, California, with his wife Lillian.

When he thinks back on East Grinstead he remembers both the advanced surgical skills as well as the ineffable spirit:

> It was a wonderful place to get Guinea Pig surgery that encompassed the technical as well as the spiritual skills that the Guinea Pigs needed.

This notion of the hospital staff acting as "parents caring for their children" is interesting. It is mentioned, in different ways, by many of the Guinea Pigs. And in Ian Ferguson's film, *Dr. Tilley and His Guinea Pigs*, Lady Connie McIndoe, widow of Sir Archie, summarizes it thus:

> They didn't need just a surgeon, and they didn't get just a surgeon.

Arthur K. Leitch

Arthur K. Leitch was a navigator with the RCAF. He was to become a Guinea Pig while on ops, but not by the traditional methods of frying or mashing. Leitch was returning to base in a shot-up plane. The icy wind blasted his face for the entire five hours it took to get back. He developed "Tic Douloureux" down the left side of his face.

Leitch spent time in East Grinstead where his personal mobility allowed him to assist other more severely debilitated patients. He was happy to help, and he extolled this as part of everyone's healing, his own included. Like many Guinea Pigs, he was impressed with the Canadian Wing.

He returned to active service, eventually being awarded the Distinguished Flying Cross. After the war he went to university, married Frances, and had a career in a construction company. Unfortunately, he suffered from rheumatoid arthritis which plagued his retirement and curtailed plans to attend Guinea Pig reunions. However, he followed the Club's activities in the newsletter and *The Guinea Pig* magazine. Arthur Leitch died in 1989.

George Wilkinson

George Wilkinson was a member of the Guinea Pig Club, having been repaired at the Queen Victoria Hospital following an injury. Wilkinson returned to Canada, married Beryl, and lived in Ottawa where he raised a family. He worked for a time for a pulp and paper company and returned to college.

Frederick S. Hiley

Frederick "Fred" Hiley was a pilot with 420 Squadron. Prior to the war he had been studying aeronautical engineering, but duty called. Hiley was well on his way to a distinguished career.

In May 1942 he was part of a raid on Stuttgart. Following the raid, the plane was hit by anti-aircraft fire. Attempting to hobble home, Hiley and crew were then engaged by a Messerschmidt 110 which caused more damage to the aircraft and killed the rear gunner. The fighter was eventually driven off, but not before it had destroyed one of the engines, the electrical system and both the pilot's and the navigator's compasses. Hiley flew the plane home and landed safely. For this he was awarded the Distinguished Flying Medal which was presented to him by King George VI at Buckingham Palace on January 18, 1943.

Sometime after this Hiley joined the Guinea Pig Club. It was a bombing run, and Hiley was taking off with a full payload. Something went wrong soon after take-off and the plane crashed. Hiley was told that the resulting explosion destroyed the aircraft completely and sent his unconscious body hurtling. He landed in a haystack, which saved his life.

But Hiley was badly burned. The first six months were, and remained, a blur to him as treatment, morphine, and trauma took their toll. He later confessed to his son that he felt "dead" for that period. But when he was able to remember, what he remembered was the kindness and care he received.

He would complete his tour of duty in Canada as both a test pilot and as a personal pilot for air force "brass." He would go on to complete his studies in aeronautical engineering and find himself in the middle of the Avro Arrow project at A.V. Roe. He would also work for Trans-Canada Airlines (Air Canada) until 1976. Fred Hiley and his wife Eleanor had seven children. He remained an avid member of the Club until his death in December 1990.

Everett Ferguson

Everett "Fergie" Ferguson was one of the characters of the group. A native of Biggar, Saskatchewan, and later a resident of Winnipeg, Fergie graduated in 1943 with the best marks ever seen in navigation and was awarded the Bud Starrat Memorial Watch. He was immediately sent overseas and posted at Market Harborough in Leceistershire.

On March 20, 1944, he was scheduled for a training run in a Wellington. But at 0130 hours two engines failed. The plane hit a tree and burst into flames. Two men were killed instantly. Fergie was thrown clear of the aircraft. The airport had been ringed with barbed wire, slowing the arrival of the rescue team to the crash site. After the delay, they arrived and determined that, among the survivors, Fergie was the most grievously injured with third degree burns to his right hand, arm, back, left knee and foot. There were also facial and scalp injuries, a fractured nose and a fractured jaw. When some two hours later the casualties were taken to the Leceistershire Royal Infirmary, Fergie was listed as "dangerously ill."

So Fergie's entry into the Club predates the opening of the Canadian Wing, but he is placed in this section due to his arrival there in September of 1944, and in honour of the unique part he played in the mythology of the Guinea Pig Club.

In order to fully appreciate the moment, a little background to the scene is required.

Since June 1944, when the first V-1 weapon fell on London, the dreaded "buzz-bombs" or "doodlebugs" were a constant menace. The V-1 FZG-76 *Flakzielgerät* anti-aircraft target device [the designation was deliberately deceptive] was coined by the Nazis the *Vergeltungswaffe* [retaliation weapon], or V-1. Particularly insidious in that they were cheap to make, the pilotless, guided, *flying* bombs were soon everywhere, their

distinctive buzzing sound signalling their arrival. Yet the sound was vastly preferable to the cessation of sound which signified that the bomb would explode within a few seconds. Squadron fighters were despatched to shoot down these oddly annoying yet

dangerous devices [see Paul Davoud's story]. Inevitably, with so many V-1s in existence, many were successful on their deadly missions. From their sites in northern France, the bombs were sent across to England.

An attack by this strange new device has been described in detail in the memoirs of Brock McElheran, in his book *V-Bombs and Weathermaps*, the story of his experiences as a meteorological officer for the Royal Canadian Navy. Posted at the naval air stations in southern England during the war, McElheran was severely injured in a V-1 bomb attack and spent time in East Grinstead for operations and treatment. McElheran states that at first it was assumed the device was an aircraft. As he listened to one close by he noted:

After several minutes I heard the engine of an aircraft, which within a few seconds became very

This page: **Damage to the Canadian Wing**

loud. It had a harsh, snarly tone very similar to a Harvard training plane.[7]

Anti-aircraft fire soon opened up on the craft, and McElheran heard it crash. Newspapers noted the large blast that occurred when it crashed and determined that it must have had a full load of bombs. Then more unusual details started coming out. The aircraft had flown in with its navigation lights on. Some people said it looked as though it had been on fire. Others noted a single white light. It had flown low and fast and—strangely—had taken no evasive action. The rumours continued:

> A buzz went around that the searchers hadn't found the pilot's body in the wreckage. This strengthened the belief that he had jumped when the aircraft caught fire and had left it on the automatic pilot.
> The next day...another buzz went around, this one behind backs of hands—there never had been any pilot. The aircraft was a robot....[8]

And East Grinstead was on the route of these robots.

But back to Fergie, who was lying in his hospital bed when a call came to clear the ward. This usually meant taking cover under the bed. Fergie was going about it at his own pace and thus was able to witness the curious phenomenon of a shell from an RAF Typhoon crashing through the new windows of the Canadian Wing in pursuit of a buzz-bomb. Fergie had a front row seat. The cannon shell took the leg off his bed before exploding in close proximity. The amazed and impressed Fergie summarized the experience this way:

> I'm the only person ever shot down out of a hospital bed.

After the war, Fergie would come into possession of a unique souvenir, a piece of his shot-up bed, suitably inscribed and presented to him by Dr. Tilley.

Dr. Tilley and staff repaired Fergie while someone else repaired the new Wing. Dr. Tilley applied a large abdominal flap to Fergie's right hand, one of the most substantial he had ever used. Tilley was truly proud of the result as Fergie regained limited use of this severely damaged limb.

Everett Ferguson went back to Canada for more surgery at Trenton, primarily on his nose. Then he went back to Winnipeg to marry his sweetheart, Mae. They would have a long happy marriage blessed with two children, Janice and Ian. Ian Ferguson, a filmmaker, would one day go on to make the documentary film *Dr. Tilley and His Guinea Pigs.*

Everett Ferguson had a successful career in advertising, working for the McKim Advertising company as vice-president in charge of large, prestigious accounts. Ferguson lived life to the fullest and died a happy man in October 1995.

Donald V. Wright

F/O Donald Wright served with RCAF 440 Squadron, first flying Hurricanes and then Typhoons. His squadron, along with Squadrons 438 and 439, formed a new Canadian wing in early 1944. They moved their base to Hurn in Hampshire in March and built up their strength. Some of their activities included anti-shipping sweeps to the Channel Islands, and sweeps to Caen and Cherbourg. The 440 Squadron then moved on to Funtingdon from where it would fly its first bombing mission.

For unlike the RAF Typhoon squadrons, which primarily used their planes as rocket launchers, the RCAF Typhoon wing was to utilize their kites primarily as fighter-bombers. They would carry either two 500 lb. or two 1,000 lb. bombs cradled under their wings, and would fly to target with much accuracy. So 440 Squadron began bombing "NOBALL" [V-1] launching sites as well as German transportation locations like bridges.

After D-Day, 440 Squadron shifted its base of operations to Normandy while concentrating its actions in Normandy, especially in the Caen area. Their most active month would be August, and throughout the summer they were hit by heavy flak. September saw operations from Brussels, and in late September they established themselves at a base in Eindhoven, Holland. By October, 440 Squadron was specializing in hitting German rail transports, an activity that they would engage in until the end of the war.

Donald Wright survived the operations but not without injury serious enough to send him to East Grinstead. There he was seen to by Dr. Tilley. After the war, Wright pursued a career in dentistry. Dr. Wright was married to Dorothy and had a family. He died in 1992.

Stanley Given

Stanley "Stan" Given joined up in early 1942. The Elmwood, Ontario, native was sent to Manning Pool in Toronto and did ITS at the Eglington Hunt Club, also in Toronto. He went on to AOS (ANS) in Crumlin, Ontario where he trained as a navigator.

It was on to England where he did Battle School in Devon, AFU coursework in Gloucester and OTU at Honeybourne near Evesham. While at OTU he participated in nickel raids on France, flying Whitleys. Then it was more battle training at Yorkshire and on to a conversion unit at Topcliffe.

Given was posted to 432 Cougar (Leaside) Squadron, which flew Halifaxes. He would eventually make thirty-three trips on two different Leaside "L" Lulus. The first was shot down over Holland while loaned to another crew. The second would take him to the Guinea Pig Club.

Stan Given was halfway through his tour of ops. On a return to the base at Eastmoor, the plane ran into trouble. Fortunately, no one was killed, but Stan Given had just become a "mashed" variety of Guinea Pig. His face was in less than perfect shape, but he was temporarily fixed up so that he and his colleagues could finish their tour as a crew. By September 1944 with thirty-three ops over Germany and France under their belts, the tour was complete and Given went on to East Grinstead and Ross Tilley's inventive hands. Tilley grafted and re-crafted Given's face.

Following the assistance he was given at East Grinstead, Given was able to be repatriated in time to be home for Christmas 1944. The rest of his war would be served in Canada, instructing navigators at Summerside, Prince Edward Island. He was discharged in November–December 1945 as a flying officer.

Stan Given went on to university (Queen's), earning a degree in metallurgical engineering which took him to careers in the steel and aluminum industries. He managed during this time to become a registered Professional Engineer (Ontario and British Columbia). He has been married for over fifty years to Vivian and they have two children.

Stan Given remembers the care he received at the Queen Victoria Hospital:

> Dr. Tilley, Dr. McIndoe, the nurses and all the staff
> were so wonderful, cheery and extremely pleasant that

one did not think one was a patient. The East Grinstead townspeople were terrific also.

He undoubtedly feels himself fortunate, noting the statistics:

> Of the twenty-one graduating navigators in our class at Crumlin nineteen went overseas, as two went on to become instructors. Seven were killed in action, one evaded, making a loss rate of 42%.

Norman A. McHolm

Norman McHolm ("McHolme" in his autobiographical memoir *The Touch of God's Hand*) was a young married man (to

Norman McHolm

wife Marg) and father of one when the war began. Although he had a job selling insurance, he had already joined a reserve squadron previously in the year, so it was no surprise that on the afternoon of September 3, 1939, the phone rang. Squadron Leader Russell of 110 Squadron was following up on McHolm's earlier interest in pilot training. Was he still interested? Norman McHolm was in.

His first stop was No. 2 TTS, a technical training school for aero engine mechanics and airframe mechanics, located in St. Thomas, Ontario. McHolm would soon become a clerk in the orderly room.

He was then posted to Camp Borden and after that Trenton. Then it was on to No. 2 SFTS at Uplands, Ottawa. There he became a corporal, but continued to dream of remustering, desiring to fly, like so many other ground crew. Here he became a sergeant.

McHolm did remuster and was sent to No. 3 ITU at Victoriaville, Quebec. More training followed at Brantford, and McHolm graduated on November 20, 1942, with his wings and a commission as pilot officer. McHolm was chosen to be a flying instructor posted to No. 1 Flying Instructors School at Trenton. Then it was on to No. 8 SFTS in Moncton and No. 3 SFTS Kingston.

McHolm received his overseas posting, and in January 1944 he sailed to Scotland, arriving January 30, 1944. He was posted to No. 15 AFU (Advanced Flying Unit) in Wiltshire, then to OTU Atherstone and then on to Dalton, Yorkshire. He had a crew by this time, and they were posted to No. 1666 Heavy Conversion Unit, Wombleton, where they were to fly Halifax Mark IIs.

It was the evening of November 8, 1944. McHolm and crew were on a cross-country exercise. The first three aircraft they had tried to take up were unserviceable, while:

> ...the fourth was an old clunker we did manage to get airborne. If we had followed our impulses, we would have cancelled the trip.

Halifax Bomber "Q" Queeny was about two hours into the flight when weather caused some icing and turbulence. They could not climb above the weather disturbance. In fact, turbulence caused the escape hatch to fly open. Now they were really freezing. Hoar frost shrouded all the instruments. They decided to make for the nearest base to repair the hatch. The navigator chose Peterhead, Scotland. McHolm elaborates:

> We proceeded to Peterhead and circled the base and called up on the emergency channel: DARKY, DARKY, THIS IS AN EMERGENCY. HALIFAX, NO DROP QUEENY YORK (our base call sign and the aircraft name). PERMISSION TO LAND, PLEASE!"
>
> We were given permission to land with the warning that the runway was only 3,500 feet long, barely enough to land or take off again. We let down through cloud and were in the clear at 800 feet. As soon as they heard us overhead they turned on the runway lights and we landed without any trouble.

The hatch was quickly repaired but there was still the problem of the abbreviated runway. The crew got into take-off position, the runway lights were reversed, and McHolm prepared for the take off:

> On the take off we had just about reached flying speed when the aircraft swung violently to the left. The port outer engine had failed. I tried to control the swing with throttle changes but without effect. As we were by then more than halfway down the runway, I shut

off the other three engines and tried to stop the aircraft. In a few seconds we were crashing through obstacles.... I found out afterwards that we had gone through a grove of trees, through a stone fence that tore off the undercarriage, down into a small river and up the bank on the other side. The aircraft burst into flames, and I was knocked out when hit by the control column when we went down to the river.

McHolm was unconscious. His wireless operator, Bob Keane, took control of the scene and radioed the base at Tholthorpe, notifying them of the crash. He did this with a fractured skull and later would not remember making the call. McHolm was also later to discover that his crew had risked their lives pulling him from the burning plane while ammunition went off all around them.

Norman McHolm woke up on the operating table to the words:

I can't do much more than staple his nose back on with the equipment I have here; he is lucky they didn't lose it when they got him out of the aircraft.

He was taken, strapped down in a windowless, claustrophobia-inducing ambulance, to a hospital in Kingseat, outside of Aberdeen. There he lay, his face smashed and his nose flattened. He could not move, and there was speculation that his back was broken. His condition was eventually determined to be herniated discs, crushed vertebrae, and torn ligaments. This, in wartime parlance, was good news.

Up and around a short time later, he was first transferred back to the base hospital at Wombleton and then on to East Grinstead, to Ross Tilley and company. The Guinea Pigs had seen worse than Norman McHolm's injuries as he was soon to discover:

I hadn't heard of East Grinstead before, but I arrived there with my face all bashed up and my nose pushed in—I thought I was a horrible sight—but when I arrived and saw some of the chaps, I thought, "My God, I shouldn't be in the place!" The few little injuries I had. I was so thankful—and so thankful to be alive—that I sat down and wrote a long letter to my mother....

The letter survives and offers a glimpse of what the Canadian Wing looked like to an injured airman arriving close to Christmas in 1944. In part, it reads:

> Dear Mom and Dad,
>
> I am not writing in reply to any of your letters this time because I have not received any recently, but to tell you about this modern fairyland where I am staying at present. Just picture a dirty, foggy wet old  England, and by walking through a door...coming out in the Private Patients Wing of the Toronto General Hospital! Every one a Canadian, everything sparkling new and clean, Christmas decorations everywhere, even a big Christmas tree loaded with lights and decorations. Everyone happy and full of good Canadian food, eggs every morning, all the fresh milk you can drink, everything and everyone working to make things comfortable.

He went on to describe some of the inhabitants:

> There are chaps here so badly burned that they are almost not human looking, and yet there is a whole village, a whole community devoting their time to convince these chaps that they are not that bad to look at, and that some day they will be able to take their place in life again.

This excerpt, indeed the entire letter, was published in the family's local newspaper at the time.

McHolm would spend Christmas in the ward and report back to active duty in January 1945, happily finding his crew intact. He would now be flying Halifax Mark IIIs.

Norman McHolm survived missions through the winter of 1944–45 although once he was listed as missing in action. He stayed in the service until January 1946. By October 1946 he and his wife Marg, who had two children, bought a twenty-acre farm in Woodstock, Ontario. He would go on to work for a large

Toronto advertising company. He has retained high praise for the staff at East Grinstead, and for the Guinea Pig Club. He also retains a kind of amazement at his good fortune in light of so many tragedies:

> Those of us who are left are puzzled sometimes, why me? Surely God has a reason. We have all had fifty or more bonus years, as each one treated at that hospital could have been killed when they crashed or were shot down, and yet we were spared when so many of our friends were killed.

Lionel E. Hastings

Lionel "Hank" Hastings, of York Township outside of Toronto, was eighteen and in the accounting department of Canada Packers when duty called. As he was in a military-exempt service position, the call must have been persistent as it necessitated his obtaining a medical certificate in order to leave the company. But duty to his family was also strong so he enroled, at his parents' insistence, in Toronto Normal School, a step that would give him a teaching certificate and a career to come home to.

Lionel Hastings

He graduated from Normal School in 1942 and immediately enlisted in the RCAF. He joined streams of young men mustering at No. 1 Manning Depot and was sent to guard duty at Fingal, Ontario. At No. 1 ITS Toronto, Lionel Hastings had the honour of receiving a gold identification bracelet for highest academic standing, Course 64, in December 1942.

Then it was off to No. 1 Bombing and Gunnery School at Jarvis for observer training. Here Hastings trained on Fairey Battles, which he notes "cut down the bush like nothing else," after which he trained on Bolingbrokes and Ansons. In these planes the practice included low (1500 ft.) and medium (6000 ft.) level bombing.

He next attended No. 10 Air Observer School at Chatham, New Brunswick, for navigation training from which he graduated in August 1943. From there training continued at No. 34 OTU at Pennfield Ridge, New Brunswick. There he experienced the Lochheed Ventura medium bomber which he found accident-prone and which had "the glide angle of a brick." This was something that stayed in the young airman's mind, as the navigator's plotting table sat directly above the main fuel tanks.

It was at Pennfield Ridge that Hastings crewed up with pilot Joe Knowlton and gunners Perry Purvis and "Killer" Curtiss. Three of the four (Curtiss would become ill prior to overseas duties) would spend the following year together.

November 1943 saw Hastings and crew sail over to Liverpool on the *S.S. Mauretania*. It was the normal routine to work at No. 6 (Observer) OTU at Staverton, then on to No. 13 OTU at Bicester to do intensive radar training on "GEE." [GEE was one of the earlier radar systems employed by the RCAF]. By mid-April 1944 he was at Finnmere for conversion to B-25 Mitchell bombers. Here he once again teamed up with Knowlton and Purvis. Needing a gunner to replace Curtiss they found "Eppy" Eppstadt, a fellow Canadian. By May 1944 they were members of 98 Squadron RAF stationed at Dunsfold, Surrey.

Squadron 98, along with two other Mitchell squadrons—180 and 320 (Netherlands)—formed 139 Wing of the Second Allied Tactical Air Force. Aside from 320 Squadron the wing was primarily Canadian, commanded by Group Captain C.R. Dunlap and operating from a Canadian airfield.

The Mitchell II was equipped to carry up to a 6,000 lb. bombload. In fact, it was a superior plane, both offensively and defensively, to either the Ventura or the Blenheim.

Lionel Hastings settled into his position of observer. This involved navigating with the aid of the GEE radar set and with intelligence reports from the French underground. Because his duties also involved that of bomb-aimer, he also made use of the Mk. XIV gyro-bombsight for daylight bombing and GEE-H for blind bombing from height. The Mitchell observer also operated the nose gun and was co-pilot of the bomber.

Hastings and crew began their sorties on May 11, 1944. Their ops involved daylight precision bombing, "circus" operations (flown as decoys to draw Luftwaffe fighters away from the main targets of a raid), "NOBALL" ops (on hidden V-1 launch sites), and "NIGHTLIGHT" operations that began on July 18, 1944.

NIGHTLIGHTS involved dropping flares for Mosquito intruders or target indicators for Mitchell bombers. Both day and night ops were dangerous. Daylight ops in close-pattern bombing meant tight formation-flying, which carried its own risks. Night flying often meant going out on one's own, which was dangerous for all of the usual reasons plus the fact that a twin-engined Mitchell bomber looked a lot like a German Dornier 17 in the black night sky.

On July 11, 1944, Hastings led his first formation. It was his twenty-sixth op, a raid on Verneuil. He went on to lead many other, larger, formations. The crew also took up newsreel coverage men and radio broadcasters. (Corporal Don Fairbairn of the RCAF's public relations unit went on an op and eventually the folks back home got to hear the en route report).

Lionel Hastings and crew would fly fifty missions between May 11 and August 13, a tribute to their considerable skill as well as their good fortune. Hastings could feel proud of the fact that no crew member had died on any mission he had led.

Following this tour of duty, the crew disbanded. Hastings was told he would be off ops for six months. Following a short posting at a non-operational unit in Norfolk, Hastings went to 2 Group Support Unit at Evere, near Brussels. This move split up Hastings and Knowlton, who had been Hastings' pilot the entire previous year.

At 2 GSU the duties included flying military personnel in and out of the field, carrying supplies and performing other communication duties. And it was back to flying Ansons to ferry "Tommies" to and from the battlefield.

It was on such a trip on October 15, 1944, that Lionel Hastings became a "mashed" variety of Guinea Pig. After having picked up their passengers, the pilot noticed a 'rev' drop on one of the engines. Although they landed and checked out the problem, it was determined that they could continue the flight. Soon afterward the engine shut down. They were only ten to fifteen minutes outside of Brussels. The pilot lowered the landing gear. As if on cue, the other engine failed. They were going down without power. The pilot was attempting to glide into Courtrai airfield when the Anson encountered some telephone wires, sending the plane into a bomb crater on the edge of the airstrip.

The passengers were fine. As soon as the second engine had failed, Hastings, the navigator, had left his seat to secure the men into crash position between the wing spars. He was just getting back into the cockpit when the Anson hit the wires. Hastings had not had time to strap himself in. He went face-first into the controls and the windscreen:

> Sometime later I woke up in a field hospital in Ghent. I remember seeing the white ceiling and thinking I was in heaven. As one of my friends told me later that is probably as close to heaven as I will ever get.

Lionel Hastings was the only person seriously injured in the crash. He was moved to various hospitals and then to East Grinstead. Ross Tilley had his work cut out for him. Hastings' medical photographs revealed a young man with thirty-two facial fractures, three spinal fractures, and arm and leg fractures. There would be months in body casts, but the key work would be on his face:

> ...in addition to other injuries I was in the process of having the upper part of my face pulled out into its proper place by the traction attached to my upper jaw at one end and to weights at the other end of the bed.

Here was the innovation typical of the Queen Victoria Hospital. Here, also, was Hastings' faith in Dr. Tilley:

> By the time you were ready for dismissal from his hospital you had gained a new sense of confidence in yourself and in your ability to cope with the world and the future. He had made you realize that it was great to be alive and you were indeed one of the most fortunate people in the world to have that privilege.

Hastings would return to flying duty in Canada at Mount Hope, a temporary position while he waited for a Far East posting. But the war ended in August, and Hastings returned to life as a civilian. He had thought about medical school, but inspired by his time at East Grinstead, he decided to specialize in dentistry and went on to have an exemplary career in the field. Dr. Lionel Hastings, D.D.S., F.P.F.A., F.A.D.I., had a practice in Thunder Bay and later in Regina. He has been an invited Clinical Instructor to the People's Republic of China.

He and his wife Mary have been very active in the Guinea Pig Club, Hastings twice serving as Chief Guinea Pig of the Canadian Wing, as well as Honourary Secretary. Dr. and Mrs.

Hastings have three children, and continue their tradition of volunteering for religious and service organizations such as the Anglican Church, Boy Scouts of Canada, the Kiwanis Club, and the Schizophrenia Society of Saskatchewan, which they helped to found. Dr. Hastings is a true leader of the Canadian Wing of the Guinea Pig Club, continuing to put out the Canadian newsletter, and keeping track of the membership.

Paul John Weber

Paul Weber was born in New Hamburg, Ontario, and studied engineering at the University of Toronto before joining up. He graduated as a P/O navigator on September 3, 1943, and was posted to Bomber Command.

During the latter part of the war (1944–45) it was often the practice to take an extra navigator on a mission. This would allow one to operate the H_2S radar while enabling the other to accurately plot the course to and from that target. Weber was the extra navigator in a Lancaster that had just completed a mission. On the return trip, with bombs well away and his work complete, Weber lay down at the back of the aircraft and fell asleep.

They had reached England when the pilot began to experience trouble with the aircraft. There was no choice but to make a forced landing. The Lancaster crashed and burst into flames. In the mad scramble to exit the plane, the crew either forgot about or simply could not reach the extra navigator.

Paul Weber awoke in an inferno. There was no way out except through a wall of flame. There was nothing to be done except pull on the burning door with both hands.

The result was dire. Hands badly burned, Weber emerged, his face—particularly from the eyebrows up—horribly fried. His right side took the brunt, as well, with burns to his right arm and upper right thigh. Something had happened to his right baby finger; it was twisted, distorted, and fused on backward.

Weber was to spend two years in hospital. While at East Grinstead he would receive the famous Tilley treatment. Guinea Pig Norman McHolm remembers Tilley foisting tickets to a show upon a reluctant Weber:

Here are two tickets, one for the train to London and one for a show.... You have an hour and a half to catch the train.

By the time he returned home, F/O Paul Weber was ready to take on the world. As his son Paul Jr., notes:

> He somehow came through all that with such a desire to win.

And win he did. After the war he married Connie and they had six children. Weber worked in the sales office of Bright's Wines and was also a real estate appraiser. In 1961 he bought a summer cottage on Sparrow Lake near Orillia. While on the long drives up to the cottage, Weber lamented the lack of roadside restaurants on the route. So in 1963 he purchased land, and on July 11, 1963, he opened *Weber's* hamburger restaurant. He believed in hiring local kids and paying them a fair wage. As a result, he had a loyal staff who worked to make the place succeed. But it didn't happen overnight. Indeed, the restaurant really only took hold in the 1970s. But Weber kept it open until it became a full-time, going concern.

There are now three *Weber's* restaurants, run by the Weber family. Paul Weber, who died in 1993, is remembered as a kind, humble man who always did the best for his family and his staff. In creating an enterprise that now employs some 140 people, he gave back to a community he had settled in and come to love.

Although physically scarred for life, Paul Weber was a man whose desire to live and to succeed made him an exemplary member of the Guinea Pig Club—he was the first Honourary Treasurer of the Canadian Wing in 1948. Weber had praise for all of the "kids" he knew as Guinea Pigs:

> The Guinea Pig meetings—it's always a joy to see the quality of the kids there. They're very substantial and they came out of it very well.

Donald B. Freeborn

Donald Freeborn was born in Millbank, Ontario, and lived in various parts of the province in his youth. After completing his first year of medical school at the University of Western Ontario he answered the call, as so many of his friends had done, and enlisted in the RCAF in North Bay. He went through Manning Depot, guard duty, ITS and Elementary and graduated as a pilot at No. 8 Service School, Moncton. He also spent some time as a gunnery pilot at Mont Joli, Quebec.

Then it was over to England where Freeborn took courses flying the Airspeed Oxford, the Wellington and the Halifax. He was posted to 166 Squadron, 1 Group RAF at Kirmington Lincs, flying Lancasters. He flew ops with 166 Squadron but was then re-posted to a new Bomber Squadron at Scampton Lincs. This squadron was in fact the revival of a World War I fighter squadron (153 Squadron). Freeborn commenced operations with the new squadron in September 1944.

Donald Freeborn was soon to become a Guinea Pig. He recalls:

> On October 19, 1944, my crew and I (flying Lancaster "D" for Dog) and a number of others were detailed to bomb Stuttgart, an industrial and railway target. It was a clear night, ideal for enemy fighters and ground defences. We observed several night fighters, but we were not attacked; however, we noticed other bombers being engaged around us. According to my log book, approximately five minutes from the target we encountered heavy flak, and the aircraft was hit in the under mid-section. Flak tore through to strike me in the left thigh, and the blast almost blew me out of the seat.

Unbeknownst to Freeborn, his intercom cord had become detached and so he was temporarily unable to communicate with his crew. It was in this interim that he decided, being so close to target, that he would ignore his injury and press on the attack. He found and reattached the intercom plug in time to hear the bomb-aimer giving him instructions to the centre of the target. Freeborn heard the bomb-aimer ask for bomb doors open and he replied, fulfilling his duties:

> Bomb doors open, bombs gone. Bomb doors closed.

Freeborn reminds us that at this stage of the war there was also the camera run to be attended to:

> ...the pilot must keep the aircraft straight and level for the camera run, that much hated eternity that will tell you how your bombs fell.

That procedure done, Freeborn and crew left the illuminated target area and dove into the night sky:

> We are now in the favourite arena of the enemy night fighter. They don't attempt to follow us into the target area since they are not interested in getting hit by their own flak guns.

It was also time to take a look at his wound:

> [The wound] was bleeding profusely. I felt as though I was seated in a mud puddle. Since I was hit on the left side there was no way anyone could assist me in applying the shell dressing and tourniquet. My brief medical training did help me to carry this out.

Now there was the worry about the trip back. England was at least three hours away. The crew decided to set course for neutral Switzerland and were preparing to parachute out when Freeborn discovered his parachute in shreds. It had apparently taken the shrapnel first. Freeborn told the crew they could bail out over Switzerland but that he would be attempting to fly the plane back to base. The crew, to a man, decided to stay with Freeborn, with a typical air force response:

> If you're going to fly back for bacon and eggs we're sticking with you!

They arrived at the English coast and had made it to the nearest crash landing field (at Manston near Margate in Kent). By this time Freeborn was about to pass out. It was dark, and the runway lighting was minimal. Freeborn somehow managed to get the wheels down and land the kite before passing out. He awoke in the Manston Emergency Drome Hospital:

> I awakened with a terrible taste of ether permeating me, and I felt so nauseous that I went back to sleep. Awakening again, I felt for my leg and knew then I had lost it. Visions of sitting on a corner in Toronto with a white cup begging for a handout overcame me, and I lay there with my eyes shut in a deep depression. Opening them after quite some time, I noticed a white

object high in the air above my bed and wondered what it was. It suddenly struck me that it was my leg in a cast, with a pin through the ankle. I later learned that it was to immobilize my leg since the main tendon had been severed. Relieved, I was happy to doze off again. When I awakened, I knew I was alive and well when I spotted my crew standing beside my bed, smiling. It did go through my mind that such a motley crew couldn't be in heaven.

After six days Freeborn was taken on the bumpy ride to East Grinstead. Here he met members of the Guinea Pig Club, and his spirits rose:

I was placed, as all new patients are, in a private room for observation. Lying there, still feeling a little sorry for myself, I was visited by two amazing people, Bill Foxley and Les Wilkins. Their terribly burned faces and hands shocked me at first, then a quiet feeling of gratitude overcame me, and I thanked the Almighty that He had preserved me from such terrible wounds. These two young men, just boys really, had the most outstanding morale I have ever seen in my life and retained that spirit through their ordeals at East Grinstead.

Donald Freeborn received a dermatome graft and some stamp grafts. While he was in bed recuperating, he received an immediate DFC for his efforts in bombing the target and saving his crew. (It was the only immediate DFC awarded to anyone in 153 Squadron in either war).

Freeborn returned to active flying and four trips later had a chance to add a bar to that DFC. The crew was shot down and forced to bail out over Holland. As luck would have it, the insistent night fighter wasn't content with the bail out and was continuing the fight. Freeborn and his rear gunner, J.G. McNamara, were still in the plane. The gunner decided to go for the fighter. Freeborn complied and positioned him. The gunner got his fighter and a DFM, and the pilot got his bar. All of the crew were alive when they left the plane, but the navigator, Argo Brodie, perished when his chute failed to open.

Freeborn's post-war career included seventeen more years with the RCAF. Together with Louis A. Bolin, he opened the first

RCAF Jet Instrument School, at North Bay, flying T-33s and CF-100s. His last RCAF posting was to Ancienne Lorette, Quebec, flying the Velvet Glove, part of a top-secret air-to-air missile program. The missile was to be mounted on the doomed Avro Arrow.

Freeborn would move on to Canadair, in the test pilot section, flying the F-86, the Argus, the Yukon, the CL-44 D4 swing-tail freighter and other aircraft. Flying the CL-44, he also trained Icelandic crews on the North Atlantic. He flew the Tutor trainer on many initial flight tests, demonstrating it at the Paris Air Show and across Europe; he tested the Convair 580; and he spent many flight hours on the CF-104, a greater than Mach II aircraft. He was also assigned to the Canadair executive aircraft, flying VIPs around. All of this led to his induction into the Society of Experimental Test Pilots.

Freeborn continued flying in the United States and returned to Canada to retire, in 1990, to a home on Manitoulin Island which he had built in 1972 for that purpose. He and his late wife Mary Lu had two children. Freeborn now spends his time writing and volunteering with the handicapped and disabled.

One final note concerns the shredded parachute. It is an example of that curious good fortune that found and preserved Guinea Pigs. Shortly before he was wounded, Freeborn had been talking to an American fellow serving in the RCAF. The man had been on a bombing run and had had to bail out of a mid-air collision. It was the custom of some bomber pilots to wear their harness but not their chutes, which would be passed over to them when needed. This near fatal experience had convinced the American that the pilots should wear the fighter-pilot type of parachute, which was strapped to the pilot's rear. Donald Freeborn made sure he acquired this model of parachute; he took possession two days before he was hit. It was this chute that saved his leg and quite possibly his life.

E. M. Lacasse

E.M. "Bud" Lacasse was born in Brockville in 1920. He attended school and worked in town before joining the RCAF in September 1940. His first posting was to Trenton where he clerked in the control tower. This posting also gave Lacasse the opportunity to play hockey, goal-tending for the Trenton Flyers. He remustered to aircrew and was sent to ITS Belleville. From there he was sent to St. Eugene EFTS and afterward was posted to Uplands Ottawa

SFTS. Lacasse had the honour of receiving his wings from Prime Minister Mackenzie King on October 16, 1942, at Parliament Hill.

From there it was a trip to Halifax and then to New York City where he joined many others heading overseas on the *Queen Elizabeth*. They docked in Grennoch, Scotland, and made their way to Bournemouth. Lacasse flew Hurricanes and Typhoons at OTU. When he had completed OTU, Lacasse volunteered for the Burma-India Theater along with his friends. They were sent to Liverpool and three weeks later sailed for Bombay, an expedition that lasted thirty-one days.

Front row left (with cast): E.M. Lacasse

After arriving in India, Lacasse received further training and was posted to 30 Fighter Squadron RAF, where he flew ops strafing airfields and bombing bridges. He continued on these missions until December 16, 1944, when his luck turned against him.

At around 1400 Lacasse was taking off in his P-47 Thunderbolt. The airfield was in Burma, near the Indian border of Ramu. Lacasse's objective: bridge bombing. There were three planes taking off, but due to the primitive nature of the runway the proper markings were not indicated. The three planes got to forty feet when suddenly the plane to the right of Lacasse veered in front of Lacasse's kite and caught him in its slipstream.

Lacasse's fighter flipped over and dropped to the airfield. It turned end on end several times and exploded in flames. The Thunderbolt was wingless, tailless. The propellers and engine were gone. What remained was burning furiously. Yet in one of those ironies known only to airmen, somehow the two 500 lb. bombs had managed to stay with the craft. The crash truck, realizing the plane was loaded, turned away from the scene and tried to warn a team of fire-fighters. But undaunted, the brave British crew pressed on, put the fire out and located Lacasse, digging him out of his half-buried cockpit. Lacasse still speaks of these men with profound respect:

[A fire-fighter] visited me in the hospital later and told me he was just doing his job.... Lucky for me he had the guts to do it.

Lacasse was severely injured with a fractured skull, and first, second and third degree burns to his right leg and forehead. He would remain in Burma in British hospitals for the next five months, undergoing grafts, before being transferred to East Grinstead.

He credits the Queen Victoria Hospital for healing not only his body but his mind. Like many burned airmen, he had had great apprehension as to how he would look to the people back home. But that changed when he entered the Canadian Wing:

When I got to East Grinstead my first impression was shock. I had never seen people so horribly burned. I felt that all I had was a bad sunburn.

Bud Lacasse returned home in July 1945 and was discharged in November. His post-war careers included lab technician and customs inspector. Like most Guinea Pigs, Lacasse is a modest man who downplays his role in the service:

I was just there to do a job like everyone else and I did it.

Words that echo the fire-fighter who saved him from a flaming Thunderbolt. Words that reflect the quiet heroism of a man who "takes life as it comes."

John Campbell Smith

John "Jack" Smith was on his second tour of operations as Christmas 1944 approached. The young pilot was part of a Coastal Command submarine patrol unit in the Channel. They were flying Wellingtons. Their objective was to search out the new U-Boat (V.I.I.C.). One such boat had recently sunk a troop ship off Sherbrooke peninsula.

On Christmas night at 2300 the crew was ready for take-off. The search patrols could last up to 10 hours, not counting the delay that occurred due to hoar-frost on the wings.

The crew took off at 0105. They were no sooner up than the starboard engine failed and caught fire. They were going to have to crash land. The dual problem of not being high enough to bail out, and not being able to jettison their depth charges due to the proximity of a populated area, made it clear that they were going to have to go in with the plane.

The crash would have been survivable had it not been for the fire in the starboard engine which turned the plane into an inferno. Smith explains:

John Campbell Smith

> If the aircraft had not burst into flames all six would have survived the crash. As it was, three crew members were trapped inside and could not get out.

Smith is in possession of part of the crash report, which offers a glimpse of the confusion and shock that followed the crash:

> ...the aircraft lost height rapidly in a turn to starboard and struck the ground in a direction back towards the aerodrome, and caught fire. The pilot was trapped when he regained consciousness and had great difficulty in getting clear with his clothes on fire.

The report goes on to note the heroism Smith displayed, something the man himself does not tend to mention:

> [Smith] again became unconscious but afterwards made a gallant attempt to rescue three members of his crew who could not be located and climbed back into the cockpit but was knocked down and out of the aircraft by a flash of fire when he lost consciousness once again.

The three survivors were the tail gunner, who was unharmed, the wireless operator, who had facial burns, and Smith, who had burns to his face and body and severe burns to his hands, particularly his left hand.

He was taken to a county hospital and then moved on to a station hospital. The next move was to prove less fortunate. On

New Year's Eve, Smith was flown by air ambulance to a burns centre in St. Athans, Wales:

> My experience at St. Athans was horrific, to say the least.

In an article written by Smith's friend Andre Browne (an RAF type who was at St. Athans with Smith and who would end up at East Grinstead with him), Browne noted the bleak outlook they possessed at St. Athans. Both men had been told that little could be done for their hands. Smith heard these words:

> Well, lad, your flying days are over. We haven't got much to work with here, but we'll do the best we can.

His prognosis was as follows: amputation of fingers of left hand and possible amputation of right hand. Browne had been told more or less the same thing. But Smith had been talking to one of the nurses who happened to have trained at the Queen Victoria Hospital under Dr. McIndoe, and she suggested Smith get a second opinion.

It was a case of the patient taking responsibility for his treatment. Browne was impressed with the way Smith refused treatment at St. Athans and insisted on a transfer to the Canadian Wing at East Grinstead. Browne decided to go along for the ride.

It was a happy day for Jack Smith. After a day-long trip by ambulance, loaded with morphine, he waited to be examined by Dr. Tilley. It was 1800, and Tilley had just finished an operation. He was still in his mask and his blood-soaked uniform. Smith continues:

> I'll never forget that moment or the ensuing conversation, particularly when he pointed to a very badly infected donor area and said, "Well, we have some work to do and we'd better get at it."

Smith was prepped and in the operating room within the hour. His hands had begun to exhibit signs of gangrene, so Tilley opted to work on both hands at the same time. Smith woke up the next morning, and Dr. Tilley was standing there. He had operated on Smith for four hours the previous night. Smith remembers the exact conversation he had with Tilley:

"How are you?" he said. I blurted out, "Have I still got my hands?" His answer: "Of course you have. You'll have a damned good pair of hands." And my question, "Will I be able to fly again?" He answered, "Of course you will. It's up to you."

And Smith's friend, Andre Browne? It was also a great day for him, for a Browne sat there with his wing commander, who had transported Smith to East Grinstead personally, Dr. McIndoe happened by. The wing commander showed McIndoe his work on Browne's hands and offered his prognosis. He was not expecting the response he got. Archie, the Maestro, had a fit, calling the hapless wing commander everything under the sun and offering to have him disbarred if he ever touched a burned airman again. The Maestro saw to it that Browne was admitted to East Grinstead, a salvation that Browne credits Canadian Guinea Pig Jack Smith with bringing about.

Smith was repatriated to Canada in August 1945. He was discharged and taken on by Veterans' Affairs for further treatment at the Christie Street Hospital, Toronto, where he had two other major operations . He married his long-time sweetheart, Margaret, in December of 1948 and pursued university studies in mechanical engineering. There were further operations, a good marriage and three children, and a long career in engineering. There was the Guinea Pig Club. Smith would turn up at reunions and Ross Tilley would examine his hands, saying: "Not bad, not bad at all."

And did he ever fly again? Smith notes that his wife had never liked him flying, and he had respected this. Following her death in 1981, he was drawn to his old love. He started lessons toward his private pilot's licence, hoping to have it in hand for an upcoming Guinea Pig reunion. At dinner on one of the nights of the reunion, Smith found himself sitting with Ross Tilley and his wife Jean. Smith recalls:

> I showed off my temporary private pilot's licence, just like a child showing his father a good report card. He looked at it, looked at me and said, "I told you you'd be able to fly again!"

Smith says it all quite plainly:

> Dr. Tilley was my salvation. For me, quite simply, he gave me back my hands.

Smith has gone on to a successful second marriage to Barbara and is enjoying his retirement. He sees his time at East Grinstead as extremely valuable:

> It was one of the most important times in my entire life. I thought I was badly burned, and [was] feeling rather sorry for myself until I began to look around at so many others who were really badly burned. My facial and lower body burns were nothing compared to the extent of the burns of others. As a matter of fact, on a number of occasions I was referred to as the one "slightly singed around the edges."
>
> In this environment depression gave way to optimism. Most of us had been dealt a poor hand but there was a chance of beating the odds against us. We were all in the same boat, one way or another, officers and NCOs alike, and this in itself established a strong and lasting bond of friendship through adversity.

The backbone of the Guinea Pig Club was strong:

> The attitude of "if he can do it, so can I" prevailed. There was compassion, understanding and support along with ribald humour when it was needed. That was and still is the true meaning of being a Guinea Pig.... It is a unique club and I am very proud to be one of this illustrious organization.

But while Jack Smith was re-mustering as a Guinea Pig, the boys in the Canadian Wing were celebrating Christmas and the end of 1944.

Norm McHolm clearly remembers Christmas on the ward:

> We started to get ready for Christmas morning. "Blackie" [Edward Blacksell, the indispensable Welfare Officer of the Guinea Pig Club] assisted by two able-bodied helpers, rolled

a barrel of beer into the Canadian Wing and set it up at one end. Then the festivities began.

McHolm retains a copy of the "Menu for Christmas Dinner, The Queen Victoria Hospital, East Grinstead—Canadian Wing—1944." The menu reads:

> Grapefruit Cocktail Maraschino
> Hearts of Celery
> Assorted Olives
> Consommé Valencia
> Roast Irish Turkey with all kinds of Dressing, giblet
>   gravy and cranberry sauce
> Roast Potatoes
> Green Peas and Cauliflower Supreme
> Christmas Plum Pudding with Rum-Cognac Sauce
> Assorted Ice Creams or Butterscotch Sundae
> Nuts and Fruit

Christmas 1944

This feast was prepared despite wartime rationing. The amazed and appreciative men could only smile. News of the feast must also have brought a smile to relatives back home who realized the extent to which their loved ones were being cared for; the gesture spoke for itself.

There was a party hosted by the Canadian Wing at Canada House in the town, and the local children were invited. Existing photographs show faces that have seen too much privation in their young lives.

Norm McHolm had prophesied to his parents in that letter home. He looked around him and saw something good coming out of a terrible situation. And it was happening in the Canadian Wing. McHolm wrote:

> I'm sure this place will be remembered forever. It makes you proud to be a Canadian and to know that

Canadian money and Canadian surgeons have made these miracles possible. There are chaps getting new faces, new noses, eyelids, lips and new fingers and toes, all through the miracle of plastic surgery and the skill and dedication of a Toronto doctor, Wing Commander Ross Tilley.

The ever-modest Group Captain Tilley would probably have objected to the word "miracle", insisting that plastic surgery was just that—surgery. But on the faces of the laughing, boisterous men in the Canadian Wing in December 1944, there was, quite possibly, something of the miraculous.

Christmas 1944

Guinea Pigs (1945)

The prospect of entering another year of war was daunting. The allies had seen Germany rally in the Ardennes at the close of 1944, but most people were convinced the European war was near an end. Yet when? How many more lives would have to be sacrificed, on both sides, before the allied victory?

J. Stuart Duncan

John Stuart "Stu" Duncan was born in Vermilion, Alberta, the son of a First War army veteran. He grew up on a farm in the Thirties and in 1941, at the age of nineteen, he went to Calgary to take a course in mechanics. He soon enlisted in the RCAF. Like many a young hopeful, he marked "fighter pilot" as his highest priority. Since the first available course was with an RAF Group, Duncan went with them and stayed with the British from then on.

Duncan was posted overseas in December 1942 to places like Ansty, Ternhill and Chetwynd. In May 1944 he was part of the Desert Air Force 112 (Shark) Squadron, flying Hurricanes, Kittyhawks and later MkIII Mustangs. The fighter-pilot hopeful had become the fighter pilot. Duncan's duties during this period included sorties into Egypt, occupied nothern Italy, the Adriatic, and Yugoslavia. He would carry 500 lb. bombs and attack shipping depots, rail bridges, ammo dumps, and the like, in liaison with the 8th Army. He also served on escort and reconnaissance missions.

Stu Duncan

Duncan was successful on these sorties. But his luck changed on January 11, 1945. The operation: bombing a rail bridge in Italy. Duncan proceeded on course but close to the site he was hit by anti-aircraft fire. The kite was damaged. The intrepid pilot headed back toward Canadian lines, managing to make it home. But the plane was on fire, and much too low to allow him to parachute out. It went down, ablaze, in an apple orchard. A seventy-year-old Italian farmer saw the scene and risked his life rescuing Duncan from the blazing

Mustang. The pilot was in bad shape with third degree burns to his face, hands and legs. He was taken to a Canadian Army base hospital where his hands were placed in balloons to prevent further tissue destruction. On May 12, 1945, he was evacuated across Europe to Basingstoke and then to the Queen Victoria Hospital and the Canadian Wing.

At East Grinstead, Dr. Tilley set to work, fashioning new eyebrows, which he made from grafts of hair from behind Duncan's ears. In fact, he built new ears using sheep's cartilage. Tilley grew a pedicle from behind Duncan's shoulder from which he would construct a new nose.

While Duncan was at East Grinstead the members of his squadron gathered cigarettes and clothing to send to the Italian farmer who had saved him. Duncan, meanwhile, was getting to know the men in the Canadian Wing and formed firm friendships. As he once stated:

You don't have to explain anything to that group.

In late 1945 Duncan went back home to Canada. As with many Guinea Pigs whose surgeries were not complete, he was sent to the Christie Street Hospital in Toronto where Dr. Tilley, who had returned to Canada in the fall of 1945, continued working on his Guinea Pigs. Many of the nurses from East Grinstead were now serving at the hospital which allowed a number of Guinea Pigs the opportunity to attend the wedding of Nursing Sister Enid Faulkner, who married a DFC air force type becoming Enid (Faulkner) Matheson.

In all, Duncan would spend some two and a half years in various hospitals. After discharge he went to a veteran's school and made up three years of credit in one year in order to enroll in the agriculture faculty at the University of Alberta in September 1948. He received his B.Sc.Ag. in 1952 and accepted a job with the Department of Extension, Alberta Agriculture, in Red Deer. From there he moved to a thirteen-year position as District Agriculturist in Wainwright, Alberta, and following this he became, for fourteen years, the Regional Director of Extension for North East Alberta, in Vermilion, a position from which he supervised an area of eight million acres containing ten thousand farms. He retired in 1980.

Duncan's obviously successful career did not overshadow a successful marriage. In 1946 he met Flora at the home of mutual friends (nurses from the Christie Street Hospital). Stu and Flora dated while he was in Toronto and began a letter-writing courtship when Duncan moved west, culminating in an engagement in 1948 and marriage in 1949. The Duncans would have six children, five daughters and a son. They would also have grandchildren.

The Duncans retired to Lacombe, Alberta. They travelled internationally, attended all the Canadian Guinea Pig reunions but one from 1972–1992, and twice went over to East Grinstead for the reunions of the parent club. Duncan, who had always been active in sports, remained so, curling and golfing in his later years. Stuart Duncan died on October 22, 1992. His widow, Flora, remembers his courage as he faced the cameras in 1961 on the weekly Farm Show. Since a terrible encounter with a stranger on a streetcar in Toronto in 1945, when he was treated as a freak, Duncan faced life head on and succeeded. Duncan's sincerity and his modesty are both evident in words he used to describe his war service and that of his fellow Guinea Pigs:

> We did our bit, small as it may have been, and we're still here. All of us know quite a few who aren't here anymore.

Two Guinea Pigs (John Harding and William Anglin)

John Harding

John "Jack" Harding was a navigator attached to the RAF. By July 1944 he had already completed two tours of operations flying Lancasters over Germany. His first tour was at 103 Squadron (Elsham Wolds) and the second was at 550 Squadron (North Killingholme). The Windsor native had already been awarded the DFC in 1944 and was scheduled to go home, shortly to be joined by his Welsh wife, Olwen, and their baby daughter, when he was reassigned and posted to 168 Squadron based at Rockliffe Airport, Ottawa, effective the 4th of September 1944.

John Harding

Crews in 168 Squadron flew Canadian Troops' mail, and sometimes VIPs, across the Atlantic. They flew Liberators and Fortresses and would take the mail to Lyneham, England,

Guinea Pigs (1945)

where it would be trucked to Biggin Hill in Kent. There, another section of 168 Squadron flying Dakotas (DC-3s) would forward the mail to the front lines in Brussels, Antwerp and Eindhoven. It was the policy to rotate crews so that after four or five months of transatlantic flying they would take their turn on the Dakota run at Biggin Hill. October 1944, saw Harding, his skipper F/O Bill Anglin and the rest of the crew settle in at Biggin Hill for their continental stint. They served on this run and were due to return to transatlantic duties on January 26, 1945, but as fate would have it, they were asked to do a familiarization flight with a new crew on January 25, the day before departure.

On January 25th at 0850, Bill Anglin was standing between the two operating pilots. Harding was beside the navigator's table with F/L Forbes. They were carrying mail destined for Antwerp. Harding explains the layout of the aerodrome:

> Biggin's topography is such that the aerodrome sits on something shaped like an inverted dinner plate. Both ends of the main runway fall away slightly. The control tower stands at the high point...the centre.

The conditions that morning were less that optimal:

> Weather conditions were as they'd been for several days. The airport was covered by an icy ground fog to a depth of 200 to 300 feet. Forward visibility was limited. We had experienced the same conditions on other mornings. We knew that once aloft, we would break out in seconds to a perfectly sunny sky above. We were using the full runway. About half-way down on the take-off roll, [the pilot], restricted in his forward visibility, must have felt he was quickly running out of useable runway. He'd only used half. To everyone's surprise, with only ninety knots on the clock, he hauled back and we staggered off, our port wing trailing low, heading straight for the control tower. Narrowly averting the tower and our speed dropping, we fell, careening into a Spitfire parked near its protective blast wall. We then bounced up to about fifty feet and fell again, this time on a young woman's NAAFI wagon where she was serving refreshments to a group of ground crew.

Bill Anglin had sensed they were going in and pushed himself and Harding to the back of the plane. What happened next was quick and spectacular. Harding explains:

> We both fell headlong, past the main bulkhead, onto the stacked mail bags. All I can recall was that giant blow-torch effect as the port inner fuel tank burst inside the fuselage. I can remember trying to shield my face with my hands...I had on neither gloves nor helmet.

Harding did manage to salvage a bit of luck from this experience. The 'luck' came when the plane crashed. It broke in two just aft of the main-plane. Harding notes:

> Like peas from a pod we were nearly all shunted out, along with the hundreds of mail bags.

Harding, however, was face down in the burning mail. Both Harding and the radio operator took cover behind a dispersal wall. It was then that Harding saw the burnt face and hands of his fellow crew member, and wondered about himself:

> I didn't realize I'd been burned but imagined somehow that I'd been scraped by the rough, unfinished interior of the aircraft. Blood was coursing down my right cheek from a laceration near my ear. Violent body trembling began to set in as shock took hold of us. Arriving ambulance men wrapped us in blankets. Bewildered, we were laid on stretchers in the snow and sedated.

It was a terrible crash. The NAAFI woman died of her burns. A ground crew member, without the aid of protective gear, pulled the pilot from the burning wreckage and was decorated for bravery. The men from the two flight crews involved were taken to a civilian hospital in Orpington. Harding was operated on to close the gash in his face, and his hands were treated, unfortunately with the outmoded gentian violet treatment.

However, it was only days later that the young men received a visit from Dr. Tilley who immediately ordered all the men sent to the Canadian Wing of the Queen Victoria Hospital. There, they were treated for burns, some of the less severely injured being released within days.

It was not to be as simple or as quick for Jack Harding and Bill Anglin. Harding remembers it like this:

> With our heads heavily swathed in surgical dressings and bandages, leaving only two eyelets and a small hole to eat and drink through, we must have presented a strange sight. Our hands were heavily dressed and bandaged. We couldn't bear to have them below the heart line, as the pain was intense. So sitting or standing, our hands were always held high, at chest level.
>
> All the hair on my head had been completely burned away. I had no eyebrows or lashes. My ears were like two potato chips. I had no distinct lip line. Most of my burn areas were first and second degree, the most painful I later learned, but the most responsive to repair with adequate treatment. I must admit that the pain was such that during the earlier days in hospital my will to live was very low.

Hours were spent in the saline baths, with attendants sloughing off dead, scaling skin around the burns with tweezers.

While all this was going on, Mrs. Olwen Harding, newly arrived in Canada with her baby, had heard nothing. Three weeks after her husband's devastating injuries she received a terse telegram informing her that her husband had been critically injured in a crash. With no details, the young wife and mother cabled her sister who was living in Chichester, Sussex, not far from East Grinstead. A quick trip to East Grinstead allowed the family to see for itself that Harding was safe and on the mend.

Jack Harding was visited by Dr. McIndoe who informed him that he would have a Thiersch graft taken from this left thigh and applied in the form of stamp grafts to the third degree areas of his hands. The Thiersch technique of "planing" a strip of skin was a widely accepted method by then. Dr. Tilley performed the operation, with Dr. Norm Park as Sandman. Unfortunately, it was only a ten-percent "take." Ten days later Harding offered his right thigh and the operation was repeated, this time with a one-hundred-percent "take." The hands were healing! Now to get the thighs to do the same.

Harding was discharged from hospital in March 1945 and said goodbye to Bill Anglin, who would remain for more operations. After a month's leave in Canada with his relieved wife, he was back on active duty in May, with a new crew, flying transatlantic operations. He would also fly penicillin to Poland, a mission which began in October 1945.

March 3, 1946, was the last mail delivery courtesy of 168 Squadron. Harding would then go on to work for No. 7 Photo Wing doing topographical work for the government. There would also be a thirty-year career as navigator with Trans-Canada (later Air Canada) flying its North American and Caribbean routes. Upon his retirement, he and his wife Olwen would take part in an unusual calling—that of puppet masters for a troupe whose mandate it is to teach tolerance to young schoolchildren. The specially-designed puppets display the effects of disease and treatment. Limb loss, chemotherapy and such realities are not shied away from. This quest for tolerance even among the most junior members of society reflects Harding's time at East Grinstead. The lessons learned in the Guinea Pig Club live on.

John Harding, DFC, has also turned his hand to writing, penning *The Dancin' Navigator*, the story of his exploits in the service. As of this writing he is working on a book about his late wife, Olwen.

William G. Anglin

As has been said, F/L William "Bill" Anglin, the other badly burned young man in the crash, was standing between the operational pilot and co-pilot. He could see that a crash was imminent and had just enough time to call to Jack Harding before they went in, shouting: "Get back, we're going to crash!" They both fell to the rear onto the mailbags.

What Anglin remembered next was lying in a pool of flaming gasoline. He had the wherewithal to roll himself in some newly fallen snow nearby. Like Harding, he was picked up and sent by ambulance to Orpington hospital and from there to East Grinstead. For the first month he was totally blind. He, too, frequented the saline baths and spent his days of blackness being read to by people he assumed were staff members. He was later to discover the readers were his fellow patients.

The grafts began. There were many, as he had a large burn area. Dr. Tilley tried to keep the young man's spirits up, mounting ski photos near his bed because he knew Anglin was athletic. Before long, Anglin was getting around with the rest of the boys, enjoying a beer and a joke. He would be several more months at East Grinstead but would return to active flying a few months after his discharge. He would eventually go on to fly for Canadair after the war, flying DC-3s and the new North Stars. He would later work for his father's construction firm, eventually starting his own manufacturing company.

Yet Anglin always stayed close to flying. He and his wife Teddy attended some Guinea Pig reunions and maintained an active lifestyle. As of the 1980s he was still flying his own Cessna 180 amphibian, running a small flying business out of Vancouver that took hunting, fishing and sightseeing parties around British Columbia. Bill Anglin died in 1999.

Kenneth Davidson

Kenneth "Ken" Davidson joined the RCAF in 1942 and was trained as a flight engineer. After completing his course he was posted to England in December 1944. He was sent to a Halifax bomber squadron in Yorkshire (Eastmoor). It was at this base in early 1945 that he became a Guinea Pig.

That day the takeoff went all wrong, and Davidson's Halifax was sent crashing into an armoury building, killing several crew members. Davidson survived the crash and was sent to the Queen Victoria Hospital for repairs. He would have several operations there before returning to Toronto in July 1945 where he would spend the next two years in and out of the Christie Street Hospital for further surgeries.

Upon his discharge from the service, Davidson joined the Canadian Government Service and worked there until he retired for medical reasons in 1970.

Davidson and his wife Florence attended several Guinea Pig reunions over the years and enjoyed life despite his health problems. He wintered in Florida and kept up with the other members of the Club. Ken Davidson died in 1987.

Raymond Tarling

Raymond "Ray" Tarling trained at the Calgary Wireless School and the Lethbridge Gunnery School. The young wireless air gunner did a year's service instructing in London, Ontario, at No. 4 AOS before being posted overseas. He arrived in Scotland

and was sent to Nottinghamshire where he was again assigned to an instructor's position. Eager to see active service, he volunteered on a Wellington mission to drop leaflets over northern France.

It was an unlucky trip from the start. The Hurricane escort they were promised had been diverted up the coast to deal with an enemy raid. The crew was told to proceed and have the escort catch up to them.

Tarling recalls that the rear gunner's last words were, "Here comes our escort!" It was an enemy fighter. The gunner was shot dead, and the fighter proceeded to strafe the plane. Tarling felt a bullet enter his right leg, but he was quickly distracted by the fuel tanks which were hit. They now ignited, and the plane was on fire. The pilot tried to feather the starboard prop, and he turned the plane back to England. Desperate to find an open piece of countryside, the crew spotted a possible landing site. But about thirty feet up, the plane dropped like a stone. The cockpit broke off and went under the plane, killing the pilot and the front gunner.

Tarling had not been in crash position. His face hit the transmitter. His eyes hit the transmitter. He felt himself beginning to lose sight. He would later discover he had narrowly missed losing his shoulder as the detached propeller sliced open the side of the kite.

Tarling tried to get up but the bullet wound in his leg kept him low. He had to crawl down the middle of the red hot plane. Through dimming eyes he looked down and could see the veins and arteries in his hands—the skin was gone. He remembers thinking, "I can't jump off like this." So he positioned himself and jumped like a frog, landing squat and using his elbows. He crawled as far as he could on his elbows before admitting, "I've had it."

Ray Tarling was taken to East Grinstead for many repairs. It would be some time before he returned home to Canada, but when he did he married Elsie to whom he had been engaged prior to his service overseas. The Tarlings have enjoyed a long and successful marriage. Ray Tarling is a loyal member of the Guinea Pig Club.

Kenneth L. Porter

Kenneth "Ken" Porter joined up in June 1942 and was sent to Manning Pool in Toronto. He attended EFTS in Toronto and was then sent to Goderich, Ontario, for training. There his early dream of becoming a pilot met reality:

After ten hours in the air, they really didn't want me to continue, as I was always trying to land ten feet up in the air. When you plop down, it's kind of hard on the undercarriage of the little Tiger Moths.

So in April 1943 it was off to Navigation and Bombing at No. 6 Bombing and Gunnery School at Mountain View. This two-month course offered Porter a chance to make thirty-eight flights, to drill in bombing (120 bombs) and gunnery (3,500 rounds over Lake Ontario.) Then it was off to No.10 AOS, Chatham, New Brunswick.

This was, for the most part, a navigational school. There was much theory, followed by practical application, and, of course, bombing: low level, high level. There was also cross-country flying, and high and low level flying, all done in Ansons. There was formation flying, meteorology, compass reading, morse code, aircraft recognition, and photography.

Porter graduated as an observer (Nav. B.) on October 15, 1943. He was now Sergeant Porter and was off, in November 1943, to No. 34 OTU Pennfield Ridge, New Brunswick. By January 1944, his skills in Venturas and Hudsons and been refined. It was then that a crew was formed: pilot Jack Ewart, Wireless/Air Gunner Jim Barclay, Air Gunner Russ Legge and Observer/Navigator/Bomb-Aimer Ken Porter. They were posted overseas in mid-January.

In February 1944 they sailed overseas aboard the *Ile de France*. On board, Porter rediscovered an old school friend and together they withstood the stormy Atlantic's ninety-foot waves.

Porter was bound for Bournemouth, where he spent six weeks. In May 1944 his crew was posted to No. 13 OTU in Bichester, Oxford. At Bichester, the crew practised visual map reading and learned how to use GEE. Now flying Mitchell B25s, the crew did all types of flying, completing thirty flights. They were posted to 180 Squadron, Dunsfold, in July 1944.

Their operational tour began with a flight to Chartres. Eventually they would make their way up the Falaise Gap: Nijmegen, Arnham, Zwolle, Venlo. They would fly into Germany, to Cologne and to Düsseldorf. Their targets were bridges, fuel dumps, ammo dumps, railway junctions, Panzer tank concentrations, marshalling yards, communication centres and the like. It was during this period that the crew was moved from Dunsfold to Brussels. Also, during this time, Porter was made pilot officer.

On February 6, 1945, they were completing their fiftieth mission. They were on their way back to base after a raid on

Wegbeg, Germany. They should have landed in Brussels, but bad weather diverted them back to their old base at Dunsfold.

After landing, pilot Ewart thought he would pick up his motorcycle which he had left at Dunsfold when they moved. With Porter on the back of the motorcycle, Ewart decided to drive around the perimeter track of the field to talk to the navigator of a plane that had just come in from France as Ewart wished to inquire about weather conditions. They were proceeding to the plane when suddenly a twenty hundred weight truck pulled out and crossed their path. There was no time to divert—the motorcycle piled into the truck. Ewart was injured and sent on to Aldershot. Porter, however, was a new member of the Guinea Pig Club:

> My face was severely crushed in, and I had a very deep laceration on my right leg, severing the nerves.

He was sent to the Queen Victoria Hospital where he was seen by Dr. Tilley:

> ...[Tilley] sutured my leg, and proceeded to reconstruct my face. I was pretty much immobile for six weeks at QVH, having facial bandages as well as my leg bandaged.

Dr. Tilley literally had to push out Porter's nose, cheeks and upper jaw. Unfortunately, this situation did not allow him easy access to other Guinea Pigs, or to the pub. But he healed well at East Grinstead. By the time Ken Porter was sent back to Canada he held the rank of flying officer.

Porter went on to marry Madeline on June 1, 1946. They had two children and have five grandchildren. Porter admits not having attended early Guinea Pig reunions, but he has attended three of them in the past several years. There is something about the people, it seems:

> The Guinea Pig Club is a great organization. The spirit in it is unbelievable. To see some of these fellows, who were literally fried, is something you never forget; however, you soon don't even think about it. Most of them are real extroverts, and have the uncanny ability to put you at ease on first meeting.

Bernard Ridding

Bernard "Barney" Ridding, of Stroud, Ontario, joined up in June 1940 and did a stint with the Motor Transport Section before remustering to aircrew in 1942. A navigator's wing and advanced training in radar navigation took him to 406 Fighter Command Squadron, at Manston, Kent, where they were flying Mosquitos.

On February 18, 1945, returning from a sortie, the pilot made a forced belly landing. Ridding was climbing out of the plane when it exploded in flames, burning his face, scalp and hands.

But this was a lucky man. He was taken immediately to East Grinstead, which undoubtedly aided his recovery. Dr. Tilley worked on Ridding, using the advantage of early treatment to save Ridding from prolonged grafting. Within two years of his return home in May 1945 Ridding had recovered with little or no sign of disfigurement, and the work done on him was one of Dr. Tilley's proudest achievements.

Bernard Ridding, like many Guinea Pigs, went back to school. In 1951 he started his own electrical contracting firm which he ran successfully for thirty-seven years. He and his wife Emily had two sons. Bernard Ridding died in 1996.

Ronald Gordon Noon-Ward

Flying Officer Ronald Gordon Noon-Ward was with 199 Squadron in RAF 100 Group. The duty of this Squadron was to provide electronic jamming screens against German radar. Noon-Ward was a navigator and had already flown fourteen operations when he qualified for entry into the Guinea Pig Club.

It was March 5, 1945. Noon-Ward took off from RAF Station Northcreake in a Stirling EX-E, bound for Metz, France. They arrived on station and were radiating their jamming signals when they heard a loud noise. The aircraft also tilted violently to port. Something had happened to the starboard wing. Noon-Ward climbed up to his astrodome and from there could clearly see that there was a hole about six inches in diameter in the wing. Fire was shooting through it. The wing was aflame! The pilot ordered the crew to bail out.

Noon-Ward removed his helmet and oxygen mask and clipped his parachute to his harness. He climbed over the spar and made for the rear of the plane. Visibility was poor due to the smoke-engulfed fuselage and also due to the mid-upper gunner's parachute which had opened inside the plane. Noon-Ward was preparing to jump:

> ...when suddenly I feel a severe stinging sensation on my face and then a tremendous pain in the groin, as if someone very large and very strong had kneed me, and the third sensation is absolute silence. Then I realize that I am floating to earth.... The aircraft has exploded.
>
> I cannot believe my situation. It is a clear moon-lit night above, heavy cloud below, no aircraft and no other parachutes in sight. My main thought is, "My God, am I the only survivor? Nobody at home is going to believe this. I think my teddy bear suit [flying suit] is smoking."

Noon-Ward was now falling through cloud and could not determine how fast he was falling. He thought he was still several hundred feet in the air when suddenly he touched down. He headed toward a light in the distance, his vision hampered by a flap of skin from his forehead which had torn loose and was slipping over his eye. He was walking over a level field in the direction of the light. As he got nearer he shouted for help. When no one responded, Noon-Ward continued walking until he was facing a steep embankment. He could see men at the top. They had guns. It was at this point that the young navigator realized he was facing a group of Americans. He also discovered he was in a mine-field. They would be happy to help him once he got out of the mine field. Noon-Ward climbed the embankment.

He was taken to a hangar-like building but had to leave because the fire that was heating the building was making his burns unbearable. The medic arrived and cut away his flying suit and then gave him a shot of morphine. He was offered a cigarette, which he accepted, but the first time he took it out of his mouth part of his lips came with it. He was taken to an American base hospital where his hands were bandaged. His head was also bandaged with only slits for his eyes, nose and mouth. Four days later he was flown in an air evacuation Dakota to Menbury, England. From there he went to Basingstoke and finally to East Grinstead and the Canadian Wing. Dr. Tilley examined Noon-Ward and decided that he needed some "trimming up." While in the Canadian Wing he was visited by two officers from his Squadron. They informed him that he had been shot down by an American anti-aircraft battery.

Ronald Noon-Ward became a member of both the Guinea Pig Club and the Caterpillar Club. After his stay at East Grinstead he returned to his base, where he learned that three others from his crew had survived.

Douglas J. Hicks

Douglas J. "Doug" Hicks was born in Toronto in 1925. His father died when he was an infant, and his mother raised the family alone. Hicks attended public school and then vocational school, studying in the machine shop. At sixteen, Hicks rode his bicycle thirty miles out to Malton airport in Toronto and took a job as a cabin cleaner at Trans Canada Airlines. But the war was on, and at the age of seventeen, with his mother's written permission, he enlisted in the RCAF. Trained as an air gunner, Sergeant Hicks was posted overseas in the summer of 1944. He was sent to RAF 550 Squadron. By winter, he was flying ops.

He was on his seventh operation, a raid on Dessau, on March 7, 1945. Hicks describes that seventh mission:

> We are now airborne. Just after reaching an altitude of a few thousand feet, the precursor of what we are going to experience this night rears its ugly head. From my vantage point in the rear of the aircraft there is very little I do not see.

What he saw was a fireworks display of destruction. The remains of burning planes were spread out on the ground below, their fires bright red, green and yellow, indicating a Pathfinder crash and burning incendiaries. He saw several such sites and noted that:

> [It is] not a good omen to see before we have reached enemy territory.

They were in a planned diversion, supposedly heading to Berlin but detouring to Dessau, a small town where it was reported the Germans were assembling the latest jet technology. About one hundred miles away from target they were hit. Hicks suspected a night-fighter.

Sparks and smoke are now visible streaming past my tail-end position. I now see tracer bullets coming from below us and just far enough behind that they are ineffective. From the cockpit comes the command we always dread hearing: "JUMP! JUMP! JUMP!" In the end of the aircraft, I now see flames streaking past my turret and increasing in intensity. I realize that this is serious and the real thing.

Hicks responded on the intercom with a "hey, it's okay, not to worry." His calmness at this point would later amaze him. He tried to remove his intercom and oxygen connectors and found that not only could he not see them, but with his heavy flying gloves on his sense of touch was deadened. He took off the left-hand glove and tried to remove the connector. There was no time for this. The aircraft was flying erratically, and the turret was beginning to get very hot.

Hicks was grateful he had chosen the seat-style parachute which made his escape easier. He propped open the turret doors with his elbows, stuck his rear out the open doors and fell backward. As per standard procedure, he was in the slipstream. Unfortunately, he was not free of the turret, and he was being towed behind the aircraft. His left foot caught, he was being dragged through the skies by a burning plane. As he was deciding whether to pull the ripcord and risk breaking his leg, or worse, in the yank from the turret, or whether to hang on and almost certainly crash in flames, the sky lit up like day. He found out later it was the moment the aircraft exploded. Suddenly, his foot was free. Hicks kept a cool head. He waited, counting to ten, and pulled the rip cord. He was floating in the air, planning his landing. "Relax, pull up your feet, bend your knees." He hit the ground and rolled. "Welcome to Germany."

Four of the seven men survived the crash. Hicks was taken prisoner and sent to a POW camp. Within a mater of weeks the Americans arrived, and Hicks was flown back to England. The burns on his forehead, in particular, needed tending to, so on April 7, 1945, Hicks found himself on his way to East Grinstead. His description of this part of the trip deserves mention:

I ride the bus to the railway station at King's Cross. I must now work my way to the other side of London to catch the train to East Grinstead.... My manner of dress should arouse suspicion, not only from any MP but from any of the civilians that I might encounter.

It does not. My uniform now consists of a blue battle dress with my air gunner's wing and sergeant stripes. My shirt is khaki in colour, and is U.S. Army issue. My boots, also U.S. Army issue, are the brown boots worn by paratroopers. Let's not forget my head. Because of my burns, I am still wearing the white paper bandage applied by the German hospital staff. It is now looking very grubby. It was decided at the RAF station that it should stay in place until I am able to get further hospital attention at my destination. Finally, my hair. It desperately needs not only a good washing but a good combing.

Upon Hicks' arrival his first request was for a bath and hair wash. He soon got comfortable in the Canadian Wing and wrote letters home. He also wrote to Irvin Airchute, the makers of his parachute, who bestowed on Hicks the award of Caterpillar. Hicks had joined not only the Guinea Pug Club, but the Caterpillar Club as well.

But there was also the other sort of letter to write, the letter to the mother of the mid-upper gunner, who was one of the three who hadn't made it out of the crash alive. Hicks recalls:

I apologized for being a survivor, and although the letter was very short I did attempt to convey sympathies which would run with and play with my mind for a long time.

But Hicks was beginning to benefit from life in the Wing:

Life in this hospital was a joy. Most of the patients were mobile; an unwritten code was that we would do most of the small chores, take care of the occupants, and generally assist to the best of our capabilities. We would fetch bedpans, help with the feeding and do a number of chores that were easy to do and would free up the hospital staff.

As with many other Guinea Pigs, Hicks remembers the spirit of the townspeople as well:

The inhabitants of East Grinstead...were well aware of the appearances of hospital patients. Those with burns were not only ugly in their appearance, but many of their features were horribly disfigured or undergoing repairs. Pedicles of skin would be hanging loosely from various parts of the body. Noses and ears would have appendages growing, skin grafts and transplants were in full evidence. Not a pretty sight. Even so, the villagers accepted us all as family.

While at the hospital Hicks not only recovered from his burns but had his nose refashioned. He also had the opportunity to go twice to London. The first time was to acquire a new uniform:

When I received a new uniform it was obviously from a pool of used ones. It was evident where they came from. They were from other airmen whose fate was unknown. Ones who did not return from one of their trips. The uniforms were used but in good shape. The one I obtained had belonged to an RAAF officer who had the rank of flight lieutenant. He was, or had been, a bomb-aimer. When I returned to hospital I wore this uniform with the rank of an officer for a few days...if I thought I would impress some of the nursing sisters, I was not successful. The sewing needle came out in a few days and I returned to flight sergeant status.

Happily, Hicks' second trip to London would be for the interview that six months later would lead to his commission as an officer.

As his time at the hospital wore on, Hicks was given the opportunity to assist in solving a little mystery. A truckload of cans had arrived at the hospital. They were from a Canadian ship that had caught fire in an English port. The cargo holds had been flooded in the fire-fighting efforts, and, as Hicks remembers: "These cans had no labels." Hicks and some of his colleagues had their mission:

Our job was to determine the contents. We attempted to decipher the serial numbers on the cans or the codes used by the manufacturer. This was not very successful. The only way we could really be positive of the content was to open them. The easiest ones to identify were the sardine cans. This exercise gave us many moments of fun and helped while away the time.

One morning Hicks remembered being awakened by the thundering roar of hundreds of DC-3 aircraft towing Horsa gliders. The last assault was underway.

On VE Day anyone mobile made their way into town. They obtained kegs of beer, took them back to the ward and tied them to the portable bed tables. They added to this bounty the bottles of stout they had accumulated over time (they were regularly prescribed stout twice a week). With their beer wagon in tow they made the rounds to the beds of the immobile Guinea Pigs; VJ Day called for another celebration, this time in town.

Hicks returned to Canada a flying officer. He went back to Trans Canada Airlines (later Air Canada) and worked for the airline for forty-two years. Upon his retirement he was Air Canada's Airport Manager at La Guardia, in New York. The airline provided him with more than a career for it was there that he met his wife Madeleine, a stewardess. They had five children. Upon his retirement, Doug and Madeleine Hicks moved to Las Cruces, New Mexico.

J.A.H.B. Marceau

Flight Lieutenant Henri Bernard "Ben" Marceau was to have a dramatic entry into the Guinea Pig Club. The young Montrealer received his gunner's wing on May 25, 1942. Sergeant Marceau was married to Marguerite when he was sent overseas on what was to be his first tour of operations with 425 (Alouette) Squadron. He flew his first raid with them on January 1, 1943. The 425 was flying Wellingtons, and by the time he was nearing the end of his tour the squadron had a loss rate of less than 2 percent. As well, by this point there were three crews for each available aircraft.

Marceau completed his first tour of duty and was screened for the nine-month period crews were given between tours. He prepared for his second tour, and by January 1, 1945, he had completed heavy conversion onto Halifaxes. Sent to 434 Squadron, he would eventually be flying Lancasters. The desired plane was the "Canadian" Lanc (a Lancaster with the new radial engines). There were many of these new planes on the base, but there was also an older Lancaster with in-line engines. Marceau's skipper, F/L R.J. Fenn, had flown these engines before, and as this was the only Lanc that was usually idle, the crew volunteered to take it up.

It was March 11 and *mitrailleur* Marceau, Skipper Fenn, and the rest of the crew were to be part of a bold daylight raid on Essen. Less than two years earlier, Bomber Harris had engineered the first thousand-plane raid; now they had grown common. Six Group was providing two hundred of the bombers on March 11 in what would prove to be the last bomber raid on the nearly-destroyed city. It was also Marceau's forty-seventh mission.

They were over the bombing run. The city below, while ruined, still had more than a vestige of its phenomenal defensive capabilities. Marceau sat scanning the skies. The last words he heard were: "Bombs gone. Keep a straight course. I want to take a good picture." There was a burst of flak. Marceau remembers thinking: "Better get out of there." Then the plane exploded.

Henri "Ben" Marceau

Marceau, alone in the rear, had no way of knowing for sure if anyone else was alive in the fireball. Isolated in the back of the aircraft, he struggled into his parachute. To the bomber crew in the plane one thousand feet behind, and above, the stricken craft, whose perspex was shattered in the blast, there was no doubt. Those men were all dead. (Marceau confirmed this assumption when he met the pilot of the other plane a year later on St. Catherine's Street in Montreal. The man could not believe that Marceau was alive).

Marceau *was* alive but badly injured. He managed to extricate himself from the fiery wreckage, as it plunged, and get his chute open. As Marceau fell, he remembered the admonition that if evasion was impossible he was to try to surrender to someone in uniform as reaction among the civilians was unreliable.

Marceau could see a small plowed hill in a treed area. There was a footpath with a footbridge and a creek. Ahead of him he could make out a thatched house. He decided that when he landed he would try to stow his gear and make for the house. But his legs collapsed when he touched down. He fell on his back and released his chute. As he had kept his gloves on, his hands were undamaged. He brought one of them to the side of his head, then put his fingers to his lips. Blood. He also had flash burns, various lacerations and a cracked skull that he didn't know about yet. There was a definite leg wound, however. And his eye was not quite in its socket.

As Marceau crawled he saw two civilians approaching, also crawling. Marceau spoke to them in French and English and even a little German, but they could not understand him. He undid his Mae West, found the package of field bandages and dressings and tried to bandage his head. At this point the civilians helped him, whereupon he offered them the items in his escape kit.

Two men appeared in uniforms that Marceau could only assume represented some kind of "home guard." They proceeded to search him three times. After this, Marceau fell into unconsciousness for four days. He was removed from the first hospital he had been taken to and sent to a hospital in Krefeld. He was now a prisoner of war.

Marceau spent several weeks in this hospital, including Easter Sunday, when to his dismay he realized that the flowers he had pre-ordered for both his wife and his mother would be delivered, sent, as he says, "from a dead man." These few words remind us of the desperate purgatory that accompanied "Missing in Action" telegrams back home.

It was also at this hospital that Marceau received confirmation of his worst thoughts. It was during a visit by the German officer of the group that had shot his plane down. The officer said:

I'm sorry, but I'm the officer in charge of the guns that shot you down.

Undeterred, Marceau replied:

Well, I've been bombing you forty-seven times now.

The officer wanted the names of the crew. Marceau asked how many bodies were found. "Six," the officer said. This was Marceau's confirmation. He was the only survivor. Marceau provided the names of F/L Fenn and the rest of the crew. Then followed a curious exchange. The officer asked, "What about the rest of the crew?" Marceau looked at him. "Rest of the crew? They're bodies! You saw them!"

The officer pressed him, wanting to know the outcome of the other three crew members.

"What do you mean the three others?"

"But you are ten in a bomber."

Marceau understood. Americans. Fortresses. They were ten.

The quick-thinking gunner answered "You didn't find any bodies? Well, they ran away. They must be far by now."

Ben Marceau would be shuffled into air raid shelters; he would be locked in his hospital room, as war in the sector wound down. One day the entire hospital staff was discharged, and Marceau was trapped in his room. The Americans arrived, however, and Marceau found himself on his way to East Grinstead. He had heard rumours of this special place where those who had been badly burned could go. He arrived in the Canadian Wing two or three days before the end of the European war. He would celebrate VE Day in a hospital bed. He would lose the eye. After repairs that included a pedicle graft, Marceau returned to Montreal. He admits that it was difficult to settle back into civilian pay, particularly as he soon had a family to support. But again he managed, and eventually he worked for the Department of Immigration. The Marceaus, who still live in Montreal, are now retired. Henri "Ben" Marceau maintains a sense of humour and a generally positive attitude that belies the hardship he has seen. Asked by a francophone interviewer once whether he was at all despairing over how things would turn out for him, particularly while at East Grinstead, Marceau replied, *"Jamais aucun doute."* (never any doubt). He is a man for whom the word "individual" seems particularly suited.

John Southwell

John Southwell was a wireless air gunner who trained at Mossbank, Saskatchewan and then did radio training in Winnipeg. He was sent overseas to No. 8 OAFU. He did his OTU at Stratford-on-Avon and his heavy conversion at No. 1664 Heavy Conversion Unit in Yorkshire. He was then posted to 426 Thunderbird Squadron, Linton on Ouse.

Although he was in action toward the end of the European war, the missions were as hazardous as ever. He and his crew had just been on a night raid over "Happy Valley" (the *Rührgebeit*) when they were caught over the Zuider Zee. Corkscrewing madly, they were nonetheless hit seventeen or eighteen times. Amazingly, they were able to make an emergency landing unscathed.

But just as the missions could be hazardous, so too could be life on the ground. Having survived the dicey trip, Southwell and his crew completed their tour. It was March 13, 1945, and they were attending their screening party on 6 Group base. Southwell, his buddy Mel Burgess and two other members of the crew were in their car, a Hillman Minx. (Combined purchases of automobiles were not uncommon while stationed overseas).

Southwell, who had been in the back seat, decided for some reason to switch to the front passenger seat. This gave him a good view as they drove around the base. It also gave him the most severe injuries when the car hurtled off course and smashed into the wall of 6 Group Headquarters. Southwell went into the windshield. He sustained horrendous lacerations. So extreme were they that at the base hospital it was determined that he be sent to East Grinstead. John Southwell had become a mashed Guinea Pig.

At East Grinstead, Ross Tilley and Archie McIndoe saw to the young gunner. Southwell would spend the rest of the war in the Canadian Wing, returning home to Canada in October 1945.

Following the war, Southwell married Kay and worked as a radio operator for Air/ Sea Rescue. He rejoined the service in 1946 as ground crew. He would serve in Sidney and Vancouver, Clinton and Centralia, Ontario, and Whitehorse. He would also be stationed in Washington, D.C., until, in 1967, he resigned from the service and was released. He had spent twenty-four years and a day in the air force. By then he and Kay had six children, five boys and a girl. It was time to think about a new career.

John Southwell

With typical Guinea Pig spirit Southwell purchased, on spec while still in Washington, a fish & chips shop he remembered in Victoria, British Columbia. The Southwells went west to the 3-bedroom house that came with the shop. They built up the business. In 1971 Southwell started his own catering business, Goldsteam Catering. Eventually, five sons and a daughter-in-law would work for the thriving business, one of the largest in B.C.

The Southwells live a good life in Victoria. John and Kay Southwell spend three-and-a-half months every year in Mesa, Arizona, and work when and because they feel like it. Southwell is loyal to 426 Squadron, attending reunions. He began frequenting Guinea Pig reunions in the 1980s, is now a regular participant, and was a key organizer in the recent 1999 "Fifty-fifth Anniversary Reunion" of the Club, in Victoria. As Southwell says:

> Our comradeship has become so strong. It is a great affinity. And it is the only time we swap lies.

Arthur James Henderson

Arthur James "Jim" Henderson was stationed at Hallowford West, in Wales. On a particularly unlucky night, while waiting for take off, Henderson and crew saw another aircraft coming in for a landing on one engine. Before they could do anything, the plane smashed into Henderson's craft, taking the port wing and engulfing the aircraft in flames.

Henderson and two other crew members managed to escape. He would spend a year in hospital, first at St. Athan's in Wales for three months and then on to East Grinstead. After many grafts to his hands and face, Henderson was invalided home to Canada for more grafts and tendon transplants. Jim Henderson married Frances and they have four children.

George Alistair Noble

Among the last entrants to the Guinea Pig Club was George Noble. Noble was born September 1, 1917. He joined the RCAF in 1942 and became a navigator. By 1943 he was married to Frieda. They would eventually have a daughter and a son.

Noble suffered burns to his hands and face on active duty, but he only arrived at East Grinstead in 1946. Following plastic surgery, he returned home to Winnipeg where he underwent further surgeries at Our Lady Hospital. Then it was on to law school where, in 1950, Noble graduated. He was in private practice from 1950–1957 after which he went to work for the Veterans' Affairs Department of the federal government, in Vancouver. He later transferred to the Department of Justice. He was also at one time the Chairman of the RCAF Benevolent Fund.

George Noble kept fit gardening, golfing and curling. He died on July 30, 1976. His widow recalled a trip they made back to England in 1974. Noble had enjoyed London and the sights but was most moved by his trip to East Grinstead, where he was welcomed and made comfortable by the medical staff. As she summarized:

I think that must have been the highlight of the trip.

John A. Pelly

Perhaps it is fitting that the final entry is from a British, now Canadian, member of the Club. John Pelly had been with the

Royal Navy College, Dartmouth, England, from the time he was thirteen-and-a-half years old. He went to sea and served in the Far East, the Mediterranean, and the Arctic and Atlantic Oceans as well as the English Channel. In August 1944, he was offered the opportunity to specialize in flying. Accordingly, he took EFTS at St. Eugene, Ontario and SFTS in Kingston, Ontario. While in Canada, he met and became engaged to Joan, herself in the service.

It was by now May 1945. Pelly continued training and March 30, 1946, he joined the Royal Navy 816 Squadron at Lee-on-Solent, flying Fireflies.

On April 25 he was attempting a deck landing aboard HMS *Theseus*. The landing was not successful, and he crashed into the sea. Pelly was picked up and taken to Gosport and then to an RN hospital, Hasler, for three months. In September 1946, he went back to Canada for a month to marry June, then it was on to East Grinstead for more operations. He was finally discharged in the fall of 1947. In 1948 he sailed to Canada where he and his wife lived first in Montreal before settling in Toronto to raise a family. He worked for the CCM company for seventeen years then opened and operated his own company, Great Circle Trading Co. Ltd., an importing enterprise, for twenty years. Pelly retired in 1988. He and his wife live in Ontario.

Pelly became a member of the Canadian Wing of the Guinea Pig Club, a membership he retains to this day. This story is a reminder of how the war moved people and altered destinies. Young men came to Canada to train. Some fell in love and settled here after the war. On the other hand, looking back to Gerry Dufort, our first Guinea Pig, sometimes a young man went overseas and stayed there, marrying and putting down roots.

The war came to a decisive end in August 1945 with the bombing of Hiroshima and Nagasaki. Years of fighting ceased, and the framework by which one had lived one's life altered once again.

The war had taken a generation of men and women and changed them fundamentally. Young kids and teenagers when they joined up, they returned home men and women, eager to take their place in society and get on with their lives.

At the Queen Victoria Hospital, preparations were being made for the turnover of the Canadian Wing. For it had been promised at the outset that the Wing would remain part of the hospital, a gift from Canada to the British people and a memorial to the patients who became Guinea Pigs during the war.

The Handing Over of the Canadian Wing

Canada's involvement at the Queen Victoria Hospital was nearing completion. The time had come to fulfil the promise and relinquish the Canadian Wing to the hospital and the people of East Grinstead.

The Handing Over Ceremony occurred on September 5, 1945. There was also a farewell party. The local newspaper, *The Courier,* reported it to have taken place the previous Saturday, but LAC William Rhode's ticket, which he kept as a souvenir, clearly states that the "Farewell Dance" was to be held at 8:00 p.m., Wednesday, September 5, 1945, in honour of the Canadians. At any rate, *The Courier* covered the event, describing how the Rainbow Ballroom, Whitehall, East Grinstead, was employed for the purpose, and that the guests included Mr. Blount, Chairman of the Board of Management of the Queen Victoria Hospital; Air Marshall G. O. Johnson, Air Officer Commanding in Chief, RCAF Overseas; and Deputy Air Commodore C. R. Godwin.

It was a formal occasion, yet in the course of the evening there was a glimpse of the spirit and the irreverence that highlighted both Ward III and the Canadian Wing.

The Siren

Ross Tilley, throughout his tenure at East Grinstead, had his quarters at Whitehall. Wherever he went, day or night, he potentially could hear the air raid siren that signalled the approach of enemy aircraft. This was especially true at his living quarters as the siren sat on the roof of the Whitehall, directly over his room. Tilley was known to say less than complimentary things about the siren and always swore that when the war was over he would "take the darn thing back to Canada."

As a gesture of affection for Tilley, official inquiries were made. Urban District Council applied to the Ministry of Home Security to grant the unusual request. They agreed. Ross Tilley would get his memento. The siren was taken from its prominent position, cleaned up, then carried that Saturday night to the Rainbow Ballroom. It was presented to a very pleased Dr. Tilley by Mr. A. J. Golding, Vice-Chairman of the Urban District Council.

Then there were toasts. Mr. Blount led a toast to the "Royal Canadian Unit of the Queen Victoria Hospital" that concluded with:

The Royal Canadian Air Force Unit established not only an atmosphere but also a tradition which it will be our effort to maintain. That building and unit will always stand as a monument to the young men of Canada. But it is, to my mind, more than that. It is a tribute to the magnificent effort made by Canada in the Forces.[9]

Ross Tilley responded, saying that they would miss East Grinstead and the hospital "more than he could say." Archibald McIndoe then stated that it was their sad duty to say farewell to "that wonderful branch and to all their good friends." McIndoe hearkened back to the early days and to his meeting with Tilley, to the link between the two men who had together lived out such a dream. Then he quoted from a plaque in the hall of the Canadian Wing:

Too low they build who build beneath the stars.

Canada, he felt, had reached the stars.

Wednesday, September 5, 1945

With *The Courier* immortalizing the event, the handing-over ceremony took place. RCAF men and women marched through the town of East Grinstead to St. Swithun's Church, site of many hospital events, including marriages, where F/L J. Stuart Duncan delivered the Canadian flag. They then proceeded to the hospital itself. The programme for the ceremony reads:

1. General Salute.
2. Inspection of RCAF Guard of Honour.
3. Address by Air Marshall G. O. Johnson, C.B., M.C., Air Officer Commanding in Chief, RCAF Overseas.
4. Handing-over by Frederic Hudd, Esq., Acting High Commissioner for Canada.
5. Acceptance by Edward Blount, Esq., OBE, Chairman, Board of Management, Queen Victoria Hospital.
6. Lowering of RCAF Ensign by Group Captain A. Ross Tilley, OBE, Officer Commanding the RCAF Wing.

7.   Raising of Union Jack and Canadian Ensign by A.H. McIndoe, Esq., CBE, FRSC.

8.   "God Save the King"

Photographs of the period show a disciplined RCAF Guard of Honour standing at attention, the cluster of dignitaries before the flagpole, and a line of doctors, nurses and patients around the perimeter of the field. What was passing through the minds of the patients, most of whom would be heading home, would be difficult to surmise. What was passing through the minds of the medical personnel was likely a mixture of elation, sadness, and pride. Many would be returning to Canada and some would continue to work for Dr. Tilley. Others would be posted elsewhere in Europe. One thing was clear—the group that had worked so well together, that had performed their special magic, was being disbanded.

Lowering the ensign

Did the Guinea Pigs wonder about their future? Archie McIndoe had always told them they would have to stick together. Would they be able to maintain their promise to one another? As the ceremony wound down, all must have been thinking of the gift itself, the Wing that had cost, ultimately, £60,000 and that had been a home to all of them, doctors, nurses and patients alike. Many of those present took pictures, and the photos have a sombre finality about them. But though they would be leaving, the Wing would bear a permanent dedication engraved on a plaque at the entrance. The plaque reads:

To the gallant young men of the Royal Canadian Air Force whose wounds have brought them here and to the Surgeons, Nurses and Staff who have cared for them, this building has been erected by the people of the Dominion of Canada.

The healing of the world is in its nameless saints.

"Comin' in on a Wing and a Prayer"

They were coming home. Guinea Pigs who had been repatriated earlier had already prevailed over their home-comings, the stares of strangers on streetcars and busses, the encounters with old buddies in the pool hall or the store. They had changed, these men. It might be argued that most veterans, particularly those who had seen overseas service, had changed. It was hard to go back home to the old ways, to the bedroom at the back of your parents' home and to rules and curfews. But the Guinea Pigs had changed outwardly as well; the war had altered their very features, tangible evidence of the changes within.

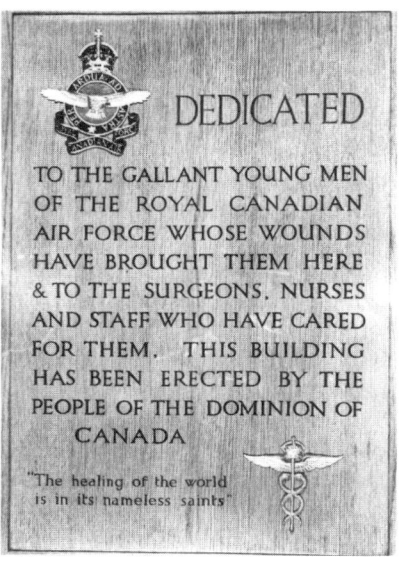

The massive homecoming in 1945 intensified a housing crisis as people came to the cities to look for work or go back to school, and others left jobs that the end of the war had made redundant. It was a large, fluid stream of people who would soon be taking over the helm of society. The Department of Veterans' Affairs would work on resettling, educating and housing the returning veterans, but it was to be a time of great change.

The Guinea Pigs were no different. Some went back to wives who had to re-learn the contours of their husbands' faces. Some went back to girlfriends who took one look at their altered men and married them. Some stayed in the air force and some went back to school, or looked for a job. And many went back to further operations.

The Christie Street Hospital

Although hospitals in other towns and cities would serve many of the returning veterans, the most famous of the early post-war Guinea Pig medical sites was the Christie Street Hospital in Toronto. Sunnybrook Hospital would not officially open for another three years, in 1948, so it was to the Christie Street Hospital that many Guinea Pigs would go for surgery.

Its official name was the Military Orthopaedic Hospital, but nobody called it that. In fact, several Guinea Pigs interviewed stated that they didn't know exactly where it had been located, only that it was on Christie Street. Its actual location was on the west side of Christie Street, north of the corner of Dupont and adjacent to the CPR rail line. It had begun its life as a National Cash Register factory. In 1918, following World War I, it was turned into the primary treatment centre for veterans of the Great War. The 400-bed facility continued its role as a convalescent military hospital during the Second World War, and it was to this place that Dr. Tilley would return to operate on his Guinea Pigs.

The Wingco Returns

It was a happy day for the Guinea Pigs when Dr. Tilley returned to Canada. Having accomplished so much at East Grinstead, he returned to Toronto with the images of the young men still with him. There would be no time for nostalgia, however, as there was work to be done. Tilley became a consultant at both the Wellesley Hospital and the Christie Street Hospital and found himself operating on some of his old friends from Ward III and the Canadian Wing. They had come home. What would happen to them now?

After the War

Dr. Tilley would watch first-hand as his Guinea Pigs made their way back into society, demonstrating Archie McIndoe's commitment that they be doctors to the men until those men had returned, successfully, to their roles as responsible members of society.

There was another admonition of Dr. McIndoe's that was undoubtedly on the minds of the Guinea Pigs and that was that they "stick together." McIndoe had told them that alone they would falter, together they would succeed. In 1944, he had written in an open letter in the Guinea Pig newsletter that he believed the club would "grow and flower with the passage of time."

But how to do this in Canada? Unlike England, Canada stretched far and wide. How to maintain contact with one another and also with East Grinstead and the British Guinea Pigs?

The Guinea Pig

Guinea Pig Magazine

One key element in the desire to keep people connected was the creation of *The Guinea Pig*. In 1947, editor Bernard Arch rolled the first issue of the magazine off the press. The impetus for the project had been the early Guinea Pig newsletters, but this thrice-yearly publication was formal and regular. Early editions of the magazine contain address lists, requests for information about certain Guinea Pigs, anecdotes, stories and humour. The magazine would have several editors over the years, all of them Guinea Pigs: Bernard Arch; Henry Standen, whose cartoon drawings regularly graced its pages and some of whose drawings are contained in this book, and Jack Toper. It was a niche publication, but to the Guinea Pigs it was cover-to-cover reading, a tangible attachment to the security and support that was the East Grinstead experience. The magazine is still being produced today, with Jack Toper at the helm, and it is still "cover-to-cover reading."

RCAF Toronto Station: The Reunion of 1948:

Armed with their copies of *The Guinea Pig*, the Canadian Pigs had an idea. Three years had passed since the war's end. It was 1948, and the Guinea Pigs figured—time for a party. A reunion of whomever they could muster, under the watchful eye of the Wingco, Ross Tilley. But such a venture would be incomplete without the Maestro, Archie McIndoe. The Maestro was contacted. He promised to attend.

A grainy newspaper photograph shows Dr. McIndoe seated at a piano. Beside him sits Dr. Tilley, the two of them as comfortable and seemingly inseparable as they had been at East Grinstead. And around them are standing a proud, smiling group of Guinea Pigs, about thirty-six in all, which was remarkable given that these were primarily the Pigs from the Toronto area, and nearly all who had been located had attended.

It was a joyous occasion and an emotional one. Yet, as always, it would serve another purpose, for it was to be the cornerstone of the eventual foundation of a Guinea Pig Club in Canada.

Dr. McIndoe reminded the Canadians that groups have a tendency to die out over time from lack of energy or lack of comradeship. McIndoe felt that merely getting together to hash out old stories would not hold the group together. He reminded the men that they had to move forward as a unit.

Ross Tilley agreed. A proto-club executive was formed with Ross Tilley as president, Paul Weber as treasurer, Donald Freeborn as secretary, and both Paul Branch and Larry Lymburner as organizing committee members.

Tilley sent a note to *The Guinea Pig* in which he asked to hear from all Canadian Guinea Pigs. (It was amazing how far and how fast some of them had flown). Everyone was aware of the difficulties that lay ahead. The wide-spread community of Canadian Pigs would make the possibility of meetings and reunions a real challenge. But impossible? Guinea Pig John Pelly wrote to the magazine citing a letter Dr. Tilley had written to him on the subject. Tilley answered Pelly's query by stating:

So far we have not been able to organize satisfactorily, but I hope to be able to rectify this in the near future. We will probably have to run on a regional basis, due to the distances involved. However, a full scale reunion ought to be possible in time.

There was the word: possible. And there was the phrase: possible in time. Prophetic it was, in that it would take some time, and that it would, indeed, be possible.

1952—All Things Are Possible

In 1952, while Guinea Pigs were pursuing careers and having children, Dr. Tilley himself took a bride, Jean Russell of Australia. Also in 1952, in an event of significance for Guinea Pigs, Frank Hubbard and George "Curly" Wilson headed across the pond for the September "Lost Weekend" reunion at East Grinstead—the British Pigs called their reunions "Lost Weekends." There they enjoyed once more the hospitality of the town. They spoke of their interest in getting a club going in Canada and came home more determined than ever. Guinea Pig President Tilley offered his heartiest encouragement, and Frank Hubbard was elected Secretary-Treasurer of the fledgling Wing. Henry Standen, editor of *The Guinea Pig*, wrote to Garnett "Tar" Moore and expressed his faith in Frank Hubbard:

> I must say that in Frank you have a first-rate fellow who, I am sure, will do everything possible to keep alive the spirit of the Guinea Pig Club as it was while you were over here with us in the hospital.

Hubbard had his work cut out for him. But armed with address lists and recent memories of East Grinstead, he wrote to the Canadians. The response was positive. Many Pigs seemed to like the idea of regrouping. Jim Hicks, however, summarized one of the problems inherent in getting together thus far:

> I guess I am like a lot of the other Canadian Guinea Pigs having become involved in the everyday business of chasing the dollar.

Yet even he was in favour of it, and the plan met with approval from a variety of Guinea Pigs including:

> •George Allen: "...was glad to hear you are organizing in Canada."

• John Pelly: "...if there is anything in the wind I hope to be there with bells on."

• Ken C. Smyth: "I hope it is a successful evening; enough to continue activities, or at least to encourage it."

• Jack Smyth: "...looking forward to a bang-up do."

• Bob Lloyd: "I earnestly hope that you will have a bang-up turnout so that the club will continue."

• Reg Harrison: "I am still interested in the Guinea Pig organization."

• Orvel Dove: "I am definitely interested in keeping the Guinea Pig organization alive in Canada."

• Howard Phillips: "I will always be a Guinea Pig and be interested in what other Pigs are doing."

• W.J. "Bill" Higgins: "I am more than interested in the Guinea Pig Club."

• Garnett "Tar" Moore: "It is good to see that somebody is at last assuming the initiative and 'sparking' the establishment of a Canadian Guinea Pig Club."

• Ivan St. John: "I'm glad someone finally took the initiative."

• Bill Tanner: "I hear that there might be some action taken to bring the Pigs back to life."

• Ken Davidson: "I am very much interested in the suggested reunion in Toronto."

• Bob Tait: "This idea of starting the Guinea Pig Club in Canada again meets with my approval 100%. I should like to hear more of the plans the club has in store for the future."

So, what better than a party? The "Roof Gardens" at Toronto's Royal York Hotel was booked for May 2, 1953. Letters continued to fly back and forth along with confirmations, ticket purchases, and questions. Ray Leupp, who would be travelling from Colombus, Ohio, wondered whether he would need a tux. Ken Smyth did as well. Karl O'Connor and his wife Frances wondered how to interpret "Dress Informal" in light of the times and the company. Clearly, excitement was mounting for this reunion.

Dr. Tilley sent around a circular on March 26, 1953, reminding Guinea Pigs of the upcoming date. And those who would not be able to attend seemed truly disappointed. The reasons included distance, work or family. Lionel Hastings and his wife Mary were expecting a child. Howard Phillips was farming in Texas. Art Doyle and his wife Helen had just had their first child, a son. Bob Tait would be attending but his wife would not "because of the youngsters."

One of the lovely unwritten stories here is that these Guinea Pigs were experiencing the typical joys and restrictions of young parenthood. It is not inappropriate to compare this fate to that of severely burned and damaged military personnel from the First War. The Guinea Pigs were married, were having families and starting businesses. These men were "in life."

So the stage was set for a bang-up do. And Hubbard and organizers did not disappoint. Dr. Tilley arrived with his wife, Jean, who was welcomed into the community. The Guinea Pigs wined and dined atop the Royal York Hotel, and the executive felt they were on their way to a bonafide club in Canada.

Death of Sir Archie

On April 11, 1960, tragedy struck Guinea Pigs worldwide. The beloved Maestro, the Boss, Archibald McIndoe, was dead. Born in 1900 he was sixty years old when he was suddenly taken, leaving his widow, Lady Connie McIndoe, to grieve his loss. She was not alone. The hospital was in mourning, and many Guinea Pigs were numb with shock. Archie, who had given them so much, had given them back their lives.... It was inconceivable that he would no longer be among them. The abject loss the Guinea Pigs experienced was evident in the next issue of *The Guinea Pig*. At the last moment the cover art was pulled, leaving a blank white space.

There were many moving tributes, for Archie had friends internationally. The Royal College of Surgeons of England wrote an In Memoriam in which McIndoe's skills as both a surgeon and a man were lauded. One of his best friends, Mr. Clifford Nauton Morgan, was moved to state:

> His personality was as scintillating as his surgery. He always had a friendly and understanding manner and instilled confidence and the certainty of success into those he met, and I feel sure, having met some of his ex-patients, that it was his personality more than anything else that made him adored by those salvaged airmen of the Guinea Pig Club.[10]

Mr. Rainsford Mowlem, FRSC, in a memorial statement, remembered Archibald McIndoe's first career choice, abdominal surgery, and praised his eventual rise in the new field of plastic surgery. He mentioned McIndoe's international accomplishments and his vice-presidency of the Royal College of Surgeons. It is a reminder of how energetic a man McIndoe was. For although he seemingly gave his all to his Guinea Pigs, the restless nature and strength of the man allowed him to continue in private practice, to travel, and to assume administrative responsibility. The Maestro was a man who would not be stopped by anything except death.

Perhaps the most poignant eulogy appeared in *The Guinea Pig*. It was called "Archie" and it was penned by "a Guinea Pig." This anonymity served to make it a universal account of the love the Guinea Pigs felt for this extraordinary man. It begins:

> It is not lacking in any respect when, in speaking with love and admiration of the best friend many of us ever had, we refer to him simply as Archie.

The anonymous Guinea Pig then went on to describe a rare occasion when Archie had spoken of the war years. The Guinea Pig was made to realize:

> ...what a terrible strain it had been for him during those hundreds, if not thousands, of sessions that he spent in the operating theatre fighting in his own way to provide us with a path back to sanity.

But McIndoe's boundless goodwill always kept him going, and his reward came from the Guinea Pigs themselves:

> ...nothing gave Archie greater pleasure than to hear of any success that one of his Guinea Pigs might have achieved. It was then that a heart-warming gleam would come into his eyes, and he would smile in that shrewd way of his, and he would nod with approval....

The Guinea Pigs would come to terms with Archie's loss, as they had with the loss of the two other members of the original Ward III operating team—anaesthetist John Hunter and operating theatre nurse Jill Mullins. With Archie's death all three were gone. It was the end of an era.

With McIndoe's death, the Presidency of the Club was open. It was filled when His Royal Highness Prince Philip agreed to serve as President of the Club, an honour he holds to this day.

The Sixties were going by. Like everyone else, the Guinea Pigs were dealing with huge social and cultural change, growing families, and career choices. The idea of forming an active club was still there, but where to find the time?

Some of the Canadians, including Bob Lloyd and Hank Ernst, travelled over to East Grinstead for the 1967 reunion. Dr. Tilley and his wife were to have attended as well, but due to a mixup of dates they arrived a week late. Still, there was a Canadian presence that kept the flame of a Canadian club alive. His Royal Highness Prince Philip, who had been notified of "The Lost Weekend," sent the following telegram:

Thank you for your message. I hope it is lost pleasantly.
—Philip.

1971—Thirtieth Birthday Celebration/Guinea Pig "Lost Weekend"

If ever there was an impetus to get the Club up and running, the events of 1971 provided it. The Guinea Pig Club was preparing to celebrate its thirtieth birthday. This was to be an especially big do, and so extra efforts were made to involve the overseas Guinea Pigs, particularly the Canadians, as Dr. Tilley had been chosen the Guest of Honour. Arrangements were made for an inexpensive flight over, and many Canadian Guinea Pigs attended who would not otherwise have done so [See Appendix A].

It was a wonderful reunion. Most of the Canadians arrived on September 23, excited and glad to be back. For many of the wives, it was their first opportunity to visit the place that had changed their husbands' lives. There was the "Eve-of-Dinner Dance" at the Ye Olde Felbridge Hotel. There was a tombola and a cabaret. The next day there was the annual dart match between the staff of The Guinea Pig, a local pub named after the Club, and the Pigs. True to form, the winners always alternated year to year, and this year it was the Pigs who won. The Annual General Meeting took place, and then it was off to the evening events—the "stag" dinner for the men, the women's dinner, followed by "Connie's After-the-Dinner-Party," Lady McIndoe's annual contribution to the festivities, which would include a giant cake with thirty candles.

Dr. Tilley presided as guest of honour over the men's dinner and was accompanied by another distinguished guest, Group Captain Douglas Bader. Chief Guinea Pig Tom Gleave made a speech stating:

> ...Tonight has a Canadian flavour and we are grateful to those who have leapt across the pond to be with us—not forgetting their ladies too—and to have our Ross Tilley and Jean with us makes our "Lost Weekend" complete.... The Club started as a means of getting together and supping ale...had it stayed that way it would have withered and died; but with Archie's dictum in our ears about sticking together we became a charity with a purpose, but even that would not have been enough, for without our 'Scientists' and 'Friends' we could not have survived....

Following several speeches Dr. Tilley stood to reply to the "Toast of the Guests." He was clearly moved by the reception the Canadians had received. He spoke of his time at East Grinstead:

> I can truthfully say that my time spent at the Queen Victoria Hospital during the war was the happiest of my life; although to use the word "happiest" in referring to the war years is perhaps not the right one, it comes nearest to what I felt....

This was a personal and solemn admission yet even here it came with the Guinea Pigs' penchant for lightness. For Ross Tilley also evoked his old nemesis, the siren at Whitehall:

> ...the chief problem was the air raid siren. It was only twenty-two feet from my pillow. I know, because I measured it.

In evoking the siren Tilley solved the mystery of what he had done with it when he took it back to Toronto:

> ...nowadays it is used as a fire alarm in the village of Rousseau, about 140 miles north of Toronto.

Tilley toasted his colleague Dr. Norman Park, who was in attendance, calling him "the best anaesthetist in Canada."

So the evening progressed. When Group Captain Douglas Bader, CBE, DSO, DFC, stood up to speak, he summarized the view of many when he said:

> It is people like the late Sir Archibald McIndoe and your Guest of Honour tonight, Dr. Ross Tilley, who have done more for other people than anyone else I know.... They have made the name of East Grinstead famous throughout the world.... May I tell you that to be here tonight as your guest is to be in the most gallant company I know....

It was a heady evening that reminded the Guinea Pigs who they were. The next morning, after a cocktail party and before departure, an informal meeting of the Canadians was held. There had to be a way to get the club to fly. Bob Lloyd was elected chairman of the Canadian Committee. He would be responsible for much that was to follow.

The Most Gallant Company

Bob Lloyd and his wife Dorothy worked hard to organize the 1972 reunion in Canada, knowing it would probably be *the* opportunity for the club. It was scheduled for June 9–10 at the Skyline Hotel in Toronto. On June 10, with Chairman Ken Allison and secretary Bob Lloyd at the helm, the meeting took place. According to two existing accounts of the meeting there were either thirty-two or forty-five Guinea Pigs present, as well as Drs. Tilley and Park. Also over from England were Chief Guinea Pig Tom Gleave, Henry Standen and other guests from the parent club.

This was it, the direct question: is it the wish of those present to form a Canadian Wing of the Guinea Pig Club?

All other questions flowed from this one. The answer was a resounding "Yea." Chief Guinea Pig Tom Gleave defined the aims of the parent Guinea Pig Club, which included concern for a member's general welfare, be it medical, financial or morale; reunions; and the continued creation of the magazine. He also outlined the job responsibilities of the various officers in the parent club.

Following this, Ross Tilley endorsed Tom Gleave's words on the aims and purposes, stressing the aims concerning morale assistance and rehabilitation. He also hoped that through time the Canadian Wing might have the financial resources to be able to assist any member in need. The slate of officers was proposed by Bob Fraser and seconded by Stu Duncan. The Chief Guinea Pig: Bob Lloyd. Treasurer: E. H. "Fergie" Ferguson. The Western Representative was Hank Ernst, while the Eastern Representative was Paul Branch. The Medical Liaison Officer was Norman Park. The membership voted that the next reunion would be in 1974 thus instituting the practice of a reunion every two years unlike the parent club which meets every year.

The reunion had been successful. They had been feted at the expense or contribution of Rothmans of Pall Mall, Canadian Breweries, and the Skyline Hotel. They would have the pleasure again in 1974.

The meeting adjourned, the reunion ended and Guinea Pigs headed home. But for Bob Lloyd and his wife Dorothy, the work had really just begun. There were many (forty-three or sixty-five) Guinea Pigs unaccounted for.

The 1974 Reunion

The 1974 reunion further established the Wing in Canada. Bob and Dorothy Lloyd had seen to most arrangements and visiting Guinea Pigs like Henry Standen (who would write up an entertaining "Diary" of the reunion for *The Guinea Pig*) were shown every courtesy, to the point of being met at the airport with a small (toy trumpet) fanfare and a six-by-six-inch red carpet. Group Captain Tom Gleave was met in a 1923 Pierce Arrow car complete with chauffeur.

The customary parties and dart matches ensued. But it was at the meeting itself that a significant moment took place. Toasts were drunk to absent friends, notably Archie McIndoe. Various people were called to the podium including Dr. Norm Park and Dr. Ross Tilley as the Wing's speaker. Following Dr. Tilley's moving speech, Guest Speaker Brigadier General W. F. M. Newson, a Guinea Pig, and a personal friend of Dr. and Mrs. Tilley, gave an amusing talk on plastic surgery.

Then it was time for the surprise. Bob Lloyd went to the microphone and announced the following:

The Canadian Wing of the hospital in East Grinstead has a memorial plaque, carrying the name and likeness of AVM Edwards of the Royal Canadian Air Force, to mark the opening of the wing in 1944.... We thought it would be a pleasant gesture to have placed opposite a similar plaque with the likeness of Dr. Ross Tilley, to mark our appreciation of his work—and that of his staff—carried out in the Wing. Suitable arrangements have been made, and this bronze replica will be fitted to the stone tablet installed in the Wing's entrance. The plaque reads:

Group Captain A. Ross Tilley OBE, MD
RCAF OC + C Chief Surgeon
Canadian Wing 1944–1945
A Truly Dedicated and Talented Surgeon and Humanitarian

This was totally unexpected by Tilley, and the man was disarmed:

I feel overcome...you do me a great honour and have made me very happy. I should like to make it clear to you: Archie and I always regarded the privilege as ours. It was not your privilege to be our patients; it was our privilege to be of service to the Guinea Pigs, and we always looked upon it as a great honour....

The soft-spoken Tilley had spoken his heart. His words echoed the very nature of the Club at its inception and the enduring power the man gently commanded.

The 1976 reunion of the Guinea Pig Club took place at the Commonwealth Aircrew Reunion in Winnipeg, in September 1976. It was the first reunion ever attended by some of the western Guinea Pigs.

The 1977 reunion took place on June 4 and 5 at the Skyline Hotel in Toronto. Little did anyone know that a scant two months later the Club would suffer a loss and go through more change.

Death of Dr. Norman Park

Dr. Tilley's enduring friendship with Norman Park was a joy to him. So it was with great sadness that the Club said goodbye to Dr. Park in August 1977. "The Sandman" had been unwell for some time and was nursed by his wife, Betty, until he succumbed to his illness on August 10.

Dr. Park had been able to attend the reunion in June, as Dr. Tilley noted in his farewell tribute:

> He died after several years of serious illness, but during this time he never lost his marvellous serenity and good nature.... To us he was always "Norm"— and he joined the Canadian Surgical Unit at East Grinstead in the fall of 1942 and was with it most of the time to the end of the war. He became a superb anaesthetist.....
>
> After the war, Norm joined the staff of the Sick Children's Hospital in Toronto and untold numbers of children benefited by his gentle, but firm administration. His colleagues frequently called on him for assistance, which was always freely given.

Art Doyle, who had been elected the new Chief Canadian Gunea Pig at the reunion, also paid tribute to Dr. Park:

> "Norm" was one of the "greats" who did much without any sort of showmanship, and in his own gently modest and unassuming way he left his own personal mark on many. It is unlikely that we will appoint a Medical Liaison Officer to succeed him.

Doyle's words were correct in that there was probably no stranger who could have moved into such a position. Dr. Park had been there with the men from their first arrival at the hospital, and since the end of the war he had consulted with them on their medical situations, offering them comfort and continuity. Who could walk in and fill those shoes?

Probably nobody, as Art Doyle implied. Yet there was one possibility.

Dr. Leith G. Douglas

Leith Douglas was a young plastic surgeon who had met Dr. Tilley early in his career. Tilley, who enjoyed a very happy marriage but was childless, took a liking to the young surgeon, while Douglas felt a kinship to Tilley. Dr. Douglas explains:

My father died when I was very young. I grew up without a father. Dr. Tilley was a father figure for me.

This particular connection reflects many of the Guinea Pigs' reactions to Dr. Tilley, when, as young men, they also looked to him for guidance and advice. As Dr. Douglas says:

Dr. Tilley was one of the first surgeons I knew. He taught me a great deal and was always there if I had a problem. I would always call on him and his vast experience. He was a very approachable person—a sympathetic, compassionate person—who treated his patients and his colleagues with respect and, again, with compassion.

Dr. Tilley told Leith Douglas all about the Guinea Pigs and their Club and even brought Douglas along to a few of the gatherings. Dr. Douglas enjoyed meeting the men and was sympathetic to them. So when Norm Park died, Dr. Tilley thought of Leith Douglas. Could he step in as the Medical Liaison Officer? Would he be accepted?

Dr. Douglas took on the role and was pleased at how well he was accepted by the men. He attributes his acceptance, at least in part, to the favour he was shown by Dr. Tilley, and his lasting attachment to the Club to the closeness he had shared with Dr. Tilley:

I like to follow in his footsteps and to do the things he did, to feel close to him in that way, and probably a little bit of that has rubbed off. People saw how fond he was of me, and I of him, and perhaps that's why I didn't have much difficulty moving into a position where they probably like me more than they would some guy who came in off the street. And I have great sympathy for people with these problems, working with them as I do. And I like service people.

Leith Douglas was the best possible choice to succeed Norm Park and has remained with the Club ever since.

As someone in Dr. Tilley's own field, Leith Douglas was in a unique position to truly understand the significance of what Tilley accomplished. In his article in *Reader's Digest*, Douglas outlined the accomplishments of Tilley's surgical team and the importance of what they had done. And in a personal interview he commented on the true importance of the work that was done at East Grinstead. Douglas saw the real innovation not so much in terms of the types of grafts done there, although that was highly advanced, but in the initial post-burn treatment that the patient received. Douglas outlined the earlier use of escharotics:

> If you had a deep burn...well, in those days they waited for the skin, which had burned right through, to die and come off. Then it would come off, and they'd put on a skin graft. People tried to find some way to protect that area from the big enemy, infection, and they devised things that were, frankly, terrible. They used to put gentian violet, tannic acid, tripple dye or silver nitrate on the burn. A thick eschar would form. It would kill tissue that would probably have been okay.

Thus Dr. Douglas pointed out an awful fact:

> If you heal it gently, it will heal up, but you put this stuff on you now convert what was going to be an okay burn into a full thickness burn.

The treatment, the standard treatment, had caused a worse burn to the patient. Dr. Douglas elaborated:

> Put this on somebody's face and the whole face is converted to leather. And all this stuff on it has to come off.

Aside from the negative aesthetic effect the treatment had, the other effect was lack of function. Mobility was limited. The patient was trapped.

Dr. Douglas noted, in particular, Dr. Tilley's comments regarding his work on the hands of patients. Douglas said, regarding the Queen Victoria Hospital practices of saline bath treatment and keeping the burn area moist:

> You were able to trim all of the dead tissue off and keep the hands moving. Dr. Tilley always used to say: if you don't lose it you don't have to get it back.

Dr. Douglas sees this as the revolutionary treatment at East Grinstead. It defied common methodology—it flew in the face of accepted methodology! Drs. Tilley and McIndoe had imposed a new method. It was next to heresy at the time.

How Tilley could have been this force for change was curious given his unpolitical, quiet nature. But Douglas echoed others when he spoke of Tilley's great authority. He was quiet but not withdrawn; he spoke softly but meant business. As Dr. Douglas noted, "I never heard him raise his voice in all the years I knew him."

In Dr. Leith Douglas, the Guinea Pigs had found another important ally, one whose link with Dr. Tilley would become increasingly valuable in the years to come.

Dr. Douglas, who currently practices at the Wellesley Unit of St. Michael's Hospital in Toronto, continues to be an advocate for the ageing Guinea Pig Club members, as well as performing his duties as the home-game medical doctor for the Toronto Maple Leafs.

By the end of 1977, Guinea Pig Art Doyle had another change to oversee. For the previous several years, then-Chief Canadian Guinea Pig Bob Lloyd, as an employee of Rothmans of Pall Mall, had managed to secure many donations (funds, sponsorship) for the Club. With his retirement in 1977, new sources of support eventually would have to be sought. His letter to Club members displays Guinea Pig optimism and humour along with a request for "your fullest participation in the present and future of your Club."

The Fourth Reunion, June 1979

The Fourth Reunion took place in June 1979. Chief Canadian Guinea Pig Art Doyle retired. Again, activities were held at the Skyline Hotel, with trips to the Carling O'Keefe Brewery for the customary darts match. At the general meeting, Dr. Tilley gave an account of his recent trip to the Far East. Lionel Hastings accepted the unanimous vote for the position of Chief Canadian Guinea Pig and asked that there be an Honourary Secretary to assist him. John Reynolds offered his services.

An important consideration under discussion was the upcoming Commonwealth Allied Aircrew Reunion which would be held in September in Winnipeg. Dr. Hastings noted that it might be possible to have a Guinea Pig Reunion there at the same time to which some of the Guinea Pigs from the United Kingdom could be invited. There was also the option of sending a large contingent of Guinea Pigs to East Grinstead in September 1981 for the Fortieth Anniversary of the parent club.

The Fifth Reunion/Fortieth Anniversary of the parent Guinea Pig Club

This reunion in England was attended by more Canadian Guinea Pigs than any other reunion in the history of the association. The Minister of National Defence, the Honourable Gilles Lamontagne, DFC, arranged for Guinea Pigs and their wives to be picked up by Service Air at Vancouver, Edmonton, Winnipeg and Trenton to be taken to the rendezvous in Ottawa where they were accomodated by local Guinea Pigs and friends for a "meet and greet."

The next day they boarded a Service Air jet with Dr. Tilley and his wife Jean and a total of sixty Guinea Pigs and wives on board. They landed in Gatwick for the largest Guinea Pig reunion ever held. The reunion was held at the Copthorne Hotel because of the recent burning of "Ye Olde Felbridge" Hotel in East Grinstead. In additon, Max Ward of Wardair provided special fares for other Guinea Pigs and friends who could not be accomodated by Service Air.

It was a spectacular occasion with live entertainment from London and many other features. It was at this reunion that most of Ian Ferguson's film *Dr. Tilley and His Guinea Pigs* was filmed.

Dr. Tilley was presented with a Waterford crystal whiskey decanter and goblets along with a card that said, simply: "Ross— With appreciation and affection from all UK Guinea Pigs."

Two other incidents of importance occurred in 1981.

Incorporation

In April 1981, Lionel Hastings received a letter from the Deputy Director of Saskatchewan Consumer and Corporate Affairs. It acknowledged Dr. Hastings' application for incorporation under the Non-Profit Corporations Act. Accordingly, The Guinea Pig Club Canadian Wing, Inc. was incorporated and registered as a charity on May 19, 1981. If there had ever been any doubt as to the official status of the club, it ended then.

Order of Canada

The other significant occurrence in 1981 was something that brought great joy to the Club. As early as 1973 Paul Branch had written to Bob Lloyd concerning the idea of nominating Dr. Tilley for the Order of Canada. Bob Lloyd nominated Tilley. Support for the nomination was submitted in letter form by Bob Lloyd, Paul Branch, Hank Ernst, George Wilson, Everett Ferguson, and Dr. Norm Park. The procedure was useful but not successful, and the Club was left wondering why someone like Dr. Tilley would not be deemed worthy of the award. The British had appointed Dr. Tilley to the Order of the British Empire back in 1944, yet although the Order of Canada had been in existence since 1967, the Canadians were still making up their minds about Tilley.

But Guinea Pigs are nothing if not tenacious. They resubmitted the application on January 9, 1981. Dr. Tilley was nominated by Dr. Leith Douglas. The Club, through Lionel Hastings, was contacted in March with a request for more information on Dr. Tilley's behalf. Yet in April they were notified that Dr. Tilley's file had been set aside again. Thus began a letter-writing campaign that ignited the fires the Guinea Pigs knew so well. Dr. Hastings was able to send along as supporting material:

- a letter of commendation by Dr. Leith Douglas
- a letter from Dr. W. K. Lindsay, Professor, Deparment of Surgery, University of Toronto
- a letter from Mr. J. W. Hamilton, QC, Chairman, Board of Directors, Wellesley Hospital, Toronto
- a letter from Dr. Neil A. Walters, Surgeon-in-Chief, Professor and Head of General Surgery, University of Toronto
- a letter from Frank E. Hanton, DFC, General Manager of Aviation, Government of Saskatchewan
- a letter from John A. Reynolds, Regina, Honourable Secretary of the Guinea Pig Club [Canada]
- a letter from Paul S. Warren, Ottawa, Eastern Representative, Guinea Pig Club [Canada]
- a letter from Robert Tait, Winnipeg, Western Representative, Guinea Pig Club [Canada]
- a copy of the tribute to Dr. Tilley in an issue of The Guinea Pig (New Year, 1981)

• a copy of the article that appeared in the September 1971 issue of *Reader's Digest*

More letters went back and forth between Rideau Hall and the Guinea Pigs, including letters from Guinea Pig George Wilson and Bruce "Dutchy" Miller, former orderly at Queen Victoria Hospital.

In November, Dr. Tilley received a confidential letter stating that he was recommended to be appointed a Member of the Order of Canada. The Guinea Pigs sent a Presentation Book to their Wingco which contained many heartfelt tributes.

Jean Tilley, Dr. Tilley's wife, wrote to Lionel Hastings thanking him and all the Guinea Pigs for their efforts on her husband's behalf. As for Ross Tilley, he was touched beyond belief by the efforts and the appointment itself, as the application had been made without his knowledge. As for their tributes:

The Presentation Book is to me the most heart warming creation that I have ever seen.

In a letter from the Director of the Chancellery of Canadian Orders and Decorations, Roger de C. Nantel, on December 4, 1981, Ross Tilley was officially appointed a Member of the Order of Canada. His appointment was publicized in the December 19 edition of the *Canadian Gazette*. It would be spring 1982 before the investiture took place at Rideau Hall under Governor General Ed Schreyer, but it had happened: Canada had recognized Dr. Tilley, surgeon, teacher, humanitarian, for his lifetime of service to his country and to his fellow man. He was the first Canadian plastic surgeon ever to receive the award. In a letter to Lionel Hastings in December 1981, Tilley commented:

The heights are now here—and I love it.

The 1980s were a time of retirement for many Guinea Pigs, a time to spend with their children and, perhaps, grandchildren or in some cases a time to start new careers. The Club had come a long way. It was an incorporated charity whose members were reaping the rewards of years of work. There was fun as well, like the 1982 reunion in Calgary that saw the Guinea Pigs, Canadian as well as British, enjoy the Calgary Stampede.

But the work was not over for the Club.

Ross Tilley Burn Centre

There would be further honours for Dr. Tilley. On Wednesday, April 18, 1984, a new burn centre opened at the Wellesley Hospital. Ross Tilley's name was chosen to grace it, and thus the *Ross Tilley Burn Centre* at the Wellesley Hospital came into existence. This was a wonderful, practical way to honour the man.

Nineteen eighty-four was also the fortieth anniversary of the opening of the Canadian Wing of the Queen Victoria Hospital. The contingent of Guinea Pigs from the United Kingdom was especially large at the Canadian Reunion that year, some forty guests arriving to take part in the weekend held on June 25–26 at the Inn on the Harbour Motel, Victoria. Guinea Pig Ray Leupp came up from the United States, and, of course, Canadian attendees were also present and accounted for in numbers. Dr. Lionel Hastings would be turning over the reins of the Club, after five years, to George "Curly" Wilson. John Southwell was the reunion chairman, a duty he would perform more than once in the years to come as the reunions tended to move progressively westward.

Among various presentations, Dr. Tilley was given an inscribed silver tankard. But the highlight of the reunion was the film *Dr. Tilley and His Guinea Pigs* by "Fergie" Ferguson's son, Ian Ferguson. Pigs present noted with delight that the film included an interview with HRH The Prince Philip, the Club's President, who was suitably clothed in his Guinea Pig tie.

The Guinea Pigs headed to Sandown Raceway for the trotting races. Guinea Pigs, en masse, were losing until the ninth race, when an unknown horse named "Come on Archie" appeared at the gate. This was too much to resist. With visions of the Maestro in their heads, they placed their bets. The horse, like the man, was a winner. The Raceway even honoured the Club by announcing one of the races as "The Flying Guinea Pigs Special."

There was much to be thankful for as the reunion wound down. Besides practical thanks to people like John and Kay Southwell, and to Maxwell Ward, of Wardair, who subsidized the Guinea Pigs' travel, there was undoubtedly silent thanks given for the longevity of their association, and for their personal stamina and strength. This strength and stamina would be called upon once again when needed.

1987 Threat to the Queen Victoria Hospital

In June 1987, there was a proposal by the South East Regional Health Authority to study the special units of the Queen Victoria Hospital. The Authority carried out an Optional Appraisal to debate the future of the burns, eye, dental and plastic surgery units, with the intention of possibly moving them to a more central location. Although the Regional Health Authority swore that the discussions marked only "the very early days" and incorporated many possibilities, and although a member of the appraisal team reassured the public that even if the special units departed there would still be a Queen Victoria Hospital to serve community hospital needs, most people saw it as an either/or situation: either it remained intact or, once decimated, it ceased to exist. Gone would be the McIndoe Burns Unit (so-named in 1964), gone the Maxillo-Facial/ Oral Surgery Unit, gone the Corneo-Plastic Unit and the Plastic Surgery Unit. The appraisal team noted that even if this came to pass, it would not take effect for another ten to fifteen years.

What was about to happen, essentially, was that the former cottage hospital, which had won an international reputation through the war years and since had become a world-class centre, would go back to being the little cottage hospital of yore.

Local spokespeople were quick to react. They noted that many small local and cottage hospitals had been shut down in recent years, and that one of the main reasons that Queen Victoria Hospital had been spared had been due to the existence of the special units. In particular, Mrs. Kitty Hutchison, a retired employee of the Queen Victoria Hospital who had worked under Dr. McIndoe and who had married British Guinea Pig Jackie Hutchison, sounded the alarm. She urged townspeople not to let their hospital go without a fight. It was time for the Guinea Pigs to give something back to the town that had done so much for them.

The Forty-Second Reunion of the parent club took place in East Grinstead, and Pigs prepared for a fight. They reminded themselves that the Blond-McIndoe Burns and Plastic Centre was built by private funding. They reminded themselves that the Canadian Wing was built and financed by Canadians, and the American Wing, which opened in 1946, was U.S. funded with monies Archie had raised on an American speaking tour. They reminded themselves that they were Guinea Pigs, men who volunteered with burn victims— children, Falklands War victims, and the like. They were bolstered by Lady Connie McIndoe, Archie's widow, who had remained close to the club since his death.

Ross Tilley got involved, along with the Canadian Pigs. The addition of Canadian support added international weight to the campaign. Dr. Tilley wrote a letter to East Grinstead M. P. Tim Renton, registering his "deep distress" at the prospect of the units being moved:

> The area which holds so many memories for me, and is a memorial to the bravery and dedication of the boys who defended our countries during World War II, is the wing where the badly burned airmen were housed. The Canadian Wing was built by the Royal Canadian Engineers and as a token of our thanks and friendship was presented to the British government after the war. It is an indication of the great esteem in which this hospital is held by all, whether patient, staff, or a surgeon like myself.[11]

Tilley continued to expound on the virtues of the hospital and the town:

> East Grinstead has always been a "Guinea Pig" town, and if the hospital goes, so does all the pride and memories, both painful and wonderful.

He concluded with an eloquent tribute to the hospital:

> The Queen Victoria is not "just" a hospital, it is a monument, a memorial, a dedication to many great and unique people—people who fought for you and me. To take away any part of the Queen Victoria Hospital would be to take away a national pride and a national shrine.

By 1990 the Queen Victoria Hospital would have a reprieve, although a new threat would surface in 1993. Again people would rise to defend it. To many people the Queen Victoria Hospital remains inviolable.

1987 Reunion

The 1987 reunion was held in Regina and was well attended despite the absence of the Wingco, who was suffering from ill health. Attendees included the Lieutenant Governor of Saskatchewan, His Honour F. W. Johnson, QC. A special salute was made to the "nurses, orderlies and other medical personnel."

Ross Tilley's ill health was not fleeting. He had been ailing for some time. The Canadian Wing was soon to suffer its most devastating loss.

Death of Dr. Tilley

Although Dr. Tilley had closed his offices in 1980, he had continued to be present for the next three years or so at the twice-weekly burn clinics held at the Wellesley Hospital. His career had been a busy one and had seen him move between the Wellesley and the Sunnybrook Hospital and, in his earlier years, to and from Kingston where he taught plastic surgery courses at Queen's University and performed surgery in town when needed. As well, he had kept up with the Guinea Pig Club, and the men. But Tilley had been waging a personal battle against cancer and other diseases, and on Thursday, April 19, 1988, he died.

This was a terrible blow to his devoted wife, Jean, to his many friends, and to the members of the Club. As with Archie McIndoe and the British Guinea Pigs, Ross Tilley had been larger-than-life in certain respects. Both doctors had wielded knives that had brought men back from the brink of death and despair. And if it is true that many people look upon their physicians as "healers" and as somehow possessing "special abilities," then in the case of the Guinea Pigs, Ross Tilley not only possessed the "doctor" mystique but had actually demonstrated these special abilities.

Mortality, from a man who had told them to live. It was a painful irony, and one that was hard to accept.

A memorial for Dr. Tilley was held on the evening of Monday, May 9, 1988. It was attended by friends, admirers, medical staff and members of the Club. Guinea Pig Paul Branch gave the address on behalf of the Pigs. In it he spoke warmly of "Ross," his powers as a surgeon, his humanitarian nature, his personal genius:

> Ross possessed not only remarkable surgical skills but
> also an uncanny ability to explain his approach to the

surgery to each patient, thereby minimizing the patient's fear and anxiety.

He ended on an eloquent note and spoke the thought of all Guinea Pigs:

> Guinea Pigs throughout the world agree that a great Canadian humanitarian and professional has departed our midst to a well deserved rest. Ross will be fondly remembered by all with whom he came into contact. Certainly among Canadian Guinea Pigs and Guinea Pigs throughout the world he will be remembered not only as a remarkable plastic surgeon but one whose dedication to the well-being of his fellow man knew no bounds.

Chief Guinea Pig Tom Gleave, in an address that appeared in *The Guinea Pig*, spoke of Tilley's compassion:

> Ross became the personal lifelong friend of every patient he treated. He was a gentle, compassionate being and his abiding commitment to his patients went far beyond surgery. He aimed at not only making them look normal again but...feel that way too. To them he will forever be their beloved "Wingco."

Gleave then mentioned the thirty-six year marriage Tilley had shared with his wife and offered her his condolences.

Perhaps the final word on Dr. Tilley should go to the man himself, who on a rare occasion spoke of his love for his field of medicine:

> I wanted to restore people to normal.[12]

At the same time he summarized a personal philosophy of medicine:

> I looked on them as friends, not as patients.

Forty-Fifth Anniversary of the Canadian Wing

The Guinea Pigs met again in 1989 for the Forty-Fifth Anniversary of the Canadian Wing. This reunion was held in Guelph, Ontario, at the John McCrae Legion Hall. Chief Canadian

Guinea Pig Jim Martin and others had organized the itinerary. Wardair was still subsidizing flights which allowed many UK Guinea Pigs to attend. The Pigs golfed, ate and drank, and, of course, competed in the darts tournament. The location of the reunion also allowed Guinea Pigs to attend the Hamilton Air Show which was a popular attraction for the members. At the general meeting, the new executive committee was named. Bill Martin [no relation] would replace Jim Martin as Chief Canadian Guinea Pig.

Members were reminded that in 1991, two years hence, it would be the fiftieth anniversary of the birth of the Guinea Pig Club and as many members as possible should try to head across the pond for the party.

Also, in October 1989, new letterhead incorporating the phrase *Cursum Perfeci* was adopted to honour the beloved Wingco. The phrase is Latin for "To Bring a Journey to a Perfect End," and it was adopted to let Jean Tilley know that Dr. Tilley would always be remembered.

Dr. A. Ross Tilley Scholarship

In 1990 the first Dr. A. Ross Tilley Scholarship was awarded. The scholarship was managed by the Dr. A. Ross Tilley Foundation, which was the brainchild of Mrs. Tilley. Following her husband's death, Jean Tilley decided to establish a scholarship in his memory that would aid young plastic surgeons. Her stipulation was that the surgeon be a specialist in reconstructive work and possess the humanitarian nature of her late husband.

The Tilley Foundation, which has received donations from the Educational Foundation of the Canadian Society of Plastic Surgeons as well as from private donors, is primarily financed by a generous donation from Mrs. Tilley. The establishment of this foundation and scholarship program has enabled representatives of a new generation of plastic surgeons to flourish. Ross Tilley would have approved.

Fiftieth Anniversary of the Birth of the Guinea Pig Club

The Fiftieth Anniversary of the founding of the Club was a smashing affair with much videotaping, interviewing, photo-opportunities and merriment. Members from all over the world travelled to East Grinstead and proved that, in Guinea Pig years, fifty was not that long a time. With both the Maestro and the Wingco gone, it was up to those present to remind the club of both its origins and its obligations. Archie and Ross had taken them a long way—they would have to go the balance on their own.

1992

The Canadians celebrated the Forty-Eighth Anniversary of their Wing of the Club in 1992. They met in Winnipeg and had a fine time there. One of the important things resolved at this meeting was the commitment to preserve the Guinea Pig papers. Honourary Secretary Lionel Hastings was authorized to sign a contract with the Saskatchewan Archives Board. The Club's archives would be housed in Regina in a state-of-the-art facility. It was another reminder of the passage of time, and of one's responsibility to the Club.

Another event in 1992 served to remind the Guinea Pigs of their responsibility to the Club, and to history.

The Valour and the Horror

One of the most controversial documentaries to have appeared since the war was the segment "Death by Moonlight—Bomber Command," part of the CBC television series *The Valour and the Horror*, a National Film Board of Canada film by brothers Terence and Brian McKenna. This film incensed a large number of air force veterans, Guinea Pigs included. In the case of the Guinea Pigs, part of their anger stemmed from the fact that as men who were burned or otherwise disfigured by the war they were the very embodiment of the sacrifices made by the allied campaign. Archie had taught them to "live for their country" and they had built a life around the fact that they had acted well and for the best. With this film, their efforts were called into question and, in effect, condemned.

Much of the debate surrounding this controversy belongs elsewhere, but what is clear is that to many veterans the film contained unsupported generalizations made by men with little comprehension of the realities of war.

The film aired first on the CBC and despite director Brian McKenna's assertion that most people loved it, a vapour trail of anger and invective followed the film. The Honourable Marcel Masse, Minister of National Defence, communicated to Dr. Lionel Hastings that he had received more complaints about *The Valour and the Horror* than all other recent items of National Defence business.[13]

Guinea Pigs were shocked, in particular, with the portrayal of burned airmen in the film. They were seen as "funny-looking monsters." This ignored what was being done at East Grinstead, both medically and spiritually. Veterans in general also noted discrepancies and inconsistencies in the use of footage. In the end this film, which by its timing might have been a fitting way for veterans to look back on their years of service, became an object of shame.

And lawsuits. A class action suit was brought by The Bomber Harris Trust (representing between 25,000 and 50,000 airmen) against the Canadian Broadcasting Corporation, the National Film Board of Canada and the writer/director team of Terence and Brian McKenna. This would drag on for years. There would also be a Senate inquiry.

The Senate Committee on Social Affairs, Science and Technology would eventually find the film "seriously flawed." It called some of the research into question and concluded by calling it a "personal film" and an "opinion piece."

History as opinion piece. Perhaps it has always been so. But television being the medium it is, and film having the power it does over an audience, each omission or discrepancy is magnified. And for the veterans, it was tantamount to a kick in the gut as thanks for their sacrifice, especially because the film was financed by the government, through the National Film Board.

There was a campaign to keep the BBC's Channel 4 from showing the film, which many veterans viewed as a national embarrassment. Veterans on both sides of the Atlantic joined in this cause, and some of the letters of protest came through the Queen Mother's office, although she did not herself write a personal letter. The effect was heartening—protest letters began appearing as soon as it was announced that the BBC would screen it.

But the film was screened in Britain where it was similarly controversial. The Bomber Harris Trust, meanwhile, lost not only its case but, eventually, its appeal. No doubt those involved in the film felt vindicated, but theirs was a Pyrrhic victory at best. And the veteran airmen, whose numbers dwindle daily, were forced to take comfort in the fact that, on both sides of the Atlantic, many people shared their version of the truth.

A sad event took place in 1993. Group Captain Tom Gleave, Chief Guinea Pig, died on June 12. Gleave had held the position for thirty-three years. One of a kind in life, he was irreplaceable in death, and the role of Chief Guinea Pig would remain unfilled.

Happier Times—The Canadian War Memorial and the Fiftieth Anniversary of the Canadian Wing

The year 1994 offered the Guinea Pigs two events which they greeted with pleasure. The first event heartened all Canadian veterans. It was the unveiling of the Canadian War Memorial in Green Park, London, England. The ceremony took place on June 3, 1994, in the presence of Her Majesty the Queen, Her Majesty the Queen Mother, His Royal Highness The Duke of Edinburgh, and Prime Ministers Jean Chretien and John Major. The monument itself which is modelled on the Vietnam Memorial in Washington, is two large sections of red Canadian granite laid out horizontally bedecked with squares of bronze emblazoned with maple leaves. Water flows over the granite. It is a permanent memorial to all veterans who fought for the allied cause.

The second event took place on August 12–24. The Canadian Wing of the Guinea Pig Club celebrated its fiftieth anniversary. They travelled to Victoria for the party. Among the darts matches, the salmon fishing and the golfing, there was the official meeting. The Guinea Pigs were delighted to have as their guest HRH The Prince Philip, President of the Guinea Pig Club, who met with them at Government House.

Several Guinea Pigs came from the UK to be present at the special anniversary. At the business meeting the Honourable Secretary's report and the Honourary Treasurer's report were presented as well as a report by Dr. Leith Douglas, Medical Liaison Officer, who commented positively on the Dr. A. Ross Tilley Scholarship. He also gave an account of the "Continuous Passive Motion Device," a $5,000 gift to the Dr. Tilley Burn Unit from the Canadian Guinea Pigs: their anniversary gesture. The device, which ran on a clockwise motor motion, allowed the stiffened joints of burn victims to be rehabilitated. It was a tangible way to celebrate the anniversary and a special way to remember Dr. Tilley.

Dr. Ross Tilley Public School

There was still more good news for the Guinea Pigs.

In January 1995, Dr. Lionel Hastings received a letter from Steve Rowland, an advanced life support paramedic from Bowmanville, Ontario, Dr. Tilley's hometown. Rowland had long admired Dr. Tilley and his work, and he had a mission. He sought first to have the Tilley home declared an historic site. But it was the second part of his letter that was of particular significance to

the Pigs. There was a new elementary school going up on West Side Drive that as yet had no name. Rowland planned to lobby hard to have it named after Tilley. Were the Guinea Pigs interested? Would they send letters of support?

Dr. Ross Tilley Public School

The Guinea Pigs did not need a second invitation. Letters were written to the Northumberland Clarington Board of Education backing Rowland's idea. It was perfect. Tilley's father had been a Bowmanville doctor, and the town had certainly been blessed by the Tilley family presence.

The campaign was successful. On Tuesday, November 5, 1994, barely a week shy of Remembrance Day, an interesting contingent officially opened the school. Present were Principal Ron Cameron, who was proud of the new school's association with Dr. Tilley; Mrs. Jean Tilley, who had actively supported the campaign and who would continue to take a personal interest in the school; Mrs. Tilley's niece; and—representing the Guinea Pig Club—Chief Canadian Guinea Pig Bill Martin, Honourary Secretary Lionel Hastings; Guinea Pigs Bert Aldridge, John Harding, and Henri "Ben" Marceau, as well as nurse Fran Oakes. Widow Ruth Kerr also attended as did Guinea Pig Friends Bea Jackson and Olga Lavalee. Dr. Leith Douglas and Mrs. Lorna Douglas were also on hand. It was a good showing by the Club, and those who attended would not have missed it.

Dr. Hastings spoke of Dr. Tilley's great talents, and his most lasting gift to his men:

> ...he taught us that it is great to be alive and the real joy is the gift of life regardless of handicaps.

Guinea Pigs would later make a cash donation on behalf of the Club, which would be used to buy books for the school library. As well, Mrs. Tilley would donate several significant artifacts to the school, which has made it clear that they wish to keep Dr. Tilley's memory alive.

Dr. Ross Tilley Public School. The emblem is a pair of spread-open hands. Ross Tilley, the ever-modest gentleman, the great surgeon of faces and hands, would have been pleased with this honour. A school. In his hometown. Young people who would be reminded of their history. It had a nice ring to it.

Fifty-Fifth Anniversary of the Parent Club

The fifty-second anniversary of the Canadian Wing should have taken place in 1996, but since this year was also the fifty-fifth anniversary of the parent club, the Canadians opted to postpone their own reunion by a year to focus on attending the annivesary in East Grinstead.

As always, it was a pleasure for Canadian Guinea Pigs to return to East Grinstead. And one of the issues raised at the meeting of the parent club was the mandate of benevolence toward any Guinea Pig in need. There was concern that some Guinea Pigs in need were not stepping forward. The mandate to help one another is near and dear to the Guinea Pigs. Also discussed at the meeting was talk of simplifying the reunions and doing away with some of the formalities, seeing as there were fewer Guinea Pigs at each reunion. There was also a suggestion by editor Jack Toper that the magazine *The Guinea Pig* be produced less frequently, but this was greeted with such dismay that he vowed to continue with the present schedule.

In other words, changes were discussed, accommodation to age, health and mobility. The Guinea Pig spirit was willing, but the flesh—which had been tried more than that of many—was weakening. However, Guinea Pigs have always gone the distance, on spirit alone if need be, so it is little wonder they vowed to keep the reunions going, even if somewhat modified.

The East Grinstead reunion, as was the custom, meant a trip to St. Swithun's Church, a ritual in which the departed Guinea Pigs, medical staff and friends were remembered. The church, over two hundred years old, flies the air force ensign, and a Memorial Chapel commemorates the dead of the two World Wars. This part of the reunion serves to remind all Guinea Pigs that they have much to be thankful for.

Guinea Pigs maintained their stamina throughout the "lost weekend." No longer young men, they nonetheless fed off the energy of seeing and speaking to one another, which brought to mind the words of Archie McIndoe: "The Weekend is important and therapeutic for my Guinea Pigs."

The Fifty-Third Anniversary of the Canadian Wing

June 5–8, 1997, saw the Guinea Pigs arrive at Mount Hope, Ontario, where they revived memories and had fun. A "pub night" was planned, and Pigs were requested to wear their World War II uniforms if they still possessed them. Several complied, and it added to the atmosphere.

There was a trip to the Canadian Warplane Heritage Museum, of great interest to the former airmen. Honoured guests at the gala dinner included Ron Cameron, principal of the Dr. Ross Tilley Public School; Dr. Leith Douglas; Dr. John Taylor, who heads the Ross and Jean Tilley Foundation; Dr. Joel Fish, a prominent plastic surgeon at the Ross Tilley Burn Centre, Steve Rowland, the paramedic who started the campaign to name the school after Tilley; and David Bogue, a patient upon whom Dr. Tilley had come out of retirement to operate. At this gathering Dr. John Taylor was appointed a "Friend of the Guinea Pig Club." Plans were also made for the next reunion which would be the Club's fifty-fifth.

One More Mission—The Tilley Burn Centre Moves

Since 1984, the Tilley Burn Centre had been in operation at the Wellesley Hospital. However, in the late 1990s a new government in Ontario enacted many policies, one of which saw the closing or relocation of many hospital services. At the Wellesley it was no different. The Wellesley, which would now become a branch of St. Michael's Hospital, would be closing its burn unit. The unit would be moved to the Sunnybrook Health Sciences Centre. The Sunnybrook Hospital had been in full operation since 1948 and had dealt with many veterans. Over the years there were additions to the facilities, and in 1990 it became the Sunnybrook Health Sciences Centre.

In 1998 when the Burn Centre was slated to move, it became clear that there was no guarantee it would retain Ross Tilley's name. This concerned Mrs. Tilley and the Guinea Pigs. After all, Tilley had worked at the Sunnybrook, and he was an inspiration in the field of burns and plastic surgery.

The Guinea Pigs once again made their presence known, writing letters and showing active interest, and they were rewarded when the unit transferred to the Sunnybrook intact. As of Thursday, November 5, 1998, the new unit at the Sunnybrook was officially the Tilley Burn Centre.

The diligence with which Mrs. Tilley and the Guinea Pigs have kept Ross Tilley's memory alive is to be commended, for they do so in the face of a culture that rarely acknowledges or even recognizes its heroes; a culture with a sometimes appalling, always embarrassing, long-term collective memory.

Roll on, Victoria—The Canadian Wing, Fifty-Five Years Young

The Victoria Reunion was held from May 18—22, 1999. It was organized by Guinea Pig John Southwell. Southwell, who is in the catering business, is an expert in the field and well-connected, so the Guinea Pigs could expect a wonderful time.

They were not disappointed. Twenty-eight guests (Pigs, family) arrived from the UK to assist in the frivolity and were greeted by an equally enthusiastic group of Canadian Pigs and their families. Local newspapers picked up on the story of these jubilant people, and articles were written about several of them. Interviews were videotaped, as well, and later made available to the Guinea Pigs. Activities included a trip to the British Columbia Aviation Museum. Guinea Pigs were surprised and pleased to spot a photograph of Guinea Pig Ed Smith taken in the post-war years when he was a Squadron Leader flying CF-100s with 428 (Ghost) Squadron. There was also a trip to the Vancouver Island Brewery for the ubiquitous dart match, as well as a shipboard meal in the evening. The reunion was generally regarded as one of the best, if not the best. And before they said farewell, they were already making plans for the following reunion, in 2001.

One other happy occurrence in 1999 was the publication of the first edition of *The Tilley Newsletter* (June, 1999). This newsletter, edited by Dr. John Taylor, highlights items of interest concerning all things to do with Dr. Tilley. It is a decidedly medical newsletter, since Tilley's name is associated with the Burn Centre, the Scholarship and The Tilley Lecture, an annual lecture to the Canadian Society of Plastic Surgeons given by the recipient of the annual scholarship. But the first issue also devoted space to the Dr. Ross Tilley Public School and, of course, to the Guinea Pigs.

Thus, "the members of the Maxillonian Club who call themselves The Guinea Pigs" closed out the year and, indeed the century, with the knowledge that others are now committed to keeping Dr. Tilley's memory, and his example, alive.

The Millennium, the Club and the Future

As all Canadians have moved into the new millenium, we have taken with us those memories that matter, those stories which sustain. The Guinea Pigs have a wealth of memories. As do their wives.

Fran Thompson, widow of Douglas Thompson, has chosen the form of poetry to express her feelings about what her husband endured. She acknowledges the influence of the Guinea Pig Club on his life, but she remembers also the hardship his injuries caused. It is a point that must never be lost, for it is what makes the achievements of these men all the more remarkable. In describing the lifelong scars and the perpetual struggle her husband went through, she is an eloquent witness to the personal sacrifice made by a man, and his family, for his country. From the poem "When Did the War Really End?" she writes:

> *When did it end for you my love?*
>   When did it end for you?
> The day you died just months ago
> The burden was lifted.
> At last you drifted on wings of freedom.
> The war was over!
> That's when it ended for you my love.
> That's when it ended   for me.

Another Guinea Pig wife also chose poetry to convey her emotional response to the Club and its members. Mary Orr Hastings' poem, "Canadian Retrospect", speaks of these men, their deeds, and their fate. She touches upon the salutory effects of knowing these unique people and makes this observation:

> ...These are the men whose special place, marked down
> In History takes but little space
> But these are the men, who for the knowing
> I am a better person...

Both women speak from experience, and with profound compassion.

Where is it going, this long-standing club of young airmen? It is getting smaller, and there are no new members to swell the ranks. It has been said that as long as there is a Guinea Pig left, there will be a Guinea Pig Club, so the organization will be around for some time.

It is strange. It was never a club anyone wanted to join. But once a person had met the requirements, it was a club he could not have done without. It is a club that has run on its own steam for over half a century as a benevolent organization and a solace to its members.

And the members of the club? Grandfathers, great-grandfathers now, elderly men with the array of problems of the elderly. But these burdens have been placed on shoulders that experienced assaults on their well-being at an early age. An extra burden maybe, but the Guinea Pigs can take it. The humour helps.

All of them achieved. There were never any suicides. Some went on to exemplary careers in the air force, professional practice or private industry, over-achieving perhaps, in part, because of their early experiences. Others lived quite ordinary lives filled with family, friends and work. Just normal lives, really, the kind most of us live.

Normal lives. One can hear Dr. Tilley's words in that phrase, and his desire "to restore people to normal." That these men have lived lives normal in every respect is the greatest possible tribute they could ever make to their Wingco, and to the Maestro, who had told them that there was nothing equal to "living" for one's country. These men have lived—no more fitting epigraph is needed.

Cursum Perfeci

A Guinea Pig Scrapbook

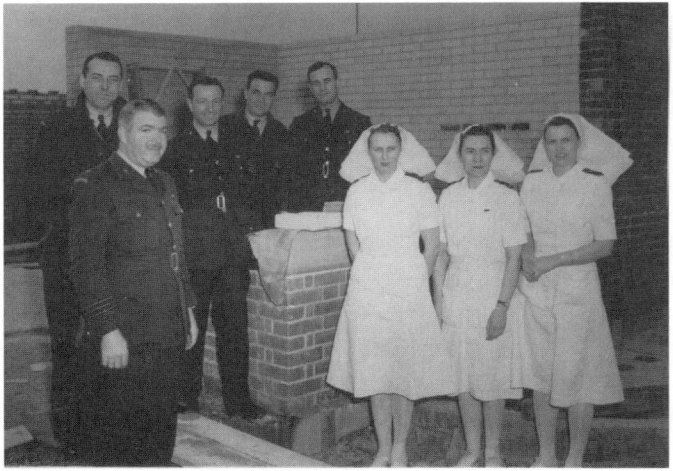

Top: Staff of the Canadian Wing, 1944.

Below: QVH photo with Dr. Tilley and nurses.
Back row (left to right): Sgt. Cornwall, an RCAF engineer, Sgt. John Ingram,
    Squadron Leader Norman Park.
Front row (left to right): Dr, Ross Tilley, Leonora Loyst, Frances Oakes, Marge
    Jackson.

Top Left (left to right): Lillian Hall and William Rhode

Top right (left to right): Bob Tait and Everett "Fergie" Ferguson

Bottom: Lionel "Hank" Hastings and the crew of H "Sneezy"
(left to right): F/O E. G. "Eppy" Eppstadt (AG); WO P. S. "Perry" Purvis (WAG);
F/O L. E. "Hank" Hastings (NavB)(Observer); F/L J. L. "Joe" Knowlton (P_lot)

Top: Graves of the crew of Hank Ernst's and George Beauchamp's plane.

Bottom left (left to right): John Southwell and Mel Burgess with ill-fated Minx.

Bottom right: Henry Standen's drawing of Bill Anglin's flying business.

Top: Entrance to the Canadian Wing.

Bottom (back row left to right): Ken Allison, Bob Tait, George Wilson, Paul
   Weber, Bill Tanner
(front row left to right): NS F. Anderson, Matron Marge Jackson, NS Midge
   Phillips, NS Marj Peacock, NS Marg Kaines, NS Enid Faulkner

Top: Wartime wedding of Leo and Ethel Lacroix, East Grinstead, 1944.

Bottom: Stu Duncan and crew in Egypt, May 1944. Duncan is in the back row third from left, on camel.

Top: Wedding of Enid (Faulkner) Matheson.
(left to right): S/Ldr Dan Gordon, DSC; S/Ldr Ken Matheson, DFC+bar;
        NS Enid(Faulkner) Matheson; NS F/L Fran Oakes

Bottom: Enid (Faulkner) Matheson at wedding party.
(left to right): Larry Lymburner, Jim Martin, Enid Matheson, Douglas
Thompson, Larry Somers. *(seated)*: Stu Duncan

Top: Dr. Tilley being presented with the air raid siren at the "Handing Over" banquet, East Grinstead, 1945.

Bottom left (left to right): Dr. Norm Park and Johnny Kerr at a Toronto reunion.

Bottom right: Ed Smith with Mynarski Lancaster, VE 50th Anniversary celebrations, Hamilton, Ontario.

Top: Same group as at Enid Matheson wedding (sans Larry Lymburner), 1972.

Bottom: 1976 Winnipeg Reunion
Back row (left to right): Frank Hanton, Hank Hastings, Hank Ernst, Jack
    Reynolds, Paul Branch, Bill Newson.
Front Row (left to right): Orvel Dove, Norm McHolm, Jim Hicks, Reg
    Harrison, Bob Tait.

Top: 1992 Winnipeg Convention
Back row (left to right): Paul Branch, Jack Reynolds, Bob Tait, Ed Cecile, Art
        Doyle, Stu Duncan.
Front row (left to right): Les Syrett (UK), Bill Martin, Jack Perry (UK).

Bottom: Mary Hastings making a presentation to Mrs. Jean Tilley, 1974.
(at left): Jack Smith; *(far right)*: Dr. Tilley .

Top: Victoria 1984. *(left to right)*: Garnett "Tar" Moore and George "Curly" Wilson.

Bottom: Victoria 1984. *(left to right)*: Dr. Tilley and George "Curly" Wilson.

Top: Winnipeg, June 1992.
(left to right): Stu Duncan, Flora Duncan and Edna Martin.

Bottom: Winnipeg, June 1992
(left to right): Bill Martin, Joyce Hanton and Frank Hanton.

Top: Hank Hastings *(left)* and Ed Smith *(right)* at the Guinea Pig Pub, East
    Grinstead, September 1996.

Bottom: Jack Reynolds, Jack Harding and Hank Ernst

Top: Olwen and Jack Harding and their special puppets.

Bottom: Guinea Pigs at the opening of the Dr, Ross Tilley Public School,
November, 1996.
(left to right): Hank Hastings, Jack Harding, Bill Martin, Henri Marceau, Bert
Aldridge

Top left: Dedication on Canadian Wing, 1944.

Top right: Lionel "Hank" Hastings with a guinea pig.

Bottom: Victoria Reunion, May 1999. Guinea Pigs at Air Museum with a
          Tiger Moth.

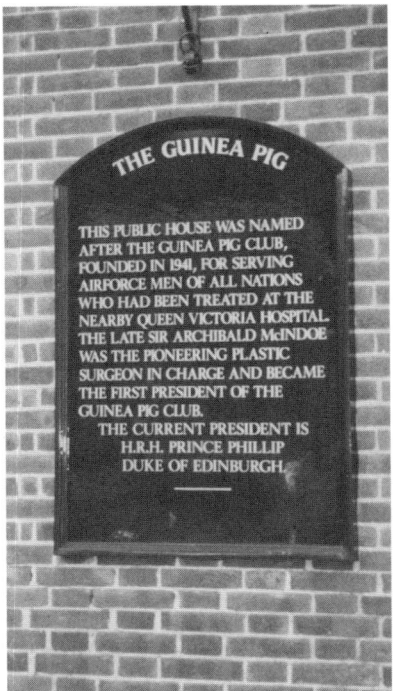

Top left: Dedication on the "The Guinea Pig" Pub, East Grinstead.

Top right: "The Guinea Pig" Pub

Bottom: "The Guinea Pig" Pub

ppendix A

The Guinea Pig Club Canadian Wing

Formation and Executive Listings

by Dr. Lionel Hastings

The Canadian Wing originated at a dinner meeting in honour of Sir Archibald McIndoe on his visit to Canada, on Monday, November 1, 1948. The meeting was held at the Officers' Mess, RCAF Station 1107 Avenue Road in Toronto (former No.1 ITS). After an inspiring address from Sir Archibald McIndoe, the Canadian Wing was formed with the following officers:

President: Dr. A. Ross Tilley, who was a Group Captain and head of the Canadian Wing at Queen Victoria Hospital, East Grinstead
Treasurer: Paul Weber
Secretary: F/O Donald Freeborn
Organizing Committee: Paul Branch, Larry Lymburner

In 1952 Guinea Pigs Frank Hubbard and George "Curly" Wilson attended the Guinea Pig Reunion in September in East Grinstead, having been flown to England courtesy of the Department of National Defence. This revived interest in the Canadian Wing, and, with the encouragement of President Dr. Tilley, Frank Hubbard became the Secretary-Treasurer of the Canadian Wing. Frank Hubbard, with the assistance of Dr. Tilley, then planned a successful reunion at the Royal York Hotel in Toronto on Saturday, May 2, 1953. At that time Dr. Tilley was pleased to introduce his charming bride, Jean Tilley.

After this successful reunion Guinea Pigs returned home to concentrate on raising their families and earning a living. As a result the Guinea Pig Club Canadian Wing entered a period of relative inactivity until 1971.

In 1971 the parent club in the U.K. made a special effort to have Canadian Guinea Pigs attend the 30th Anniversary of the Guinea Pig Club in East Grinstead, at "Ye Olde Felbridge Hotel", September 24, 25, and 26. Special arrangements were made for a flight from New York courtesy of Loftleider Airline at a cost of $78.00 return. It was indeed a fantastic reunion with teelve Canadian Guinea Pigs (nine with their wives) accompanied by Dr. Ross Tilley and Dr. Norman Park and their wives in attendance.

Following the Sunday morning party around the pool, a group of seven Guinea Pigs held an impromptu meeting to discuss the possibility of reviving the Canadian Wing of the Guinea Pig Club. Because he had a pen and was seated close to a table, Bob Lloyd was elected as secretary for the meeting. The decision to revitalize the Canadian Wing was unanimous.

The effort of Bob Lloyd after the meeting, with the assistance of Rothmans of Pall Mall, was tremendous. We will be eternally grateful to Guinea Pig Bob Lloyd for making the revitalization of the Guinea Pig Club possible. In addition, a special effort was made to relocate Canadian Guinea Pigs who were still alive. A reunion was planned by Bob Lloyd for June 9 and 10, 1972, with a total of 90 to 120 Pigs, wives, and friends planning to attend. The reunion proved to be an outstanding success and a business meeting was held at the Skyline Hotel on June 10, 1972 with thirty-two Guinea Pigs, Dr. Tilley and Dr. Norman Park in attendance. Chief Guinea Pig Group Captain Tom Gleave and Honourary Editor Henry Standen were guests from the parent Guinea Pig Club in the United Kingdom. The meeting was chaired by Guinea Pig Ken Allison with R. T. "Bob" Lloyd as secretary.

After the completion of thanks to those who had made this successful reunion possible, Chief Guinea Pig Tom Gleave was called upon to outline the aims and purposes of the parent club with regard to the welfare and rehabilitation of Guinea Pigs. He stressed the value of the *Guinea Pig* magazine and their annual reunions. This was followed by an outline of the officers of the club of which H. R. H. Prince Philip was the President with Group Captain Tom Gleave as the Chief Guinea Pig acting as Secretary and Co-ordinating Officer. Other officers were indicated by their titles such as Henry Standen who was in attendance as Honourary Editor of *The Guinea Pig*. These remarks were reinforced with "Wingco" Dr. A. Ross Tilley stressing the importance of rehabilitation and morale assistance for Guinea Pigs.

Chairman Ken Allison then called upon those Guinea Pigs present to suggest a slate of officers. After a short discussion, the following slate of officers was proposed by Bob Fraser and passed unanimously. You will note that at this time the Chief Canadian Guinea Pig also acted as secretary:

Guinea Pig Executive 1972–1977

President: Dr. A. Ross Tilley, OBE
Chief Canadian Guinea Pig   R. T. "Bob" Lloyd
Treasurer: E. H. "Fergie" Ferguson
Western Representative: H. "Hank" Ernst
Eastern Representative: Paul Branch
Medical Liaison Officer: Dr. Norman Park

This executive remained in office with reunions in 1974 and in June 1977 when Chief Canadian Guinea Pig Bob Lloyd decided to resign in order to provide the necessary care and attention for his son Brent who was seriously injured in a car accident. The thanks of all Canadian Guinea Pigs go to Bob and Dorothy Lloyd for their outstanding contribution in revitalizing the Canadian Wing, with the assistance of Rothmans of Pall Mall Canada Limited.

At the June 1977 Reunion at the Skyline Hotel, the following executive was elected:

Guinea Pig Executive 1977–1979

President: Dr. A. Ross Tilley, OBE
Chief Canadian Guinea Pig: Edward A. Doyle
Honourary Treasurer: Norman McHolm
Western Representative: Dr. Lionel E. Hastings
Eastern Representative: Paul S. Warren
Medical Liaison Officer: Dr. Norman Park

Please note that Chief Canadian Guinea Pig Edward A. Doyle also acted as Secretary.

At the 1979 Reunion in June, also held at the Skyline Hotel in Toronto, the following executive was elected and remained in office for reunions in 1980, 1981, 1982, and 1984 in Victoria (1979–1984). Dr. A. Ross Tilley received notification of his Member of the Order of Canada award in December 1981.

The Guinea Pig Executive 1979–1984

President: Dr. A. Ross Tilley, OBE
Chief Canadian Guinea Pig: Dr. Lionel E. Hastings

Honourary Secretary:	John A. Reynolds
Honourary Treasurer:	Norman McHolm
Western Representative:	Robert Tait
Eastern Representative:	Paul S. Warren
Medical Liaison Officer:	Dr. Leith Douglas

Dr. Leith Douglas was appointed in November 1979 after the death of Dr. Norman Park on August 10, 1977.

At the reunion in Victoria, British Columbia, in June 1984 the following executive was elected.

Guinea Pig Executive 1984–1986

President:	Dr. A. Ross Tilley, OBE, CM
Chief Canadian Guinea Pig:	George A. Wilson
Honourary Secretary:	W. E. "Bill" Martin
Honourary Treasurer:	Norman McHolm
Western Representative:	Robert Tait
Eastern Representative:	Paul F. Branch
Medical Liaison Officer:	Dr. Leith G. Douglas

This executive remained in office until Feb. 26, 1986, when Chief Canadian Guinea Pig George A. Wilson resigned. Approximately two months later in April 1986, Dr. Lionel E. Hastings was reappointed Chief Canadian Guinea Pig for 1986–1987 until the reunion in Regina in 1987. The following executive was elected:

President:	Dr. A. Ross Tilley, OBE, CM
Chief Canadian Guinea Pig:	J. "Jim" Martin
Honourary Secretary:	Edward A. Doyle
Honourary Treasurer:	Norman McHolm
Western Representative:	Robert Tait
Eastern Representative:	F. Paul Branch
Medical Liaison Officer:	Dr. Leith C. Douglas

President Dr. A. Ross Tilley, OBE, CM, passed away on May 19, 1988, in Toronto. This position will never be replaced in recognition of his outstanding contribution to humanitarian and surgical skills to all Guinea Pigs. Several years later the title of *"Cursum Perfeci"* was added to our stationery in his honour.

At the reunion in Guelph on June 17, 1989, the entire executive resigned and the following executive was elected.

Guinea Pig Executive 1989–1995

Chief Canadian Guinea Pig:	William E. Martin
Honourary Secretary:	Dr. Lionel E. Hastings
Honourary Treasurer:	Frank E. Hanton
WesternRepresentative:	Robert Tait
Eastern Representative:	Mr. Edgar G. Cecile
Medical Liaison Officer:	Dr. Leith G. Douglas

The executive remained intact until October of 1995 when Edgar G. Cecile moved west from the state of Michigan to the state of Washington on the west coast. As a result Mr. Paul Branch was appointed eastern representative in early 1996. There were no further changes until May 1999 at the reunion when Frank E. Hanton resigned as Honourary Treasurer after ten years of faithful service. At the business meeting on May 21, 1999, in Victoria British Columbia, Mr. Kenneth R. Fisher was elected Honourary Treasurer and as of that meeting the following executive is presently serving.

Guinea Pig Executive 1999-present

Chief Canadian Guinea Pig:	William E. Martin
Honourary Secretary:	Dr. Lionel E. Hastings
Honourary Treasurer:	Kenneth R. Fisher
Western Representative:	Robert Tait
Eastern Representative:	Paul Branch [deceased July 2000]

ppendix B

Friends of the Guinea Pig Club

Mrs. Eileen M. Angly	Vancouver, BC
Lt. Col. Robert V. Cade	Regina, SK
Mr. Ron Cameron (I)	Bowmanville,ON
Mrs. Sue Cawston	Armstrong, BC
Mr. J. R. Danaher*	Regina, SK
Air Marshall Larry Dunlap	Victoria, BC
Dr. Leith Douglas	Toronto, ON
Mr. Ian Ferguson	Nun's Island, PQ
Dr. Joel Fish (I)	Toronto, ON
The Lord of Uffington, John Fordham, Esq.	Bedford, NS
Lt. Col. Ken Garbutt	Regina, SK
Mr. Kenneth W. Harrison	Regina, SK
Mrs. Shirley Hubbard	Sardis, BC
Mrs. Bea Jackson	Willowdale, ON
Mrs. Olga Lavallee	St. Laurent, PQ
Col. George Miller	Langley, BC
Professor William Rodney	Victoria, BC
Mr. Steve Rowland (I)	Bowmanville,ON
Mrs. Heather Southwell	Victoria, BC
Dr. John R. Taylor	Mississauga, ON
B/Gen. Cliff A. Walker	Regina, SK
Mrs. Nancy Ward	Sidney, BC
Mr. W. H. Whitwham	Brampton, ON

* Deceased
(I) Induction at 2001 Meeting

Appendix C

Canadian Guinea Pigs for Whom No Stories Are Available

J. Cyril Anderson
Harold Avery
Douglas R. Bacon
J. H. Bain
V. Banks
William D. Barber
Gerry E. Bernier
L. F. Berryman

Gordon A. Biddle
Alan C. Bowes
Eric Bristow
W. R. Burton
E. A. Cain
B. Campbell
Louis-Philippe Catellier
Maurice J. D. R. Charbonneau

R. Cleland
R. Colver
Arthur G. Cooke
H. N. H. Curwain
G. Dakin
James Ferguson
G. Forbes
Robert Garvin (or "Garwin")

William H. Golding
Les Goodson
J. Grill
J. Grudzien
Neville Gunnis
W. J. Higgins
Roy Hocking
R. Houston

D. H. Lanctot
Albert Lander
John E. Levi (or "Leui")
C. M. Lipsett
A. J. Lord
Jimmy Love
Joseph L. Lymburner
C. "Chuck" Maclean

Donald S. MacNeill
T. D. McKeown
Kenneth C. Mclennan
D. C. McNeill
Bruce S. Mitchell
Marc Monpetit
Jimmy Morrison
J. Delmar Mufford

Lawrence Muir
T. Nichols
Gordon Alistair Noble
G. S. O'Brian
Harold A. Ogden
L. Phillips
J. Rickard
S. Round

D. Schultz
G. L. Spackman
Ivan St. John
D. Stultz (or "Stults")
J. B. Sullivan
J. Thomas
B. Vincent

Appendix D

Searching for Family Personnel Service Records

The National Archives of Canada holds the Personnel Service Records for both the First and Second World Wars and for the Korean Conflict. Should you wish to locate the files of a family member you may follow one of the following two procedures:

Post-First World War Records–Formal Access: The *Privacy Act* and the *Access to Information Act* govern formal access to the military personnel files of regular force personnel serving after the First World War, as well as those on active service during the Second World War and the Korean Conflict. Persons seeking a complete copy of their own service records may wish to apply under the *Privacy Act*. Those wishing to obtain a complete copy of a veteran's file may wish to apply under the *Access to Information Act*. The veteran must have been deceased for more than 20 years, and proof of death must be provided unless he or she died in service. Such formal requests should be sent to the Personnel Records Section, Access to Information and Privacy Division, National Archives of Canada, Ottawa, ON, K1A 0N3. Fee: $5.00. Photocopy charges may be assessed.

Informal Access: If an individual wishes to receive copies of specific documentation, rather than a complete file, informal access to these records may be obtained by sending a written request to the Personnel Records Unit, Researcher Services Division, National Archives of Canada, Ottawa, ON, K1A 0N3. Although no fee is charged for this service, photocopy charges may be assessed.

In the case of a living veteran, his or her signed consent is required for the release of personal information. If the veteran has been deceased fewer than 20 years, limited information may be released directly to a member of his or her immediate family in reply to a written request, if accompanied by proof of death and relationship. There are no restrictions placed on information relating to individuals who have been deceased for more than 20 years; however, proof of death is still required.

You may also wish to consult the web site of the National Archives of Canada at: http://www.archives.ca

This information provided by the National Archives of Canada.

Notes

1. (p. 18) Dennison, E. J., *A Cottage Hospital Grows Up*. London: Baxendale Press, 1996, p. 82.

2. (p. 36) Berkowitz, Jacob. "The English Patient." *The Ottawa Citizen*, Wed., Mar. 25, 1998, p. C1.

3. (p. 50) Harris, Sir Arthur T. *Bomber Offensive*. New York: Macmillan, 1942, p. 144.

4. (p. 82) "Cardston Pilot Relives World War II." *The Chronicle*, (Cardston) Tues., May 7, 1945.

5. (p. 89) Gray, Donald. "When a Tour Equals 19 Trips." *Air Force*, Vol. 17, no. 2, 1993, pp. 46-47.

6. (p. 134) Barber, Charles. "Rebuilding Faces the War Blew Away." Cityscape. *Monday Magazine*, July 5-11, 1984.

7. (p.173) Brock McElheran. *V-Bombs and Weathermaps: Reminiscences of World War II*. Montreal-Kingston: McGill-Queens University Press, 1995, p. 37.

8. (p. 173) ibid, p. 38.

9. (p. 223) "Canada's Name Will Live For Ever in Hearts of East Grinstead People." *The Courier* (East Grinstead) Sept., 1945.

10. (p.231) Extracted from Annals of the Royal College of Surgeons of England, May, 1960, reprinted in *The Guinea Pig*.

11. (p. 247) "Canada Joins Fight for QVH." *The Courier* (East Grinstead), 1987.

12. (p. 249) Figuera, Nancy. "Toronto's Dr. Tilley: Surgeon and Friend." *Graduate*, University of Toronto Alumni Magazine, Vol. VI, 102, Nov/Dec 1983, p. 10.

13. (p. 251) Hastings, Lionel, "Who Will Speak on Our Behalf?" *The Guinea Pig*, New Year's, 1993.

Glossary

Air Forces and Branches and Units

RAF	Royal Air Force
RAAF	Royal Australian Air Force
RCAF	Royal Canadian Air Force
RNZAF	Royal New Zealand Air Force
USAAF	United States Army Air Force
WD	Womens Division (RCAF)
B.Cmd	Bomber Command
6 Grp	6 Group (RCAF)
PFF	Pathfinder Force
A/S/R	Air Sea Rescue
DAF	Desert Air Force
BCATP	British Commonwealth Air Training Plan
CDB	Coastal Defence Battery
PRU	Photographic Reconnaissance Unit

Ranks

A/M	Air Marshall
A/V/M	Air Vice Marshall
A/C	Air Commodore
G/C	Group Captain
W/C	Wing Commander
S/L	Squadron Leader
F/L	Flight Lieutenant
F/O	Flying Officer
P/O	Pilot Officer
W/O	Warrant Officer
F/S	Flight Sergeant
Sgt	Sergeant
Cpl	Corporal
LAC	Leading Aircraftsman
LAW	Leading Aircraftswoman
AC1	Aircraftsman First Class
AC2	Aircraftsman Second Class
AG	Air Gunner
AOC	Air Officer Commanding
BA	Bomb-Aimer

CO	Commanding Officer
FE	Flight Engineer
MO	Medical Officer
MU/AG	Mid-upper air gunner
WO	Warrant Officer
NCO	Non-Commissioned Officer
ORs	Other Ranks (erks)
POW	Prisoner of War
RG	Rear Gunner
WAG	Wireless Air Gunner
W/O	Wireless Operator
WOp/AG	Wireless Operator/Air Gunner

Various Divisions

AFU	Advanced Flying Unit
ANS	Air Navigational School
AOS	Air Observer School
B &GS	Bombing and Gunnery School
CFB	Canadian Forces Base
CFS	Central Flying School
CGS	Central Gunnery School
EFTS	Elementary Flying Training School
FIS	Flight Instructors School
FTS	Flight Training School
HCU	Heavy Conversion Unit
ITS	Initial Training School
MD	Manning Depot
OTU	Operational Training Unit
SFTS	Service Flying Training School
TTS	Technical Training School

References (including slang)

ack-ack	anti-aircraft fire
aerodrome	station, base, airport
airman's burn	a flash burn of the face and hands from intense dry heat
ammo	ammunition
Apron	tarmac around a hangar
A.S.I.	air speed indicator
astro	astro-navigation, astrograph: concerning the calculation of position by sun or stars. Astrodome: the perspex-covered device on top of the fuselage where the navigator can fix his sights
AWOL	Absent Without Leave
bail out	parachute departure from an in-flight aircraft (also "bale out")
bandit	enemy aircraft
belly landing	a wheels-up landing
bogey	an unidentified aircraft
bought it	shot down; killed in action; "bought the farm"
Brass	senior officers; refers to gold oak leaf clusters on peak of cap (see also "scrambled eggs")
briefing	aircrew instructions prior to an operation
Bumf	leaflets dropped from aircraft (nickel)
Buzz bomb	V1 flying bomb (doodlebug)
Caterpillar Club	a club whose members have been forced to bail out of an aircraft using a parachute.
circuits and bumps	landing practice
Circus	fighter-escorted, short range bombing raid
CB'd	confined to barracks
chop	get the [chop]: be killed
coned	caught in the crossed beams of searchlights
contact flying	flying close to the ground
corkscrew	to take extreme avoidance action, port and starboard, to elude enemy

DC	depth charge
deck	ground level or sea level
DFC	Distinguished Flying Cross
DFM	Distinguished Flying Medal
dicey	risky; chancy (see 'shaky-do')
dispersal areas	several far-flung areas around an airfield where planes are parked as a precaution against a concentrated air attack
ditch	a forced sea landing
diversion	an operation designed to lead the enemy off track and away from main attack target
do	an event; can refer to a social situation or an air operation. In air operation, if the mission was hazardous, reference is to a 'shaky-do.'
dog leg	several short course alterations designed to lose time yet bring crew back to original course
DR	Dead Reckoning: calculating a position using courses flown and airspeed flown
drogue	long, narrow cloth sleeve towed behind aircraft and used as a target in gunnery training
DSO	Distinguished Service Order
E/A	enemy aircraft
egg	bomb
ETA	estimated time of arrival
E/V	escort vessel
evasive action	extreme measures taken to evade enemy aircraft (see "corkscrew")
feather	turning the blades of a malfunctioning propellor to give some resistance to airflow; to bring the propeller blades in line with the flight of the aircraft
fire the colours	to shoot the daily authorized colour recognition flare
flak	ack-ack
flap	a commotion

flarepath	the line of lights indicating the runway for night flying aircraft
flash burns	airman's burn: short exposure to intense heat and flame
flip	a short flight
for the slab	going for a medical operation; also "slabbing" (Guinea Pig slang)
48	48 hours free of duty
Flight	nickname for Flight Sergeant
fried	burned in an aircraft fire (Guinea Pig slang)
gardening	mine laying
GEE	a medium range radio aid used for target identification and navigational purposes
Gen	information, usually reliable; intelligence
George	automatic pilot
glycol	coolant for liquid-cooled engines
G.M.T.	Greenwich Mean Time, used in navigation
going for the chop	proceeding to a medical operation (Guinea Pig slang)
Goldfish Club	a club restricted to those who have bailed out, crashed or ditched over water
gone for a Burton	bought it; killed
gongs	military decorations for aircrew (ex.: DFC)
Groupy	nickname for Group Captain
Guinea Pig	injured airmen at the Queen Victoria Hospital, East Grinstead; members of the Guinea Pig Club
Halibag	Halifax aircraft
Hang-up	bomb that does not release over target; a stuck bomb
hash brown	fried and mashed (Guinea Pig slang)
hat trick	to do the; three successes in a row
high-tail	to depart from a situation at top speed (derived from the fact that the tail of a plane at full speed is higher than its nose)

hit the silk	to parachute
H2S	a pulse reflector (air/ground/air)
IC	incendiary bomb
ID	identification
immediate award	a decoration granted on the spot for a specific action
jammed	garbled communication due to radio interference
Jerry	German
jink	take evasive action
KIA	Killed in Action
kite	aircraft
leg	an aircraft's route between two turning points
Leigh Lights	special highly powered searchlights mounted on planes for use in discerning submarines
live	fused; ready to explode
LMF	Lack of Moral Fibre
Mae West	inflatable vest named after the actress
marshalled	the arrangement of aircraft in order of take off on the perimeter track at the head of the runway
marshalling yards	freight yards; area where trains are made up
mashed	crushed and maimed in an aircraft crash (Guinea Pig slang)
Met	meteorological or weather forecasting
MIA	Missing in Action
MiD	Mention in Despatches
mission	sortie, operation
M/S	minesweeper
MT	Motor Transport
M/V	merchant vessel
NAAFI	Navy, Army & Air Force Institute
NFS	National Fire Service
Nickel	propaganda leaflets (i.e. a nickel raid)

Office	cockpit; or rear gunner's turret
on the deck	flying low
Ops	operations, sorties, missions, raids
pancake	crash land with wheels up
pack up	cease to function
Pathfinder	elite crews who are trained to precede the bomber force and mark the target
perspex	shatter-proof material used in windscreen, in cockpit and turret covers
piece of cake	easy; a cinch
pinpoint	to fix the location accurately
prang	to crash
rookie	recruit; a new member of a crew
QVH	Queen Victoria Hospital, East Grinstead
radar	RDF: radio direction finding equipment
recce	reconnaissance
RT	radio transmitter
satellite	secondary airport
Scientists	doctors, surgeons, medical personnel (Guinea Pig slang)
scrambled eggs	military decorations on uniforms
screened	completion of a tour
scrub	call off a mission; to cancel
S/E	single-engined
shaky-do	dangerous op; risky
shoot a line	as in "it was a real line-shoot"; to exaggerate; to embellish
singed	burned, but not too badly (Guinea Pig slang)
split-ass turn	a half-circuit of the airfield before landing
sprog	green; new (as in sprog crew)
stood down	inactive for the night
stooge	a stand in
Sty	Ward III, Queen Victoria Hospital (Guinea Pig slang)

Tail-end Charlie	rear gunner
Tannoy	public address system used on military bases
T/E	twin-engined
TI	target indicator
Tour	number of operational trips required of Bomber Command aircrew; thirty trips on first tour, twenty on second
VE-Day	Victory Europe Day (8 May 1945)
VJ-Day	Victory Japan (14 August 1945)
V1	flying bomb (doodlebug; buzz bomb)
V2	A4 artillery rocket
Wimpey	A Wellington aircraft
Window	strips of metal deliberately dropped from aircraft to confound enemy radar
W/I	wireless transmitter
Wingco	nickname for Wing Commander
Wizard	anything "first class"
Write-of	an aircraft crashed beyond repair

Bibliography

Selected Books

Bishop, Edward. *The Guinea Pig Club*. London: New English Library, 1973.

Brown, David. *Aerodromes in North Yorkshire and Wartime Memories*. David Brown Publishing. Stockton-on-Tees, England, 1995.

Dennison, E.J. *A Cottage Hospital Grows Up: The Story of the Queen Victoria Hospital, East Grinstead*. London: Baxendale Press, 1996.

Dunmore, Spencer and William Carter. *Reap the Whirlwind*. Toronto: McClelland & Stewart, 1991.

—*Wings for Victory*. Toronto: McClelland & Stewart, 1994.

Formánek, Vítek. *The Stories of Brave Guinea Pigs*. East Sussex: J & KH Publishing, 1998.

Gleave, Tom, *I Had a Row with a German*. Putman, 1942.

Harding, John, DFC, *The Dancin' Navigator*. Copyright 1988.

Harris, Sir Arthur T. *Bomber Offensive*. New York: Macmillan, 1947.

Harvey, Douglas, *Boys, Bombs, and Brussels Sprouts*. Toronto: McClelland & Stewart, 1981.

- *Laughter-Silvered Wings: Remembering the Air Force II*, Toronto: McClelland & Stewart, 1984.

- *The Tumbling Mirth: Remembering the Air Force*, Toronto: McClelland & Stewart, 1983.

Hillary, Richard. *The Last Enemy*. London: Wyman & Sons, Ltd., 1942.

Hills, Wallace H., *The History of East Grinstead*. East Grinstead: Farncombe & Co., Ltd., 1906.

McHolme, Norman A. *The Touch of God's Hand*. Copyright 1993.

McElheran, Brock. *V-Bombs and Weathermaps*. Montreal: McGill-Queen's University Press, 1995.

Morton, Desmond. *A Military History of Canada*. Edmonton: Hurtig Publishing, 1985.

Page, Geoffrey, DSO, DFC, *Tale of a Guinea Pig*. Canterbury: Wingham Press, 1981.

Peden, Murray. *A Thousand Shall Fall*. Stittsville, ON.: Canada's Wings, 1981.

—*The RCAF Overseas*. 3 vols. Toronto: Oxford University Press, 1944, 1945, 1949.

Simpson, William, DFC. *The Way of Recovery*. London: Hamish Hamilton, 1944.

—*I Burned My Fingers*. London: Putman, 1956.

Williams, Peter and Ted Harrison. *McIndoe's Army*. London: Sphere Books Ltd., 1991.

Selected Articles

Alford, Jane. "The Guinea Pig Club" [booklet] Coombe Dean School, England. n.d..

Allighan, Garry. "Flight Sergeant Dufort is Beneficiary of Work by Red Cross in U.K.," [re. Gerry Dufort] n.d..

Arch, Bernard. "The Story of the Queen Victoria Hospital, East Grinstead—'The Little Town with the Big Heart'" [booklet] March, 1945.

Barber, Charles. "Rebuilding Faces the War Blew Away". Cityscape. *Monday Magazine*, July 5-11, 1984.

Barnes, Alan. "Paul Weber Sr. started famous hamburger haven." *The Toronto Star*, Sat., Oct. 15, 1994.

Bell, Jeff. "Wartime ties bring 'Guinea Pigs' to Victoria reunion." *Times-Colonist* (Victoria), Monday, August 15, 1994.

Berger, Bob. "Vet Happy to be Guinea Pig No. 207."[re. Bill Martin] *Calgary Herald*, November 11, 1988.

Berkowitz, Jacob. "The English Patients" [re. Edward Smith]. *The Ottawa Citizen*, Wed., Mar. 25, 1998, pp. C1-C2.

"Burn Victims Pay Tribute to Famous Plastic Surgeon at Official Opening of School." *The Canadian Statesman* (Bowmanville), Wed., Nov. 13, 1996, pp. 1 & 3.

Calder, Mark. "Just over there to do a job." [re. E. M. Lacasse] *Recorder & Times* (Brockville), n.d.

"Canada's Name Will Live For Ever in Hearts of East Grinstead People. Air Force Wing Officially Handed Over. Plastic Surgery of World Fame." *The Courier* (East Grinstead), September 1945.

"Canadians Join Fight for QVH." *The Courier*. (East Grinstead), June, 1987.

"Cardston Pilot Relives World War II." [re. Bill Tanner]. *The Chronicle* (Cardston, Alberta), Tuesday, May 7, 1985.

Chapman, Frank. "World-wide members" [re. Pea-Nut Club]. *The Courier* (Kent & Sussex), March 13, 1998.

Chow, Wanda. "Guinea Pig Club: Pioneers of plastic surgery were 'mashed and fried' vets." *Sunday Free Press*, Winnipeg, November 26, 1995, p. D1.

Cole, Arthur. "Man of Many Faces: 35 He Helped Rebuild Greet Sir Archibald, Guinea Pigs' Maestro." *The Globe and Mail*, 1948.

"The Courier's Aunt Agatha Dies at 85." *The Courier*. (Kent & Sussex), n.d.

Douglas, Leith G. M.D., with George Ronald. "Ross Tilley: The Immortal Wingco." *Reader's Digest*, September 1971, pp. 67-71.

"Dr. Lionel Hastings: One Cool Customer." *The Windsock*, March 11, 1993. The Roland Groome Chapter, Canadian Aviation Historical Society.

"Dr. Ross Tilley" (obituary), *Daily Telegraph*, London, April, 1989.

"Dr. Tilley's Ex-Patients are Special Guests at School." *The Canadian Statesman*, n.d., 1996.

"Ex-Airmen marking 40th Anniversary of the Battle of Britain." *The Leader-Post*, Regina, Saturday, September 13, 1980.

"The Few Fight for QVH." *The Courier* (East Grinstead), October 1, 1987.

Figuera, Nancy. "Toronto's Dr. Tilley: Surgeon and Friend." *Graduate*, The University of Toronto Alumni Magazine, Vol XI, no. 2, Nov/Dec., 1983, p. 10.

"Flying boat veterans return for crash service." [re. A.M. Platsko and George Allen]. *The Impractical Reporter and Farmer's Journal*. (district Fermanagh, N. Ireland) Sept. 1, 1994, p. 12.

"From office girl to editor's chair: Mrs. Gordon Clemetson Retires." [re. Aunt Agatha]. *The Courier* (Kent & Sussex), n.d.

"Former PoW was a man of boundless energy." {re. Ken Smyth]. *St Catharines Standard*, Oct. 26, 1999.

Gray, Charlotte. "Profile: Dr. A. Ross Tilley." *Canadian Medical Association Journal*, Vol. 129, July 15, 1983.

The Guinea Pig (magazine), 1947-present. Various editors: Bernard Arch, Henry Standen, Jack Toper.

"Guinea Pigs to Gather at 447 Wing Club." *Glanbrook Gazette*, June 5, 1997, p. 5.

"Hands Off the QVH." *The Courier* (East Grinstead), Thursday, October 8, 1987.

"History of the R.C.A.F. Plastic Surgery and Jaw Injury Unit: Queen Victoria Hospital, East Grinstead, Sussex, England." *Journal of the Canadian Medical Services*, Vol. 4, 90-94, 1946.

"Hospital aid more than peanuts." *Warwick* newspaper, n.d.

"How NHS bowed to Pea-Nut power." *The Courier* (Kent & Sussex). May 29, 1981, p. 14.

Lees, Nick. "Guinea Pig Club: Think of These Boys as Human Beings." *The Edmonton Journal*, Sunday, October 2, 1988, p.D6

"The Lost Weekend for Heroes." 1965 [unidentified]

Mandel, Charles. "Plane Obsession." [re. Stanley G. Reynolds]. *Canadian Geographic*, Jan./Feb. 2000, Vol. 120, no. 2, pp. 50-56.

Murphy, Patrick. "The Guinea Pigs: Reunion Brings Back Recipients of Experimental Wartime Surgery." *Times Colonist* (Victoria), May 18, 1999.

"The nutty joke that swept the world." *The Courier*. (Kent & Sussex), May 29, 1981, p. 13.

Patterson, Lon. "Dr. Hastings Was Part of 'Guinea Pig Club'." *The Chronicle-Journal*, (Thunder Bay) November 1, 1971.

"Pea-Nut Club" [booklet]. Courier Co., Ltd., Tunbridge Wells, 1948.

Pennington, Bob. "50 War-Scarred Airmen Meet for Joyful Weekend." *The Toronto Star*, Friday, June 9, 1972.

"'Pig' Spirit Salves Burn Horror." *The Vancouver Sun*, Thursday, July 15, 1982, p. B8.

Powley, A.E. "Healing by Sculpture." *Macleans Magazine*, January 1, 1945.

"QVH Shock." *The Courier.* (East Grinstead), June 25, 1987.

Richards, Laura J. "Opening Ceremonies Honour Life and Work of Dr. Ross Tilley." *The Canadian Statesman* (Bowmanville), Wed., Nov. 13, 1996, p. 3.

Ronald, George. "The Guinea Pigs' Lost Weekend." *Reader's Digest,* 1971, pp. 116-200.

Saunders, Carolyn. "Airmen had psychological wounds, too." *The Leader-Post* (Regina), n.d.

"She Helped Badly Burned Airmen Back to Normal." [re. Matron Marge Jackson]. dateline: Torquay, Sept. 27. No newspaper name, n.d.

"Spitfire 'Guinea Pig' reunion-bound." [re. Frank Hanton] *The Leader-Post* (Regina), June 17, 1989.

Standen, Henry. "This is the Guinea Pig Club." *Royal Air Force Association* Annual, 1952.

Tait, Mark. "Guinea Pigs passed the test." [re. George Wilson and the Guinea Pigs]. *Calgary Herald,* 1981.

Tait, Mark. "Wartime burn victims here for reunion." *Calgary Herald,* July 5, 1982.

"Warning Over QVH." *The Courier.* (East Grinstead). June, 1987.

"Wartime Plastic Surgery 'Guinea Pigs' Gather in Regina." *The Leader-Post,* Sat., June 27, 1987.

Wilton, Peter. "WWII 'guinea pigs' played crucial role in refining plastic surgery in Canada." *Canadian Medical Association Journal* 1998; 159: 1158-9.

"With the RCAF in England." *Canada's Weekly,* September 14, 1945.

- Zurowski, Monica. "Burned vets recall healing hands, hearts." [re. Hank Ernst, 45th reunion]. *Calgary Herald,* November 8, 1986.

Films/Videos

Comrades in Arms. Videotape. An interview with Guinea Pig Reg Harrison. Interviewer: Austin Willis. Saturday, January 18, Branch 86 Royal Canadian Legion, Produced and directed by J. Barry Hill, Wetaskiwin, Alberta, 1998.

Dr. Tilley and His Guinea Pigs. An Ian Ferguson film. Avantage Productions. Written and directed by Ian Ferguson, 1984. 28 minutes.

The Guinea Pig Club. A Thames Television Production. Producers: Robert Fleming, Peter Williams. Director: Robert Fleming. Writer and Narrator: Peter Williams. 19.56 minutes.

L'Heure Juste. Television interview with Guinea Pig Henri Bernard Marceau. Animateur Jean-Luc Mongrain, 1991.

New Faces Come Back. (also entitled *New Faces for Old, The Comeback.* and *New Face Comes Back.*) RCAF. Filmed on location in 1944, featuring British Guinea Pig Jack Allaway. National Film Board of Canada, 1946. 28 minutes.

Videotapes of the Guinea Pig Reunions, 1980, 1997, 1999, and other short clips from privately produced videos for television news, etc.

Index